A System Verilog Primer

A System Verilog Primer

J. BHASKER

eSilicon Corporation

BSP BS Publications

An Imprint of BSP Books Pvt., Ltd.

4-4-309/316, Giriraj Lane,

Sultan Bazar, Hyderabad - 500 095

A System Verilog Primer
***by* J. Bhaskar**

Reprint 2025

First Indian Ed. 2010

Published by :

BS Publications
An Imprint of **BSP Books Pvt. Ltd.**
4-4-309/316, Giriraj Lane, Sultan Bazar,
Hyderabad - 500 095
Phone: 040 - 23445688
e-mail: info@bspbooks.net
www.bspbooks.net

In arrangement with
Star Galaxy Publishing
1058 Treeline Drive, Allentown, PA 18103
Phone : 610-391-7296

For sale in India, Pakistan, Srilanka, Bangladesh, Nepal, Maldivies and Maynmar only.

WARNING - DISCLAIMER

The author and publisher have used their best efforts in preparing this book and the examples contained in it. They make no representation, however, that the examples are error-free or are suitable for every application to which a reader may attempt to apply them. The author and the publisher make no warranty of any kind, expressed or implied, with regard to these examples, documentation or theory contained in this book, all of which is provided "as is". The author and the publisher shall not be liable for any direct or indirect damages arising from any use, direct or indirect, of the examples provided in this book.

Library Congress Control Number: 2010901999

Price: Rs. 795.00
ISBN: 978-81-7800-280-4 (Paperback)

Contents

CHAPTER 8

Advanced Verification Topics 189

CHAPTER 9

Assertions 225

❑

Foreword

More than a decade ago, it was noted that the completion of an electronic system was not related to how designers were able to create electronic functions, rather on how they were able to verify that they were done testing those functions and ready to commit the design to silicon. The electronic design automation market responded with proprietary tools and single source languages to address what the most challenging designs were showing us - an inability to close the verification process with certainty.

In a design world of standard languages that ensured data portability, reuse of training and engineering skills, and increased design reuse, the verification process was one that relied on a nascent set of tools used by few, ill-fitting proprietary techniques not reliably sharable, and verification pressures that were only getting worse with each process node. Design complexity was the bane of verification completion. And it was not just that there was no standard language for verification, it was often difficult for the designer to understand the whole design since larger designs were created from reused design blocks that they were unfamiliar with. Schedule pressures to keep design time constant flew in the face of long debug cycles that often led to not just delayed verification but incomplete verification.

At that time, research into formal methods to address the design complexity issue was underway. Market research was also indicating that the age of "Intelligent Testbench" was needed to solve the verification challenges. The formal methods research resulted in numerous groups examining the use of design properties to both statically and dynamically determine if properties held or were violated under certain conditions. The design properties, or assertions as we may also call them today, were applied to many designs to find hidden bugs lurking in deigns that were already committed to silicon. The whole area of Assertion-Based Verification (ABV) took hold and many designs were better tested when they applied this new technique to verify.

To better use assertions, a proprietary Hardware Verification Languages (HVL) was added to their language set to make the Intelligent Testbench that more intelligent. The other "intelligent" part of the testbench was to allow the computer to create tests to cover the design space rather than the engineer. The most popular of the computer generated test schemes was the use of random tests. And Constrained Random Testing (CRT) allowed more tests to be generated and run than what could be created by a verification engineer directly. CRT often found failure conditions that would be hard to reach or never attempted by the engineer alone.

While I was the chair of Accellera, we recognized the need for an industry standard language that would allow all of this information to be expressed in a standard language. This would permit design and verification engineers to share techniques, to learn from each other and to make skills portable such that techniques used on one design in one company would work on another design in another company. SystemVerilog was invented to this end.

With assertions as a key element of the SystemVerilog language and constrained random testing as a major element to automate testbench development, SystemVerilog became the first standard Hardware Verification Language. Beyond that, it also built on the popular Verilog HDL language. The decision to create a standalone language or one that was based on a popular Hardware Design Language (HDL) was well debated. In the end, it was clear we thought the design community would find it easier to adopt incremental language features than a whole new language that had limited relations to any current design language. We started to build on the popular IEEE 1364™ design language to create SystemVerilog, which went on to become IEEE 1800™. The first version of the IEEE

1800-2005 referenced IEEE 1364 and the most recent IEEE SystemVerilog version, IEEE 1800-2009, subsumes IEEE 1364 into it.

IEEE 1800 is a language which has taken hold and is firmly the industry's most popular design and verification language. The users of the language continue to grow. The language has rooted many popular verification methodologies and is set for wider adoption by the design and verification community.

As a wider community of users is set to adopt SystemVerilog, an easy to read book, much like *A Verilog HDL Primer* is needed. *A SystemVerilog Primer* follows the same simple to read style of *A Verilog HDL Primer* and is a good companion for those who own the first book and is a must have for those who will immerse themselves in SystemVerilog now.

The no-nonsense and simple writing style offers examples with each syntax item described to better illustrate and bring to life the SystemVerilog language. The *SystemVerilog Primer* sets the stage for advanced application of the language by describing the new building blocks and additions to the language over Verilog HDL. Building on this, the primer then tackles advanced extensions for improved structural modeling, code management using packages and advanced verification topics to name a few. The primer closes with succinct description of the SystemVerilog assertions.

Dr. Bhasker has done it again and I believe *A SystemVerilog Primer* will be found to be a necessary companion for many teams of engineers who are dealing with advanced System-on-Chip design issues today and tomorrow to help them survive the design complexity and verification challenges of modern electronic system design.

Dennis B. Brophy
Mentor Graphics Corporation
Wilsonville, Oregon

❑

Preface

SystemVerilog is a fairly enriched language that is derived from the best features of other design and verification languages. Because of its complexity, I decided to write the SystemVerilog Primer to explain the language in simple terms using a style that explains the syntax followed by examples and guidelines. In this book, I address the basic and very important features of the language, including items that make SystemVerilog very unique and useful for design and verification of chips. However, some very specific high-end features of SystemVerilog are not covered; these include DPI (Direct Programming Interface) and VPI (Verilog Programming Interface) as they are beyond the scope of this book.

This book is a companion to the book *A Verilog HDL Primer, 3rd edition*. The style and readability of the companion book has been maintained in this book as well. While the companion book describes the Verilog HDL features, this book focuses on the extensions and enhancements made to the Verilog HDL language that is part of the IEEE Std 1800-2009 SystemVerilog standard. Thus, I assume that you are knowledgeable about Verilog HDL when you read this book.

SystemVerilog is an IEEE standard and is an unified language for hardware design, specification, and verification. It is a combination of two main languages: design and verification. SystemVerilog contains many features of VHDL that were not in Verilog HDL, and in addition includes many C++ features that help in writing more advanced behavioral testbenches. SystemVerilog also includes an assertion language as part of its repertoire. Advanced testbench features such as randomization, coverage and interprocess communication are also part of the language.

SystemVerilog supports modeling for design and verification. A basic knowledge of C++ would be helpful in understanding the concepts of classes and inheritances, though I have attempted to explain these using examples. As I see it, SystemVerilog borrowed many concepts and features from the following languages:

i. Basic Verilog HDL extensions (e.g. new operators, built-in methods)
ii. C (e.g. typedef, struct, union)
iii. C++ (e.g. classes)
iv. VHDL (e.g. enumeration types, break, continue, return)
v. Assertion language
vi. Coverage language
vii. Interprocess communication features (e.g. semaphores, mailboxes, events).

So it is a BIG language. Having a language with so many features, it sometimes becomes necessary to have a methodology. Otherwise if not used carefully, it would hurt to use the wrong set of features for a given application. Thus many verification methodologies were born - OVM and VMM, to name a few. In my opinion, all of these serve the same purpose, though each one is peddled by a different simulation vendor. At the time of writing of this text, there appears to be a consensus to combine all of the verification methodologies and to create a standard verification methodology that is open source so that it can easily be ported across multiple simulation platforms. This text does not discuss any of the verification methodologies as there are already many books on this topic.

This book is intended as a starter book to allow new users to get up to speed on the application of SystemVerilog. It also would make a great reference for professionals who want to see examples in action - syntax and semantics based on small examples. This book is intended for hardware designers as well as circuit and system designers, software tool developers, and those interested in learning to model hardware and verify hardware using SystemVerilog. The book can also be used as an introductory text in a first university course on computer-aided design, hardware modeling, verification or synthesis. It is well suited for working professionals as well as for undergraduate and graduate study. Designers and verification professionals can use this book as a reference manual on the application of SystemVerilog. Students and professors will find this book useful as a teaching tool for hardware design and for hardware verification.

The book assumes a basic knowledge of digital hardware design as well as some familiarity with a high-level programming language such as C. It also assumes that you know the Verilog HDL language.

Finally, I would like to comment that it is impractical to learn a language by reading alone. Typing out examples from this book and compiling and simulating them on a SystemVerilog simulator is the best way to gain a complete and thorough understanding of the language. Once you have mastered this book, look to the IEEE standard for complete information on SystemVerilog.

Book Organization

Chapter 1 provides a brief history of the language and describes its major capabilities. Chapter 2 describes the basic elements of the language. This includes literals, data types including enumeration types, enhancements to array types, user-defined types, queues and strings, amongst others.

Chapter 3 describes the composite types in SystemVerilog, namely, structures, unions and classes.

Chapter 4 is devoted to expressions. An expression can be used in many different places in a SystemVerilog description, including in a delay specification. The chapter also describes the various kinds of operators and operands that can be used to form an expression.

Chapter 5 describes extensions to the behavioral modeling style. It describes the three new kinds of procedural constructs and enhancements to loop statements, if statements, case statements and parallel blocks. It also describes enhancements made to continuous assignments.

Modules and interfaces are the topics of Chapter 6. Enhancements to module declarations, port lists, and port connections are explained in detail. The concept of interfaces is introduced and its usage is explained with examples.

Chapter 7 describes packages and the notion of compilation units. Numerous enhancements to tasks and functions are detailed in this chapter.

Advanced verification topics are described in Chapter 8. These include constrained-random generation and interprocess communication. To describe each and every feature of these topics would involve a complete chapter or a book by itself. However, basic concepts and features are described. The notion of program blocks and clocking blocks is also introduced. Coverage features are beyond the scope of this text.

Chapter 9 describes the assertion specification capability of SystemVerilog. This includes specification of sequences and properties. Numerous examples of assertions are provided to help in understanding the variety of operators and mechanisms that are available in describing assertions.

Finally, Appendix A contains a complete syntax reference of the SystemVerilog language. The grammar is described in Backus-Naur Form (BNF) and the constructs are all arranged alphabetically for easier search.

In all the SystemVerilog descriptions that appear in this book, reserved words, system tasks and system functions, and compiler directives are in **boldface**. In syntax descriptions, operators and punctuation marks that are part of the syntax are in boldface. Optional items in a grammar rule are indicated by using non-bold square brackets ([...]). Non-bold curly braces ({...}) identify items that are repeated zero or more times. Occasionally ellipsis (. . .) is used in SystemVerilog source to indicate code that is not relevant to that discussion. Certain words are written in *italics* to identify its SystemVerilog meaning rather than its English meaning such as in *and* gate.

All the examples were tested on ModelSim SE v6.5 simulator.

Acknowledgments

It is with great pleasure that I acknowledge the assistance of the following individuals who offered their valuable time and energy to review drafts of this text despite their very busy schedule: John Aynsley, K.V. Balamurugan, Alan Fitch, Tom Fitzpatrick, Mark Glasser, Shankar Hemmady, Preetham Lakshminathan, Francoise Martinolle, and Ambar Sarkar.

I especially thank Ben Cohen, author of several VHDL and SystemVerilog books on assertions and VMM, for reviewing and providing a very detailed feedback on the draft.

This book has improved substantially as a result of their detailed comments and constructive criticism. I am gratefully indebted to them. Thank you very much!

This book would not have been possible without the support of my wife, Geetha, and my three Rajahs, Arvind, Vinay and Vishnu.

J. Bhasker
Allentown, PA
May 2010

❑

Chapter 1

Introduction

This chapter describes the history of the SystemVerilog language and its major capabilities.

1.1 Why SystemVerilog?

Over the years, several design and verification languages were created to satisfy certain needs. For example, we have VHDL and Verilog HDL for design and some verification; Vera, Specman e for verification; PSL for formal verification. However, there was a need to have a unified language for doing design and verification, all encompassed using a single language. In addition, today's complex designs are getting too big for a hardware description language such as Verilog HDL to keep up with, for handling both design and verification complexities. Hundreds of pages of design code is not uncommon, which implies that all of this design code needs to be verified as well. More code implies more bugs. So a need has been there to enable designs to be expressed at a higher level of abstraction, thereby allowing for more concise descriptions, and also allowing verification to be performed at this level of abstraction. Describing designs at the register-transfer level (RTL) gave a big boost to productivity as compared to the former schematics approach. Similarly, SystemVerilog is intended to provide a major boost in productivity in terms for writing more concise design descriptions and to enable verification to be performed at a much higher abstraction level.

There exist many different languages for different functionalities, each with its own style and semantics. See Figure 1-1. There are the hardware description languages (e.g. VHDL, Verilog HDL) for design, the hardware verification languages for verification (e.g. e, Vera), assertion language for formal property checking (e.g. PSL) and C/C++ for verification at abstract behavioral level. Each language has its own set of tools and nuances and doing a system-on-chip design that requires each of such features requires a cumbersome interface causing inefficient communication.

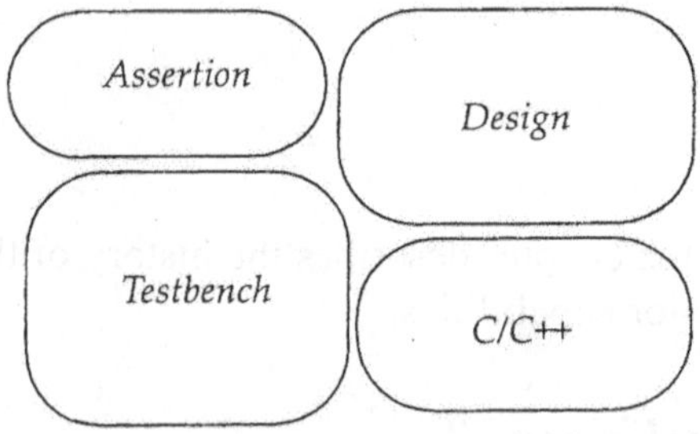

Figure 1-1 Different languages used in a design process.

SystemVerilog addresses all of these issues by providing a single language for modeling, design and verification. It is a *hardware description and verification language* (HDVL) - a single language that can be used for both design and verification of large complex designs. More importantly, SystemVerilog provides a single platform that can be used to accomplish all the design tasks, be it synthesis, simulation or formal verification; this reduces the overhead of learning different tools and different languages. It eliminates the communication overhead of multiple languages. A single language allows for a standard methodology to be developed that can enhance productivity. SystemVerilog supports higher abstraction levels for architectural and algorithmic design, and for advanced verification.

SystemVerilog improves productivity, readability and reusability of the design code. The language enhancements provide for more concise hardware descriptions, support for directed and constrained-random test-bench development, coverage-driven verification and assertion-based verification.

1.2 Brief History

SystemVerilog was first developed by the Accellera standards group[1]. The language was based upon Co-Design's[2] SUPERLOG language that was donated to Accellera by Co-Design in 2001. In addition, Synopsys[3] donated the Vera technology to be included in SystemVerilog, which included Open Vera Assertions (OVA). Accellera approved a SystemVerilog 3.0 version in 2002. In 2003, Accellera announced SystemVerilog 3.1 after integrating many new features, primarily directed at advanced verification and C language integration.

It was approved as an IEEE standard in 2005 as IEEE Std 1800-2005. This standard was described as an extension to the IEEE Std 1364-2001 Verilog HDL. Later, a proposal to merge the IEEE Std 1364 and IEEE Std 1800 into one language was completed and the new standard IEEE Std 1800-2009 that describes the entire SystemVerilog language was published in 2009. Since Verilog HDL is strictly a subset of SystemVerilog, this text describes only the extensions that were added to Verilog HDL to form SystemVerilog.

1.3 Major Capabilities

SystemVerilog has all the features of Verilog HDL - it is defined as an extension of Verilog HDL. And it has technology included based upon DirectC API and coverage API, SUPERLOG, Vera, C, C++, VHDL, OpenVera assertions and PSL assertion language. All of these integrated together is what makes SystemVerilog. See Figure 1-2.

1. http://www.accellera.org.
2. Used to be Co-Design Automation, since acquired by Synopsys.
3. http://www.synopsys.com.

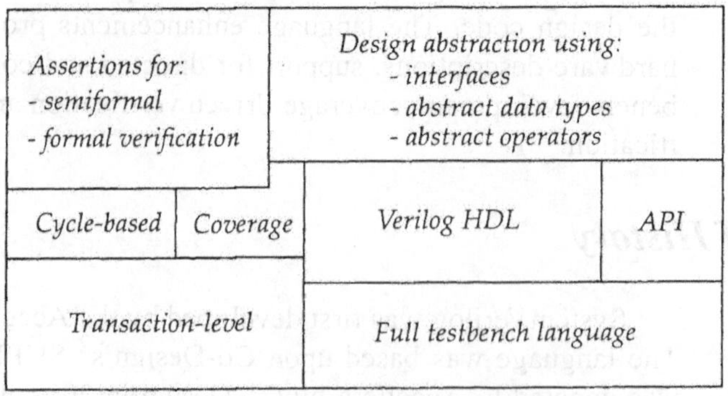

Figure 1-2 Components of SystemVerilog.

SystemVerilog has the Verilog HDL syntax, flavor and spice. This includes:

- basic data types (such as bit, integer)
- basic programming (for, if, while)
- gate-level modeling and four-state logic
- event handling and ordering
- hardware concurrency and switch-level modeling
- ASIC timing and state strengths
- mixed register-transfer / gate / switch level modeling

In addition, SystemVerilog includes all the powerful higher level data types and management functionality that VHDL has.

- packages and configurations
- simple assertions
- multi-dimension arrays
- dynamic memory allocation
- pointers and record types
- automatic variables
- signed numbers
- enumeration types

SystemVerilog also includes programming features of C++. This includes:

- C-like data types
- user-defined data types using typedef
- void type
- unions and type casting
- programming (do-while, break, continue, ++, --, +=, . . .)
- pass by reference to tasks and functions

SystemVerilog adds:

- interprocess communication
- interfaces to encapsulate communication and protocol checking
- assertion language
- new kinds of procedural statements, such as always_comb, always_latch, always_ff
- priority and unique case and if statements

Advanced verification and modeling features include:

- classes, associative arrays and dynamic arrays
- coverage monitoring
- random number generation
- semaphores, mailboxes and queues
- strings
- coverage and assertions
- external compilation unit scope

To be clear, SystemVerilog is based upon Verilog HDL - it extends Verilog HDL - so it has the same look and feel of Verilog HDL.

In summary, SystemVerilog has all the features of a hardware description language, a hardware verification language and high-level behavioral modeling encompassed within. In essence:

```
SystemVerilog = HDL + HVL + C++
```

SystemVerilog has higher level data structures that provide for concise coding with no loss of control. It provides several features to facilitate the use of the language at various level of abstractions. For example, it provides an interface definition that allows for block-based communication between design blocks and the testbench. Using interfaces guarantees that a block in a design is connected correctly. Interfaces also have public and private data, so that visibility can be provided to some internal processes to allow for built-in protocol checking. In addition, interfaces allow the use of embedded assertions to specify and verify their proper applications wherever the interfaces are instantiated.

SystemVerilog includes key verification components. See Figure 1-3. This includes writing transaction-level tests, generating constrained-random stimulus, protocol checking, functional coverage feedback and concurrent process control.

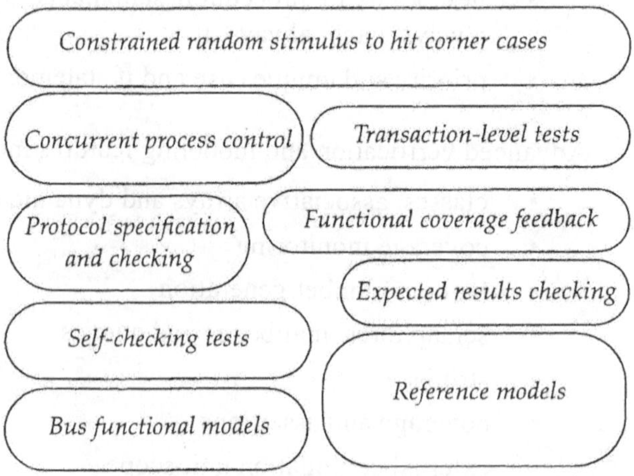

Figure 1-3 Verification components in SystemVerilog.

SystemVerilog can be used for design and verification at either the block level or at the system level.

❑

Chapter 2

Language Elements

SystemVerilog inherits the variable and type system from C. And it has additional types that are useful for system design and verification that go beyond C and Verilog HDL.

2.1 Logic Literal Values

The following unsized single bit value can be used for any arbitrary base size with automatic expansion.

```
'0         : fill all bits with 0.
'1         : fill all bits with 1.
'z or 'Z : fill all bits with z.
'x or 'X : fill all bits with x.

wire [15:0] lu_ctl;

assign lu_ctl = '1;        // Fills all 16 bits with 1's.
```

All bits of the target are set to the bit specified and treated as unsigned if the signedness cannot be determined from the context.

2.2 Basic Data Types

The following basic data types are defined in SystemVerilog.

i. *2-state type*: Has bit value 0 or 1.

- **int** : 32-bit signed integer
- **shortint** : 16-bit signed integer
- **longint** : 64-bit signed integer
- **bit** : 1-bit
- **byte** : 8-bit signed integer

ii. *4-state type*: Has bit value **x**, 0, 1 or **z**.

- **logic** : 1-bit

Here are some examples of variables declared using these types.

```
bit pwr_flag;                  // 1-bit.
logic [3:0] r_vector;          // 4-bit.

byte part_code;                // 8-bit signed integer.
int stk_ctr, stk_ptr;          // 32-bit signed integers.

shortint sh_cnt;                 // 16-bit signed integer.
longint keep_ptr, mem_ptr;       // 64-bit integers.
```

Here are the 4-state basic data types inherited from Verilog HDL.

- **reg** : 1-bit
- **integer** : 32-bit signed integer
- **time** : 64-bit unsigned integer

Type *logic* is equivalent to the *reg* type and they can be used interchangably. The only reason to use the *logic* type is that it does not directly implicate hardware, as *reg* type appears to, which is thus a more intuitive keyword to use in modeling designs.

```
// Both are equivalent:
reg sum;
logic sum;

// These are also equivalent:
reg [3:0] sw_low;
logic [3:0] sw_low;
```

The difference between *int* and *integer* data types is that the *int* type is a 2-state type while the *integer* type is a 4-state type. A 2-state type typically simulates faster and takes up less memory.

```
int fdx;             // 32-bit signed integer with
                     // each bit either 0 or 1.
integer t_min;       // 32-bit signed integer with
                     // each bit 0, 1, x or z.
```

A 4-state type defaults to the value **x** at beginning of simulation, while a 2-state type starts simulation with a value of 0. From the previous example, *sw_low* defaults to **x** since it is of type *logic* which is a 4-state type, while *fdx* defaults to 0 since it is of type *int* which is a 2-state type.

Care should be exercised when using 2-state types since they start simulation with a value of 0 and may not trigger an event, for example, on active-low signals. It is recommended that 4-state types be used for active-low signals and for other design signals that require an explicit transition upon start of simulation. This is because 4-state types cause explicit events to get generated at start of simulation that go from **x** to a known logic value.

A 4-state type can be assigned to a 2-state type; the values **x** and **z** translate to a 0.

```
bit [3:0] p_vector = 4'bxx1z;   // Gets value 0010.
bit error_handle = 'x;          // Gets a 0.
```

Figure 2-1 shows the classification of 2-state and 4-state types and integer and bit types[1] in a tabular form.

Type	*2-state*	*Bits*	*4-state*	*Bits*
Integer	**shortint** **int** **longint** **byte**	16 32 64 8	**integer** **time**	32 64
Bit	**bit**	1	**logic** **reg**	1 1

Figure 2-1 Integer and bit type classification.

By default, the integer types are signed, while *bit*, *reg* and *logic* types and arrays of these types are unsigned.

```
byte sense;              // 8-bit signed.
logic [3:0] trig;        // 4-bit unsigned.
```

However, the default signedness can be changed by using the keyword modifiers **signed** and **unsigned** in a type declaration.

```
byte unsigned result;          // 8-bit unsigned.
bit signed [31:0] d_bus;       // 32-bit signed.
```

2.2.1 Other Types

There are three additional types defined in SystemVerilog.

- **void** : This type indicates no storage. It is used in tagged unions and to define functions that do not return any values.
- **shortreal** : 32-bit single-precision floating point (note that the type *real* in Verilog HDL stores a double-precision value).

---

1. "Bit types" refers to type *bit*, *logic* and *reg*. *bit* type (note italic) refers only to the type *bit*. Similarly, "integer types" refer to type *shortint*, *int*, *longint*, *byte*, *integer* and *time*, while *integer* type (note italics) refers only to type *integer*.

- **chandle** : This type is used to store pointers passed using the DPI (Direct Programming Interface). The size of the data type is platform-specific.

```
chandle x_dim;
function void print_header;
  . . .
endfunction
```

The types *real* and *realtime* are already defined in Verilog HDL.

2.3 Data Objects

SystemVerilog makes a distinction between the kind of object and its data type. An object has a data kind, *net* or *variable*[1], and a data type. A data type has a set of values and a set of operations that are legal for that data type. Here are some object (net and variable) declarations.

```
wire logic flag, check_bit; // Two nets that
                            // hold 4-state logic type.
var logic [7:0] read_bus;   // 8-bit 4-state variable.

var bit resetn;             // 1-bit variable.
wire logic [7:0] clear;     // 8-bit net.

bit npreset;          // 1-bit variable by default.
logic qn;             // 1-bit 4-state variable by default.

var [7:0] din;              // Defaults to 8-bit logic type.
wire qout;                  // Defaults to a logic type.
```

Guideline: When a signal is driven by multiple drivers, declare the signal as a net.

A net or a variable defaults to a *logic* type if no type is specified. If neither the **var** keyword nor a net type keyword is present, then the object by default is a variable. More details on the differences between variables and nets are described in Chapter 3.

1. In Verilog HDL, these were referred to as *net* type and *variable* type.

2.4 User-defined Types

New data types can be created using the typedef feature in SystemVerilog. New type names can be created based upon existing types. In the following example of a *typedef declaration*:

```
typedef int t_myint;
```

a new type name *t_myint* is declared which is a synonym for the type *int*. The new type name, *t_myint*, can be used in exactly the same way as the original type, *int*.

```
// Following both are equivalent:
int p_addr;
t_myint p_addr;
```

Note that the typedef declaration does not create a new type; it only creates a new alternate name for an existing type. It is more like a **`define**, except that it is interpreted by the compiler rather than the preprocessor.

```
typedef logic [31:0] t_address;
  // t_address is a new type name.
t_address apb_dbus; // apb_dbus is a 32-bit logic type.
```

The typedef features provides for a design description to be parameterized for portability and enhances readability and provides for better documentation. We shall later see examples of such cases where creating a typedef of a structure makes readability easier.

Sometimes it may be necessary to define the type before the contents of the type are defined. A *forward typedef declaration* (also sometimes referred to as an *incomplete type*) can be used in such cases.

```
// Forward typedef declaration:
typedef t_ptr;
. . .
// Use the forward type:
t_ptr fifo_full;          // fifo_full is of type t_ptr.
. . .
```

```
// Define the complete typedef declaration later:
typedef t_bool t_ptr;
// t_bool is an enumeration type declared elsewhere.
```

Type *t_ptr* is an enumeration type, same type as *t_bool*. The complete typedef declaration must occur in the same scope as the forward typedef declaration. Such forward user-defined type declarations can be defined for enumeration, structure, union and class types only.

A typedef declaration can appear internal to a module or externally in the compilation-unit scope (outside of a module, interface or program block). It can also be part of a package (packages are explained in more detail in Chapter 7).

```
package p_type_select;
  `ifdef SIGNED_OPD
  typedef int signed t_opd;
 `else
  typedef int unsigned t_opd;
 `endif
endpackage: p_type_select
. . .
p_type_select::t_opd tx_data, rx_data;
```

Depending upon the value of *SIGNED_OPD*, the type of *rx_data* and *tx_data* are either both signed or both unsigned integers. The type *t_opd* is directly referenced from the package *p_type_select* using the *scope resolution operator* (::).

To import a type declared in a package into a module, an *import declaration* can be used.

```
module reset_blk;
  import p_type_select::t_opd;
  t_opd tx_data, rx_data;
  . . .
endmodule
```

2.5 Enumeration Types

An *enumeration type* declares a set of enumeration literals (named constants) that belong to the type.

```
enum {FAST, MEDIUM, SLOW} clk_speed;
enum {S0, S1, S2, S3, S4, S5} fsm_state;
```

The variable *clk_speed* is of an enumeration type which can only have one of the values *FAST*, *MEDIUM* or *SLOW*. The variable *fsm_state* is of an enumeration type that can have one of the values *S0*, *S1*, *S2*, *S3*, *S4* or *S5*.

The above two enumeration types are examples of *anonymous* enumeration types as no type name was explicitly defined. A type name can be explicitly declared for an enumeration type using a typedef declaration.

```
typedef enum
  {ZERO, ONE, DONTCARE, UNKNOWN, HIGHIMP} t_logic5;
var t_logic5 dma_interrupt;
```

Guideline: Use named enumeration instead of anonymous enumeration. This helps separate the data type from the data object.

The type *t_logic5* is an explicit enumeration type, called a *named* enumeration type. This type is then used in the declaration of the variable *dma_interrupt*. Here is another example.

```
typedef enum {FALSE, TRUE} t_boolean;
// t_boolean is a named enumeration type.

// Declare two variables:
t_boolean cpu_ready, cpu_wait;

// Assign a value:
cpu_ready = FALSE;
```

2.5.1 Importing Enumeration Types

If an enumeration type is declared in a package, then importing an enumeration type from a package imports only the type, not its literals.

```
package p_compute;
  typedef enum {ADD, LOADA, LOADB, STORE} t_instruction;
endpackage: p_compute

import p_compute::t_instruction;
// Can only use the type t_instruction, not one of
// its literals such as ADD.
```

To import all the enumeration literals including the enumeration type, use the wildcard import, or list all literals and the type explicitly in an import statement.

Guideline: When there are enumeration types present in a package, use the wildcard import.

```
import p_compute::*;
// Makes the enumeration type and its literals
// available for use.

// Alternate way:
import p_compute::t_instruction, p_compute::ADD,
       p_compute::LOADA, p_compute::LOADB,
       p_compute::STORE;
```

2.5.2 Shorthand Notation

SystemVerilog provides a shorthand notation to specify enumeration literals in an enumeration type declaration when they are in a sequence. So an enumeration literal such as:

```
CMD[5]
```

is interpreted as:

```
CMD0, CMD1, CMD2, CMD3, CMD4
```

and enumeration literals of the form:

```
BYTE[3:7], LEND[5:2]
```

are interpreted as:

```
BYTE3, BYTE4, BYTE5, BYTE6, BYTE7, LEND5, LEND4, LEND3,
LEND2
```

The following enumeration type declaration:

```
typedef enum {FLAG[6:8], DBIT[3], COMP[1:0]} t_alucode;
```

is equivalent to:

```
typedef enum {FLAG6, FLAG7, FLAG8, DBIT0,
    DBIT1, DBIT2, COMP1, COMP0} t_alucode;
```

An enumeration literal cannot be overloaded in one scope; that is, the same enumeration literal used in different types cannot be visible in the same scope.

```
enum {YES, . . .} is_scan;
enum {. . ., YES, . . .} is_reset;
// Both declarations cannot be in same scope.
```

2.5.3 Enumeration Literal Values

Each literal of an enumeration type has an implicit value associated with it. By default the values are of type *int* (32-bit 2-state type). The integer values are assigned left to right starting from 0 in increasing order. In the following enumeration type declaration,

```
typedef enum {ADD, SUB, MUL, DIV} t_alu_op;
```

the enumeration literals are of type *int* and *ADD* has a value of 0, *SUB* has a value of 1, *MUL* has a value of 2 and *DIV* has a value of 3.

It is possible to override the default values assigned to enumeration literals.

```
typedef enum {ADD = 2, SUB, MUL = 8, DIV} t_alu_op;
```

Now *ADD* has a value of 2, and *MUL* has a value of 8. It is not necessary to specify values for all the enumeration literals. If a value has not been explicitly specified, the value of the enumeration literal is 1 plus the value of the literal to the left of it. Thus in the example above, *SUB* has the value 3 and *DIV* has the value 9.

Type casting (we shall see more of this later) can be used to convert from an integer value to an enumeration literal, and from an enumeration literal to its integer value. Here are some examples.

```
t_alu_op cpu_cmd;
int inst_value;

cpu_cmd = t_alu_op'(2);
  // ADD is assigned to cpu_cmd.
inst_value = int'(MUL); // 8 is assigned to inst_value.
```

Two enumeration literals in an enumeration type cannot have the same value.

```
enum {S0, S1, S2, S3, S4 = 2} fifo_state;     // Error.
```

Literals *S2* and *S4* both have the value 2 which is not allowed.

2.5.4 Typed Enumeration

The type of enumeration literal values can be explicitly specified. The default is of type *int*.

```
enum logic [2:0] {S0, S1, S2 = 3'b101, S3} fsm_state;
typedef enum bit {FALSE, TRUE} t_boolean;
```

Variable *fsm_state* is of an enumeration type whose literals have 3-bit logic values. Literal *S0* has value 3'b000, *S1* has value 3'b001, *S2* has value 3'b101 (explicitly specified), and *S3* has the value 3'b110 (1 more than the previous value). Enumeration type *t_boolean* has literals whose values are of type *bit*. Literal *FALSE* has the value 1'b0 and literal *TRUE* has the value 1'b1. Any explicit value specified for an enumeration literal must match the type specified.

Values **x** and **z** can also be used in specifying the value of a literal. However, the subsequent enumeration literal must have an explicit value specified as it is not allowed to auto-increment a value that contains an **x** or a **z**.

```
enum logic [3:0]
  {FRI, SAT = 4'b00xz, SUN = 4'b0101, MON} week_state;
```

Literal *FRI* has value 4'b0000, *SAT* has value 4'b00**xz**, which is explicitly specified and has an **x** and **z**, and therefore the next literal *SUN* must have an explicit value specified, in this case, 4'b0101. Consequently, literal *MON* has the value 4'b0110.

The initial value of a 2-state enumeration type is 0, while that for a 4-state type is an **x**. So use the 2-state enumeration type with caution as it may not create an event at simulation startup; for example, if the literal being assigned also has the value 0, in which case no event will get created.

2.5.5 Assigning Enumeration Types

An object of an enumeration type can only be assigned a literal from its type or a value from another object of the same enumeration type, or by type casting into the object's enumeration type.

```
typedef enum bit [1:0]
  {S0 = 2'b00, S1 = 2'b01, S2 = 2'b11, S3 = 2'b10} t_gray;
t_gray fsm1, fsm2;

fsm2 = S1;
fsm1 = fsm2;

fsm1 = 2'b00;                      // Not allowed.
fsm1 = t_gray'(2'b00);             // Allowed.

int fsm_int = fsm2 + 1;            // Automatic casting.
fsm2 = t_gray'(fsm1 + 1);          // Explicit cast.
```

Literals when used in expressions automatically use their values. However, a cast may be required to assign such a value back to a variable of an enumeration type, as shown in the above example. A variable of an enumeration type can only be assigned a value within its range of values, unless an explicit type cast is used.

Enumeration literals can be printed as text or as its value.

```
fsm2 = S2;
$display ("%s", fsm2);            // Will print "S2".
$display ("%d", fsm2);            // Will print "3".
```

It is worth noting that an object of an enumeration type can have values outside of their defined range. One such case is as follows.

```
typedef enum bit [2:0]
  {HOLD = 3'b110, RUN = 3'b010, WALK = 3'b100} t_fstate;
t_fstate fifo_state, next_state;
```

Upon start of simulation, *fifo_state* will have value 3'b000, which is outside its defined list of enumeration literals. It can also get such a value by an unintended assignment.

```
fifo_state = HOLD;
next_state = t_fstate'(fifo_state + 2);
```

Dynamic casting can be used to ensure that only legal values are used; an assertion can also be written to check if such a variable holds only legal values; we examine these later.

2.5.6 Built-in Methods

Built-in methods[1] are provided to operate on objects of enumeration types. These are:

- *variable*.**first** : returns the first literal of the enumeration type.
- *variable*.**last** : returns the last enumeration literal.
- *variable*.**next**(*N*) : returns the *N*th next literal (wrapped around).
- *variable*.**prev**(*N*) : returns the *N*th previous literal (wrapped around).
- *variable*.**num** : returns the number of literals in the type.

---

1. A method is similar to a function except that it is called using the dot (.) notation - this is explained in the next chapter.

- *variable*.**name** : returns the literal in string form.

Here are some examples.

```
enum {RED, BLUE, GREEN, YELLOW, ORANGE} color;

color.first             // returns RED.
color.last              // returns ORANGE.

color = GREEN;
color.next              // returns YELLOW.
color.prev(2)           // returns BLUE.

color.num               // returns 5.

color = RED;
color.name              // returns the string "RED".
$display ("%s", color.name, " has value %d", color);
  // Prints the literal and then its integer value.
```

Enumeration types provide a convenient way to associate constant values much like **`define** with the advantage that the values can automatically be generated. In addition, a debugger may be able to print the enumeration literals in their symbolic form making debugging easier.

2.6 Arrays

An *array type* is a collection of elements all of the same type, and an element in an array can be accessed using an index. The element type can be of any type, including user-defined types, structure types and enumeration types.

```
bit [7:0] mem_a [63:0];

typedef enum
  {MON, TUE, WED, THU, FRI, SAT, SUN} t_weekday;
t_weekday month [1:31];

typedef bit [7:0] t_reg8x3file [0:2];
t_reg8x3file rf8x3;
```

```
typedef logic [15:0] [1023:0] t_frame;
t_frame frm_a;

typedef logic [31:0] t_addrbus;
t_addrbus paddr;
```

The variable *mem_a* is of an array type. It is an array of 64 elements, with each element being an 8-bit type. The variable *month* is also an array type; it has 31 elements, with each element being a user-defined enumeration type. The array type *t_reg8x3file* is a user-defined type and *rf8x3* is a variable of this type; this variable has three elements, each element being a 8-bit value. Another user-defined array type is *t_frame* and *frm_a* is a variable of this type; this variable is an array of 1024 by 16 logic values. The variable *paddr* holds a 32-bit logic value.

Packed and Unpacked

An array type can be an *unpacked* or a *packed* array type. In an unpacked array, each element of the array can be stored independent of the others, and the storage of elements is not defined by the language. A range specified after the variable name (or type name for a user-defined type) is treated as an unpacked array. The following is an example of an unpacked array (since the range is specified after the variable name).

```
bit count [3:0];                // Unpacked array of bits.
```

In a packed array, all elements are stored in contiguous bits. Any range specified before the variable name is treated as a packed array.

```
bit [3:0] cnt_r;                 // Packed array of bits.
```

A packed array provides a mechanism for subdividing a vector into subfields that can be accessed as array elements using a contiguous set of bits.

Figure 2-2 shows how unpacked and packed arrays are stored physically. Since all elements of a packed array are stored as consecutive bits, it can be treated like a vector and thus vector operations can be performed on it.

Unused	*count[0]*
Unused	*count[1]*
Unused	*count[2]*
Unused	*count[3]*

(a) Unpacked

cnt_r[3]	*cnt_r[2]*	*cnt_r[1]*	*cnt_r[0]*

(b) Packed

Figure 2-2 Unpacked and packed arrays.

Dimensions specified before the object name are packed dimensions. Dimensions specified after the object name are unpacked dimensions; an object can be a multi-dimensional packed array. Here is another example. In this case, *mem_b* is an unpacked array of 1024 elements, with each element a 16-bit packed array type.

```
bit [15:0] mem_b [1023:0];
```

An array definition in Verilog HDL is treated as an unpacked array in SystemVerilog. Here are examples of such unpacked array declarations.

```
wire [7:0] sym_tcm [4:0];
wire qam [63:0];
integer hitmatrix_a [7:0][7:0], hitmatrix_b [7:0][7:0];
```

Here are some more examples.

```
reg full_flag [0:63];  // 1-dimensional unpacked array,
                       // each element is a 1-bit.
logic [0:7] push_data [0:31]; // 1-dimensional unpacked
       // array, each element is a packed array of 8 bits.
int ptr [0:3][0:7];    // 2-dimensional unpacked array.

wire [3:0] req;             // 4-bit packed array.
wire [3:0][10:0] channel; // 2-dimensional packed array.
```

```
// Cannot create a packed array from unpacked elements:
typedef bit t_addr [7:0];
t_addr [3:0] haddr;           // Not allowed.

// Cannot have packed arrays of integer type:
byte [31:0] preg;             // Not allowed.
int [7:0] msize;              // Not allowed.
```

When accessing an array element, the packed dimensions follow the unpacked dimension.

```
object <unpacked dimensions> <packed dimensions next>

// Example:
push_data[30][0:2]        // First is the unpacked index,
              // second part-select is from the packed range.
```

Implicit Range

An array can be declared with just the size information (instead of a range). In such a case, the range by default is from 0 to (*SIZE* - 1).

```
int zero_flag [16];
  // 16-element unpacked array, each element of
  // type int and the index range is from 0 to 15.

reg [7:0] p_table [4][256];
  // Implies ranges 0:3 and 0:255, respectively.
```

A size value cannot be specified for packed arrays; a range has to be explicitly specified.

```
wire [3:0] coeff_sel;
  // 1-dimensional packed array.

wire [31:0][7:0] sram_data;
  // 2-dimensional packed array.
```

Consider an array that contains both packed and unpacked dimensions.

```
reg [0:7][0:15] even_hits [22][1024];
```

The 0:15 dimension varies more rapidly than the 0:7 dimension. And the 0:1023 dimension varies more rapidly than the 0:21 dimension. So in:

```
even_hits[5][220][3][8]
```

the 5 is from the 0:21 dimension, the 220 is from the 0:1023 dimension, the 3 is from the 0:7 dimension and the 8 is from the 0:15 dimension. Here is another example.

```
int vco [8][32];           // is equivalent to:
int vco [0:7][0:31];
```

Base Type

A packed array can be used to model an *N*-bit integer. Since the size of a packed array may be limited by an implementation, packed arrays can only be made up of bit types - *bit*, *logic*, *reg*, and recursively of other packed arrays and structures.

```
bit [7:0] hcount; // Packed array models a 8-bit integer.
```

Integer types with predetermined width cannot have packed arrays, which are *byte*, *shortint*, *int*, *time*, *longint* and *integer*. However, they can be treated as a single dimensional array in which the rightmost index is 0.

```
byte depth;           // is equivalent to:
bit [7:0] depth;

integer rd_addr;                // is equivalent to:
logic signed [31:0] rd_addr;
```

While a packed array can only be formed from a bit type, an unpacked array can be of any type, including object handles and events. For example, a packed array of structures is not allowed.

```
t_struct [7:0] str_b;      // Not allowed: 1-dimensional
                           // packed array of structures.

t_struct str_b [7:0];      // Allowed: unpacked array
                           // of structures.
```

Operations

Since a packed array is stored in contiguous bits, vector operations such as bit-select, part-select and bitwise operations, can be performed on objects of such a type.

```
wire [3:0] coeff_sel;

coeff_sel[3:2]
coeff_sel << 1
```

It is an error to access a part-select using a range direction which is different from the range direction in its declaration. A packed array can be treated as an integer depending on the context, as in:

```
int_a = coeff_sel + 3;
```

Since packed arrays behave like vectors, they can be assigned just like vectors.

```
wire [31:0][7:0] sram_data;

coeff_sel = sram_data[1][5:2];
```

A packed array can be assigned to a packed array since they are treated just like vectors - truncates or extends as the case may be.

```
coeff_sel = sram_data[2];          // Truncated.
sram_data[3] = coeff_sel;          // Extended.
```

An unpacked array can be assigned to another unpacked array if both the array sizes and element types are equivalent; each element of source unpacked array is assigned to the corresponding element in the target unpacked array. An unpacked array cannot be assigned to a packed array directly. Also a packed array cannot be assigned to an unpacked array. To assign an unpacked array to a packed array and vice versa, use the bit-stream operator (bit-stream operator is explained in Chapter 4).

A packed array can be assigned to another packed array even if the sizes do not match. The result is truncated or extended appropriately.

A complete unpacked or packed array can be written to or read. In addition, a variable slice of a packed or an unpacked array can be read or written to. Also arrays can be compared using the equality operator.

```
bit crc_mem [255:0][15:0], fsm_mem [255:0][15:0];
bit [1023:0][15:0] rd_fifo;

// Can read and write entire array:
crc_mem[8] = crc_mem[60];
fsm_mem = crc_mem;

always @(ck)
  rd_fifo = ~ rd_fifo; // Can operate on entire memory.

// Can read and write constant slice of unpacked array:
crc_mem[3:2] = crc_mem[2:1];
crc_mem[0:4]         // Error - cannot access a part-select
                     // whose direction is different from
                     // that in its declaration.

crc_mem[5][15:8] = "0111_1101";           // Range can
  // also be accessed. A value such as 8'h7D cannot be
  // assigned since the value represents a packed array
  // and it cannot be assigned to an unpacked array.

logic [0:7] stk, pix;
stk = {1'b0, stk[1:7]};        // Can copy, slice and dice.
```

The size of a part-select or slice must be a constant but the position can be a variable.

```
// Read and write variable slice of a packed array:
fsm_mem[i+:4] = fsm_mem[j-:4];

// Read and write element of array:
crc_mem[4] = crc_mem[21];

if (crc_mem == fsm_mem)
  . . .

if (pix == 8'b011)       // Can also be used in a compare.
  . . .
```

```
typedef bit [7:0] t_regfile [0:2];
t_regfile config_rf = '{3{'hA0}};
  // Can assign a constant literal.
```

A part-select of a packed array or any equivalent integer type is allowed. A *slice* selects one or more elements of an array. A *part-select* selects one or more bits of a contiguous packed array.

```
reg [63:0] wdata;
reg [7:0] byte2;

byte2 = wdata[23:16];  // 8-bit part-select from wdata.
```

A single element of a packed or an unpacked array can be selected using an indexed name.

```
bit [3:0][7:0] pty;       // 2-dimensional packed array.
bit [7:0] wrback;         // 1-dimensional packed array.

wrback = pty[2];
  // Select a single 8-bit element from pty.
```

A slice or a complete array can be copied using a single assignment as long as the unpacked array type on the left hand side and the right hand side have the same sizes.

```
hitmatrix_a = hitmatrix_b;            // Array copy.
hitmatrix_b[3] = hitmatrix_b[2];  // Array slice copy.
```

For purposes of assignment, a packed array is treated as a vector. Any vector expression can be assigned to a packed array. The packed array bounds are immaterial.

```
bit [3:0][7:0] test [1:10]; // 10 entries of 4 bytes
                            // packed into 32 bits.
test[9] = test[8] + 1;         // 4-byte added.
test[7][3:2] = test[6][1:0];   // 2-byte copy.
```

To summarize, the following operations can be performed on all arrays - packed or unpacked.

- Read and write an array :
```
arr1 = arr2;
```
- Read and write a slice of an array :
```
arr1[i:j] = arr2[n:m]; // i, j, n, m are
  // constant expressions (also in the following).
```
- Read and write a variable slice of an array :
```
arr1[x+:i] = arr2[y+:i];
```
- Read and write an element of an array :
```
arr1[i] = t;
t = arr2[j];
```
- Use equality operators on an array or a slice :
```
arr1 == arr2
arr1[i:j] == arr2[n:m]
```

Following operations are allowed only on packed arrays (not on unpacked arrays).

- Assignment of an integer :
```
packed_arr1 = 8'hff;
```
- Treatment as an integer in an expression :
```
packed_arr1 + 3
```

Signedness

An array of bit type (*logic*, *bit* and *reg*) defaults to unsigned values. If a packed array is declared as signed, then the entire vector is signed. An element of a packed array is unsigned unless the element is explicitly marked to be of a signed type. A part-select of a packed array is unsigned.

```
logic [3:0] fsm_state;        // Unsigned packed array.
bit signed [0:7] mark_count;  // Signed packed array.
logic signed shift [7:0];     // Signed unpacked array.

mark_count[2:4]             // is unsigned.
shift[2]                    // is signed.
```

If an unpacked array is declared as signed, then each element in the array is signed.

Using the 2-state Type

When accessing an out-of-bound element of a 2-state type, a 0 is returned which is dangerous, as it may be a real value. So be careful. A 4-state type out-of-bounds access returns an **x**.

```
bit [31:0] pri_reg;
logic rd_tail [0:7];

pri_reg[56]      // is 0 since pri_reg is a 2-state type.
rd_tail[10]      // is x since rd_tail is a 4-state type.
```

2.6.1 Array Literals

An array literal is a value of an array type. Such values are specified using '{...}.

```
logic [3:0] count = '{0, 1, 1, 0};
bit mdata [1:0][0:2] = '{'{0, 0, 1}, '{1, 0, 1}};
```

The 3rd element and the 0th element of *count* get value 0, and the 2nd element and the 1st element get a value of 1. Each value corresponds to the array index by position; such an association is called *positional association.*

The replication operator ({{}}) can also be used.

```
int hit_tbl [0:1][1:5] = '{2{'{3, 4, 5, 4, 5}}};
```

An array literal can be qualified by its type if necessary - for example, in cases where it is not apparent what the type of the literal is.

```
count3s (t_list'{0, 1, 0});
```

Each element of an array can be explicitly specified in the array literal by using its index or by using the **default** keyword. This is also referred to as *named association*, since a value is specified for each array element using its index explicitly.

```
int corr [0:7];
corr = '{0:6, 2:5, default:2};
```

The 0th element gets the value 6, the 2nd element gets the value 5 and the rest of the elements in the array get the value 2. Here are some more examples.

```
'{default:1}
   // All elements of array get a value of 1.

'{31:1, 21:2, 15:1, default:0}
   // All elements of array get a value of 0, except
   // the 31st element gets a 1, the 21st element
   // gets a 2 and the 15th element gets a value of 1.

'{2, 3, 4, 5}
   // Positional association used.

'{12{1'b0}}
   // Replication operator used - literal has 12
   // elements, each element of 1 bit.

'{4{'{3{4'b1001}}}}
   // Replication operator used - literal has 4x3
   // elements, each element being the 4-bit value 1001.
```

Packed arrays can be initialized using an assignment in its declaration, just like regular vectors in Verilog HDL.

```
logic [4:0] sleep = 5'h0;
bit [7:0] enable_reg = '{default:1'b0};
wire [7:0][1:0] wr_data = 16'hFF;
```

Unpacked arrays can be initialized in its declaration using an array literal specified using '{...} for each array dimension.

```
int sw_state [1:0][0:3] = '{'{7,3,0,5}, '{2,0,1,6}};

int sub_val [0:1][2:0] = '{2{1, 0, 1}};
  // Replication operator used.
```

```
int put_arr [7:0][3:0] = {default:12'h0A2};
    // Assigns all elements of array to same value.

bit [3:0] ram_a [1023:0] = '{default:4'b0};

logic [1:3] rd_data [0:1] = '{3'b001, 3'b010};
int rd_addr [0:1][0:15] = '{default:4'h5};
  // Initializes all elements to have a value of 5.

int flush [1:2][1:3] = '{'{0, 1, 2}, '{3{4}}};
```

2.6.2 Built-in Array Functions

The following built-in array functions are defined in the language.

- **$dimensions** (*array*) : returns the total number of dimensions (packed and unpacked) in the array.
- **$unpacked_dimensions** (*array*) : returns the total number of unpacked dimensions in the array.
- **$left** (*array, dimension*) : returns the leftmost index (most significant bit) of the specified array dimension.
- **$right** (*array, dimension*) : returns the rightmost index (least significant bit) of the specified array dimension.
- **$low** (*array, dimension*) : returns the smallest index of the specified array dimension.
- **$high** (*array, dimension*) : returns the largest index of the specified array dimension.
- **$size** (*array, dimension*) : returns the size of the specified array dimension.
- **$increment** (*array, dimension*) : returns 1 if **$left** >= **$right** and -1 if **$left** < **$right**.

The slowest varying dimension is numbered first, and dimension numbering starts with 1. Unpacked dimensions are numbered before packed dimensions.

```
logic [1023:0][15:0] hit_tbl [0:2][8:4][3:0];
```

Since the array has both packed and unpacked dimensions, the unpacked dimensions are numbered first. Dimension 1 is 0:2, dimension 2 is 8:4, dimension 3 is 3:0, dimension 4 is 1023:0 and dimension 5 is 15:0.

2.7 Dynamic Arrays

A *dynamic array* is an unpacked array whose size is specified only at runtime.

```
logic cor_arr [];
integer mem_code [];
```

The storage for the dynamic array does not exist until it is created at runtime. The function *new* can be used to allocate storage for a dynamic array during runtime.

```
mem_code = new[50];
  // Allocates 50 elements to the array.
```

By default, the elements in a dynamic array are initialized to the default value of the type of array. However, another array can be used to initialize a dynamic array by providing it as an argument to the *new* function.

```
integer init_arr[19:0];
. . .
mem_code = new[50](init_arr);    // Initialize first 20
  // elements with values from init_arr. Use the type
  // default value for remaining elements.
```

Another option for the initial value argument is to use another dynamic array of the same type, but not necessarily of the same size. In such a case, the values from the argument are copied as the initial values in the target.

```
mem_code = new[100](mem_code);
```

The dynamic array code size is increased to 100 elements and the initial values of first 50 elements are preserved.

A dynamic memory can be of any type and can have any number of dimensions.

```
bit [3:0] crc [];        // Dynamic array of 4-bit vectors.
integer hamm_addr [];        // Dynamic array of integers.

hamm_addr = new[120];                // Creates a 120-element
                 // array initialized to their default value.

int rfx [] []; // Two-dimensional dynamic array.

t_boolean flg [] = new[50]; // Function new can be called
  // in the declaration of the dynamic array also.
```

The method *size* returns the current size of the dynamic array and returns 0 if the array is not yet created.

```
j = mem_code.size;              // Returns 100.
```

The method *delete* deletes the array - it has 0 elements after the statement is executed.

```
mem_code.delete;
```

2.8 Associative Arrays

An *associative array* is like a lookup table. The index type is used as a lookup key. The array index can be of any arbitrary type. Here is a variable declared as an associative array.

```
typedef logic [7:0] t_data;
var t_data sym_tbl [int];
```

The associative array is *sym_tbl*. The type of the array element is *t_data*, and the index type is *int*. Associative arrays are useful when the arrays are sparse and there is no need to store all redundant values. Also an associative array does not have any storage allocated until the array is used.

Here are some more examples.

```
typedef enum {MON, TUE, WED, THU, FRI} t_weekday;
bit [3:0] lookup [t_weekday];
  // Associative array of 4-bit vectors, index is
  // an enumeration type.

logic [7:0] ia_matrix [*];
  // An associative array of 8-bit logic values.
  // Index type is unspecified; in this case, the array
  // can be indexed by an integral expression of
  // arbitrary size.

int blk_config [string];
string dictionary [string];

typedef bit signed [4:1] t_slice;
int buffer [t_slice];  // Index is a 4-bit signed value.
```

Storage is created as and when required. The first time an element is written to, it is created. The array maintains all elements that have been assigned values based on their index type.

```
lookup[MON] = 4'hF;
ia_matrix[52] = 8'b00110011;
blk_config["bond"] = 7007;

sym_tbl[2] = sym_tbl[6] + 1;
```

Associative arrays are treated as unpacked arrays; so they can be copied and compared, but only elements can be used in expressions. In addition, an associative array can be assigned only to itself or to any other associative array of a compatible type.

An associative array can be initialized using array literals with named association.

```
int blk_config [string] = '{default:12};
string names [string] =
  '{"First":"James", "Last":"Bond", "Middle":"007"};
```

The **default** keyword does not cause any new elements to be created. However when a non-existent array element is accessed, the default value is returned.

```
string emp_id [int] =
  '{20:"Bob", 10:"Paul", default:"Dummy"};
```

2.8.1 Built-in Methods

Here is a list of built-in methods provided to operate on associative arrays.

- *assoc_array*.**num** : returns number of elements.
- *assoc_array*.**delete** (*index*) : removes the specified element; if no index is specified, then all elements of the array are deleted.
- *assoc_array*.**exists** (*index*) : returns 1 if element exists, else 0.
- *assoc_array*.**first** (*index_variable*) : assigns the value of the first index to *index_variable*; returns 0 if array is empty, 1 otherwise.
- *assoc_array*.**last** (*index_variable*) : assigns the value of the last index to *index_variable*; returns 0 if array is empty, 1 otherwise.
- *assoc_array*.**next** (*index_variable*) : finds the next index after the index specified in the *index_variable* and updates the *index_variable* with the new value; returns 1 if a next element is found, else 0 is returned and *index_variable* is not changed.
- *assoc_array*.**prev** (*index_variable*) : finds the index prior to the index specified in the *index_variable* and updates the *index_variable* with the new value; returns 1 if a previous element is found, else 0 is returned and *index_variable* is not changed.

Here are some examples of using these methods.

```
lookup[MON] = 4'hF;
lookup[THU] = 4'h3;

lookup.num      // is 2.
```

```
lookup.delete(THU); // Removes element with index THU.
lookup.delete;      // Deletes all elements from array.

lookup.exists(WED)  // Returns a 0 as there is no
                    // element with this index.

blk_config("cpu") = 21;
blk_config("dma") = 15;
blk_config("wdog") = 7;
string dstr;

blk_config.first(dstr)    // Returns a 1 as array is not
  // empty and dstr gets the value "cpu", which was the
  // first index assigned in the array.

blk_config.last(dstr)    // Returns a 1 as array is not
  // empty and dstr gets the value "wdog", which was the
  // last index that was assigned.

dstr = "dma";
blk_config.next(dstr) // Returns a 1 since the next
  // entry exists and dstr gets the index "wdog".

dstr = "cpu";
blk_config.prev(dstr)   // Returns a 0 as there is no
  // previous element. dstr remains unchanged.
```

An associative array with a wildcard index cannot be used with the *first*, *last*, *next* and *prev* methods. Here is an example of reading and writing an associative array.

```
module cache_memory
  ( input logic clk, wr,
    input logic [7:0] wr_data,
    input logic [4:0] addr,
    output logic [7:0] rd_data
  );

  int cache[*];              // Associative array.
```

```
// Write to cache:
always @(posedge clk)
  if (wr)
    cache[addr] = wr_data;

// Read from cache:
always @(posedge clk)
  if (cache.exists(addr) && !wr)
    rd_data = cache[addr];
endmodule
```

2.9 Queues

A *queue* is a variable size list of ordered elements that are all of the same type. The type is specified in the queue declaration. Here is an example of a queue declaration.

```
byte q_a [$];
```

q_a is a queue that stores values of type *byte*. A queue can represent a LILO (last-in last-out), FIFO (first-in first-out), LIFO (last-in first-out) or other types of queues. Here are some more examples.

```
int q_pdata [$];              // Queue of int values.
bit [7:0] q_b [$:64];         // 64 is the max size of queue.
```

A queue is like a one-dimensional array that can grow and shrink dynamically. Thus queues can be used with indexing, slicing, concatenation and equality operators.

Elements can be added or deleted from a queue either from the beginning of a queue or at the end of a queue. Elements in a queue are indexed with the first element having index 0 and the last one having index $. A queue can be initialized using an array literal or using an unpacked array concatenation. Here are some examples of operations on queues.

```
// Declare two queues that hold integer values:
integer q_send [$], q_rec [$];
```

```
// Declare a queue and initialize it with three values
// using an array literal:
int q_c [$] = '{3, 2, 7};

// Declare a queue and initialize using an
// unpacked array concatenation:
string jtag_code [$] = {"TM001", "GT792", "HP119"};

// Add first element to queue:
q_send[0] = 6;
// Add at end:
q_send = {q_send, 2};

// Copy a queue:
q_rec = q_send;
// Delete all elements in a queue:
q_rec = {};
// Delete first element in queue:
q_send = q_send[1:$];

// Access first and last element of queue:
temp = q_send[0] + q_send[$];
// Insert element elem at position pos:
q_rec = {q_rec[0:pos-1], elem, q_rec[pos:$]};
```

The following methods can operate on queues.

- *queue*.**size** : returns number of elements in queue.
- *queue*.**insert** (*i*, *e*) : inserts element *e* at position *i*; equivalent to:
  ```
  queue = {queue[0:i-1], e, queue[i:$]};
  ```
- *queue*.**delete** (*i*) : deletes element at index *i*; equivalent to:
  ```
  queue = {queue[0:i-1], queue[i+1:$]};
  ```
- *e* = *queue*.**pop_front** () : gets element in front and removes it from queue; equivalent to:
  ```
  e = queue[0]; queue = queue[1:$];
  ```
- *e* = *queue*.**pop_back** () : gets element from back and removes it from queue; equivalent to:
  ```
  e = queue[$]; queue = queue[0:$-1];
  ```

- *queue*.**push_front** (*e*) : pushes element in front of queue; equivalent to:
```
queue = {e, queue};
```
- *queue*.**push_back** (*e*) : pushes element at end of queue; equivalent to:
```
queue = {queue, e};
```

2.9.1 Additional Methods for Arrays and Queues

Here are the *locator methods* that can be used to operate on both arrays (unpacked) and queues. Their format is:

```
queue_or_array . methodname [ with ( expression )]
```

All of these methods return a queue. Methods that return an index return a queue of *int*; for an associative array, the type of queue returned is the same as the index type of the associative array. Non-index methods return a queue of the same type as the array or queue.

The *with* clause is required for the following methods.

```
qa.find(e) with (e > 20 && e < 100)          // Returns
      // all elements satisfying the expression.
qa.find_index(e) with (e == 0 || e == 4)     // Returns
      // indices of all elements matching expression.
qa.find_first(e) with (e > 2) // Returns the first
      // element that matches the expression.
qa.find_first_index(e) with (e == 2) // Returns index
      // of the first element matching the expression.
qa.find_last(e) with (e < 20 && e > 10) // Returns the
      // last element that matches the expression.
qa.find_last_index with (item != 5) // Returns the index
      // of the last element matching the expression.
```

The *with* clause is optional in the following methods.

```
qa.min with (item > 15)             // Returns smallest
                        // element satisfying the expression.
qa.max                             // Find largest element.
qa.unique(e) with (e != 32)        // Returns all elements
                                   // with unique values.
```

```
qa.unique_index          // Returns indices of all
                         // elements with unique values.
```

In all the above methods, an argument, if specified, can be used to form the *with* expression. For example, *e* is used as an argument in many of the above examples and then *e* is used in the *with* expression. If such an argument is not specified, such as in the *find_last_index*() and *min*() methods, a default argument called *item* can be used in the *with* expression. Similarly, a method called *index* can be used with an item; this method returns the index value of the element and can be used in the *with* expression, for example as *e.index*, *item.index*.

The following *ordering methods* are supported for queues and arrays.

- *qa*.**reverse** : reverses the vector; *with* clause is not allowed.
- *qa*.**sort** : sorts the unpacked array in ascending order; optional *with* clause.
- *qa*.**rsort** : sorts the array in descending order; optional *with* clause.
- *qa*.**shuffle** : randomly orders the elements in array; *with* clause is not allowed.

The following *array reduction methods* can be used on any unpacked array to generate a single value which is the same type as the array element type. An optional *with* clause can be specified.

- *qa*.**sum** : returns sum of elements.
- *qa*.**product** : product of all elements.
- *qa*.**and with** (*expr*) : bitwise-and of elements.
- *qa*.**or with** (*expr*) : bitwise-or of elements.
- *qa*.**xor with** (*expr*) : bitwise-xor of elements.
- *qa*.**element_index** : returns index value of element.

2.9.2 An Example

Here is an example of a simple FIFO using a queue. The width and depth of the FIFO are controlled using parameters. The queue methods are used to post and pop data in and out of the queue.

```
module FIFO
  #( parameter int DEPTH = 256,
     parameter int WIDTH = 16
  )( input logic [WIDTH-1:0] idata,
     input logic clk, rstb, wenb, renb,
     output logic full, empty,
     output logic [WIDTH-1:0] odata
   );

  logic [WIDTH-1:0] mem [$:DEPTH];

  // FIFO write:
  always @(posedge clk or negedge rstb)
    if (!rstb)
      mem = '{};
    else if (!wenb && mem.size() < DEPTH)
      mem.push_back(idata);

  // FIFO read:
  always @(posedge clk)
    if (!renb && mem.size > 0)
      odata <= mem.pop_front();

  assign empty = (mem.size() == 0) ? 'b1 : 'b0;
  assign full = (mem.size() == DEPTH) ? 'b1 : 'b0;
endmodule
```

2.10 Strings

The *string* data type stores string values. Variables of type *string* are dynamic in their length.

```
string my_name;   // Variable my_name is of type string.
         // It can hold an arbitrary number of characters.

string his_name = "bond";        // Initializes a string.

// To specify an empty string:
my_name = "";                    // It is of zero length.
```

A single character of a string is of type *byte* and indices are numbered from 0 to (*N* - 1). So *his_name*[0] is 'b' and *his_name*[3] is 'd'. Characters in a string can be accessed using their indices.

```
byte tb = my_name[2];
```

To convert integer and bit-vectors to a *string* type, use a type cast.

```
string str_bit = string'(10'b11_0001_1100);
  // Padded with 0's and made into multiple of 8.

string str_int = string'(52);
  // Stores the bit pattern of 52 as a string.
```

Here are examples of string operations.

```
str_int == str_bit        // Compare equality of strings.

str_int != str_bit      // Compare inequality of strings.

str_int > str_bit
  // <, <=, >, >= compares using lexicographical
  // ordering of the characters in the string.

{str_int, str_bit}        // Concatenation.

{num_rep{str_int}}
  // Replication; num_rep can be a variable.

{{3{str_int}}, str_bit}
  // Concatenation and replication.

str_int[i]          // Index; returns a byte.
```

2.10.1 String Methods

A number of string methods are available.

```
function int len();
  // str.len() returns length of string.
```

```
task putc (int i, byte c);
  // str.putc(i, c) replaces ith character with c.

function byte getc (int i);
  // str.getc(i) returns the ith character in string.

function string toupper();
  // str.toupper() : all characters are converted
  // to upper-case.

function string tolower();
  // str.tolower() : all characters are converted
  // to lowercase.

function int compare (string s);
  // str1.compare(str2) : compares str1 to str2.

function int icompare (string s);
  // str1.icompare(str2) : case-insensitive compare of
  // two strings.

function string substr (int i, int j);
  // str.substr(i, j) returns a new string from ith
  // to jth position.

function integer atoi();
  // str.atoi() generates an integer representation of
  // the string; "123" becomes 123.

function integer atohex();
  // str.atohex() generates a hex representation of
  // the string.

function integer atooct();
  // str.atooct()generates an octal representation of
  // the string.

function integer atobin();
  // str.atobin() generates a binary representation of
  // the string.
```

```
function real atoreal();
  // str.atoreal() generates a real representation of
  // the string; "1.23" becomes 1.23.

task itoa (integer i);
  // str.itoa(i) : reverse of atoi method.

task hextoa (integer i);
  // str.hextoa(i) : reverse of atohex.

task octtoa (integer i);
  //str.octtoa(i) : reverse of atooct.

task bintoa (integer i);
  // str.bintoa(i) : reverse of atobin.

task realtoa (real r);
  // str.realtoa(i) : reverse of atoreal.
```

2.10.2 An Example

Here is an example of a function that checks if a string is contained as a substring in another string.

```
// Returns 1 if s2 is a substring of s1.
function bit is_substring (string s1, s2);
  int len1, len2;

  len1 = str1.len();
  len2 = str2.len();

  if (len2 > len1)
    return 1'b0;

  for (int i = 0; i < len1-len2+1; i++)
    if (s1.substr(i, i+len2-1) == s2)
      return 1'b1;
endfunction
```

2.11 Event Data Type

A variable can be declared to be of an *event* type. Such an event variable can be waited upon or explicitly triggered.

```
event avail;          // avail is a variable of event type.
event e1, e2;         // These are also event variables.

always @(avail)       // Wait for an event.
   . . .

@(avail);            // Wait for an event.

// Events are triggered using the -> operator:
-> avail;            // Create an event on avail.
```

An event variable can be assigned to another event variable. Such an assignment causes both events to be aliases of each other. Events that occur on one variable are visible on the other variable and vice versa. Note that only subsequent event controls after the assignment are affected.

```
e1 = e2;
  // Events on e1 appear on e2 and events on e2 appear on
  // e1 as well. Events are merged due to the assignment.
```

An event can be assigned the value **null**. This ensures that no event can occur on the variable.

```
avail = null;
```

2.12 Time Units

A time unit can be specified as part of a time value.

```
assign #5ns clock = ~clock;
#2.56ps;
// No space between value and unit.

#1ns init = clr;
empty = #2ns init;
```

The following units can be specified:

```
s, ms, us, ns, ps, fs
```

In addition, the language allows for a time unit and time precision to be explicitly specified within a module. This is done using the time unit and time precision declarations.

```
module test;
  timeunit 1ns;
  timeprecision 100ps;
  . . .
```

If present, the time unit and time precision declarations must be the first statements in the module, that is, right after the port list but before any other declarations or statements.

Time unit and time precision declarations can also be specified as part of the compilation-unit scope (outside of a module declaration) and must come before any other declaration. Here is another example.

```
// Top of file.
timeunit 100ps;
timeprecision 10fs;
. . .
```

Given that there are many mechanisms to specify a time unit, the following search order is used:

- the unit as part of the value,
- the unit specified in module or interface,
- the unit specified in a parent module,
- use **`timescale** when module is compiled,
- else use the time unit defined in the compilation-unit scope,
- else use the simulation default time unit (simulator-specific).

The explicit time unit and time precision declarations removes the file order dependency problem that occurs when using the equivalent compiler directives.

2.13 Signed and Unsigned

The keywords **signed** and **unsigned** can be used to override the default definition of types.

```
reg [7:0] part;    // By default, it is an unsigned type.
logic signed [3:0] cnt;         // This is a signed type.
```

The new types in SystemVerilog such as *byte*, *shortint*, *int* and *longint* are signed by default. However, the default behavior can be changed by using the **unsigned** keyword.

```
int s_int;                    // Signed 32-bit by default.
int unsigned u_int;           // Unsigned 32-bit.

typedef bit signed [7:0] t_signed_bv;
typedef int unsigned t_unsigned_int;
byte unsigned ubyte;
```

2.14 Compilation Directive - `define

SystemVerilog allows the text substitution to include special characters such as " (double-quote). This is accomplished by escaping the " by the ` (back-tick) character.

```
`define my_print(arg) $display (`" arg`", pval);

`my_print(rgb);
```

generates:

```
$display ("rgb", pval);
```

Two consecutive `` (back-ticks) can be used to detect a name without introducing any additional white space. This allows for two or more names to be concatenated to each other.

```
`define statename(arg) bit for``arg;

`statename(5)
```

will create:

```
bit for5;
```

Structure, union and class types are the topics of the next chapter.

❑

Chapter 3

Composite Types

This chapter describes the composite types such as structures, unions and classes.

3.1 Structures

A collection of elements of different types can be represented as a single data type called a *structure*. Structures help organize data by helping to group related data, even of different types, into one unit. An example of such a type is:

```
struct {
  bit sign;
  bit [2:0] ms_digit;
  bit [2:0] ls_digit;
} two_digit;
```

The variable *two_digit* is of a structure type. The structure consists of three elements, *sign*, *ms_digit* and *ls_digit*. Here is another example.

```
struct {
  int x;
  int y;
} coordinate;
```

The above declaration defines a variable *coordinate* to be of a structure type that has two variables *x* and *y*. The elements that comprise the structure are called *members*.

Individual members of a structure can be accessed using the dot (.) operator, which is of the form:

```
structure_name . member_name
```

Here are examples of member accesses.

```
perimeter = 2 * (coordinate.x + coordinate.y);

two_digit.sign = 0;
sum = two_digit.ls_digit + two_digit.ms_digit * 1000;
```

Each structure member can be accessed individually and used in expressions and assignments. A structure literal can be used to assign a constant value to a structure.

```
two_digit = '{0, 3, 8};

// is equivalent to:

two_digit.sign = 0;
two_digit.ms_digit = 3;
two_digit.ls_digit = 8;
```

Notice that in the declaration of the variable *two_digit*, there was no explicit type name. Such a declaration is called an *anonymous structure* declaration. An *explicit structure* type can be declared using the typedef declaration. This type can then be used to declare a variable.

```
typedef struct {
  int id_num;
  string last_name;
  string first_name;
} t_personal;

t_personal keep_id;
```

The structure type is *t_personal*. It has three members and *keep_id* is a variable of this type. Here are some more examples of structure types.

```
typedef struct {
  int i;
  real j;
} t_complex;                              // Structure type.

typedef struct {
  real float0, float1;
  int int0, int1;
} t_reg_bank;                             // Structure type.

typedef struct {
  logic [3:0] opcode;
  logic [7:0] opd_a;
  logic [7:0] opd_b;
} t_command;

t_command inst_reg;          // Variable of structure type.

// Variables of structure types:
t_complex xa, xb, xc;
t_reg_bank reg_a, reg_b;

// Net of structure type:
wire t_command inst_bus;
```

A variable or a net of a structure type can be assigned either in a procedural assignment or in a continuous assignment, respectively.

```
always @(negedge clk)
  begin
    xa = xc;        // Structure can be read and assigned.
    xb = some_function(xc);      // Can be an argument.
  end

assign inst_bus = '{4'hA, 8'hCD, 8'h3A};
```

An entire structure can be assigned using a single assignment or individual members of a structure can be assigned individually.

```
xa.i = 16;
xc.j = 2.3;
xb.i = xa.i * 2;
```

Structures can be nested. That is, a member of a structure can be of another structure type.

```
typedef struct {
  int x;
  int y;
} t_point;

struct {
  t_point pt1;
  t_point pt2;
} rect;
```

Variable *rect* has two members, each member is of another structure type. Members of this variable can be accessed using the same notation.

```
rect.pt1.x
rect.pt2
rect.pt2.y
```

A structure can be assigned to other structures of the same type. In addition, they can be passed to functions, tasks and as module ports.

```
typedef struct {
  int red, green, blue;
} t_rgb;
```

```
const t_rgb BLUE_VAL = '{0, 0, 255};
  // BLUE_VAL is a constant of a structure type with
  // the specified values for its members.

t_rgb frame [15:0][31:0];
  // frame is an array of structures.
frame[2][5] = BLUE_VAL;          // Assign to a structure.

t_rgb pix_in;
assign found = (pix_in == BLUE_VAL);
  // Structure can be compared.

module compress (output t_rgb pix_out, . . .);
  // Module port can be a structure type.
  . . .
```

Each member of a structure type can be assigned a default value (a constant expression) by using an initial assignment.

```
typedef struct {
  bit [3:0] opcode = 4'b0010;
  bit [7:0] opd_a = 8'hFF;
  bit [7:0] opd_b = 8'h0F;
  bit [7:0] result;
} t_instruction;                 // Structure type.
```

An initial value can also be assigned during the declaration of the variable.

```
t_instruction ir_cpu = '{4'h8, 8'hFF, 8'h2c, 8'h27};
```

Such a variable initialization overrides the initial value of a member specified in the structure type declaration, if any. One exception to the initial value of a member in a structure is a net declaration such as in the following example.

```
typedef struct {
  logic [7:0] src_addr = 8'h01;
  logic [7:0] dest_addr = 8'h56;
} t_packet;

wire t_packet ird;
```

In this case, the initial values are ignored for the object *ird*. Note that a net that is of a structure type must have elements of 4-state type.

A member of a structure could be a constant as well. We'll see later how to declare such constants.

3.1.1 Structure Literals

Here are more examples of structure literals. A structure literal has a similar form as an array literal. The type of literal is determined from the context in which it appears.

```
t_complex sync_str;
sync_str = '{0, 0.0};
  // Literal is same type as sync_str.

struct {
  t_complex a, b, c;
} pdu_str;
pdu_str = '{'{6, 2.3}, {2{'{25, 9.4}}}}; // A structure
  // with three members, each member in turn a structure.
```

The values in a structure literal can be listed explicitly by member name using named association.

```
two_digit = '{ls_digit:12, sign:1, ms_digit:22};
```

In addition, the keyword **default** can be used to initialize all members of a structure to a specific value.

```
'{default:4}        // Set all members of structure to 4.

'{a:1, b:2, c:3, default:0}
  // Member a has value 1, member b has 2, member c has
  // value 3 and the remaining elements are 0.
```

Of course, the values must be compatible with the member type.

If the member types are different, then a default for each type can be explicitly specified in the structure literal.

```
'{int:1, real:1.0}

'{real:1.0, default:0}
  // All real members are set to 1.0, others are set to 0.
```

Type and member names can be mixed in a structure literal, if needed.

```
'{real:1.0, default:10, f0:3.14}
```

The default value has the lowest precedence followed by type-specific defined values that can be overridden by member explicit values.

The replication operator ({{}}) can also be used.

```
'{3{1}}                    // is same as '{1, 1, 1}.
```

3.1.2 Assignment Patterns

An *assignment pattern* is very similar to a structure literal except that in addition to constant literals, general expressions are also allowed for members. Such assignment patterns can be used to assign to structures as it specifies a correspondence between patterns and structure members. Here are some more examples.

```
// Using named association:
sa = '{default:PI};
sb = '{31:a+b, 21:a-b, 15:a*b, default:c};
sc = '{a:2.0, b:3};

// Positional association:
sd = '{flag1, 2, 4, flag5};
se = '{1, pages-2};
sf = '{2{fq_cnt%5}};
sg = '{2{'{3{data_rd0}}}};
```

Assignment patterns are also allowed for arrays. Here are some such examples.

```
logic [31:0] rd_latch, jtag_addr;
logic [3:0] data_cs;
logic sgrant, sreq, pon;
```

```
parameter logic INVALID = 1'bz;

// Using named association:
rd_latch = '{default:INVALID};
rd_latch = '{21:sgrant ^ sreq, 10:sgrant & sreq,
            2:sgrant | sreq, default:pon};

// Positional association:
data_cs = '{req0, 1'b0, req1, req5};
rd_latch = '{31{^jtag_addr}};
jtag_addr = '{8{data_cs}};
```

3.1.3 Packed and Unpacked Structures

In an unpacked structure, which is the default, members of a structure are treated as individual variables and constants. The storage of such members of a structure is not defined by the language.

In a packed structure, the keyword **packed** is used, all members of a structure are stored in a set of contiguous bits in the specified order. Such members can thus be represented as bit-select or part-select of a vector. And since such a structure can be represented in a vector form, vector operations can be performed on it.

```
struct packed {
  bit valid;
  bit [7:0] tag;
  bit [15:0] addr;
} entry;

itag = entry.tag;
iaddr = entry.addr;
ivalid = entry.valid;

// A packed structure represents an
// equivalent packed array:
reg [24:0] entry_array;
`define VALID 24
`define TAG 23:16
`define ADDR 15:0
```

```
itag = entry_array['TAG];
iaddr = entry_array['ADDR];
ivalid = entry_array['VALID];
```

One or more bits of a packed structure can be accessed as if they were a packed array using index ranging from (N - 1) to 0. Thus:

```
entry[23:16]      // is tag.
```

A packed structure provides a mechanism for subdividing a vector into subfields that can conveniently be accessed as members.

A packed structure and an equivalent unpacked structure example is shown in Figure 3-1. In a packed structure, the entire structure is packed into a single vector.

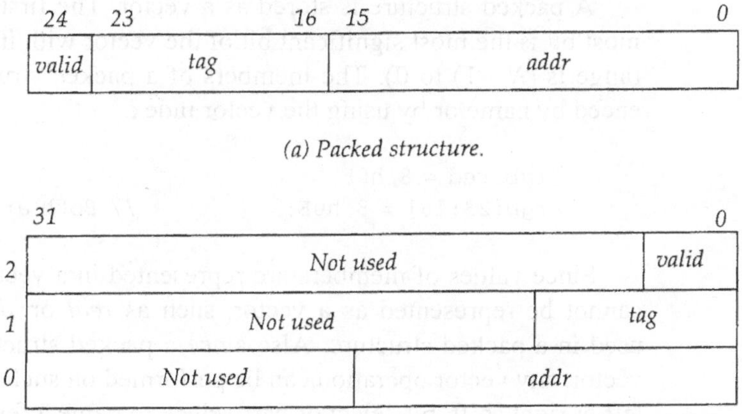

(a) Packed structure.

(b) Unpacked structure.

Figure 3-1 Packed and unpacked structures.

A packed structure may contain members of other packed structure or packed array types. However, unpacked arrays cannot be members of a packed structure.

```
typedef struct packed {
  bit [7:0] red, green, blue;
} t_rgb;
```

```
t_rgb rgb;

// Packed array:
bit [23:0] pixel;
  // pixel and rgb are effectively the same size object.

module alu (input t_rgb rgb);
  . . . // Packed structures can be passed into a module.

pixel = rgb;                    // 24-bit value copied.
pixel = {rgb.red, rgb.green, rgb.blue};
  // Both above assignments are effectively the same.

alu u_alu (rgb);
  // Can pass packed structures through ports.
```

A packed structure is stored as a vector. The first member with leftmost bit is the most significant bit of the vector with index (*N* - 1) (vector range is (*N* - 1) to 0). The members of a packed structure can be referenced by name or by using the vector index.

```
rgb.red = 8'h0E;
rgb[23:16] = 8'h0E;             // Both are equivalent.
```

Since values of members are represented in a vector form, types that cannot be represented as a vector, such as *real* or *shortreal*, cannot be used in a packed structure. Also since a packed structure behaves like a vector, any vector operation can be performed on such a structure, such as left or right shift, bit-select or part-select, to name a few.

```
rgb >> 6;
rgb[8:3] = rgb[21:16];
```

Also arithmetic and logical operations can be carried out upon such structures by treating them as vectors. Here is another example.

```
typedef enum {ADD, SUB, MUL, DIV} t_opcode;
typedef struct packed {
  t_opcode opcode;
  logic [7:0] opd1, opd2, result;
} t_ir;
```

```
t_ir ir_a, ir_b;
logic [25:0] ir_arr;

ir_a = ir_b;             // Can assign complete structure.
ir_arr <= ir_a;          // Can assign to a vector.

// Can access members or write to members of a structure:
ir_a.opcode <= ADD;

ir_b[7:0] = ir_b.opd1 + ir_b.opd2;
  // Same as writing to result member.
```

A packed structure can be assigned an aggregate literal similar to an unpacked structure.

```
'{a, b, c}
```

A packed structure can be declared as a signed type; by default, it is unsigned. An unpacked array cannot have a signedness property. Since a packed structure is a vector, it can be declared as signed or unsigned and compared.

```
typedef struct packed signed {
  logic [3:0] x;
  logic [3:0] y;
} t_coord;

t_coord plot_a, plot_b;

plot_a + 1
plot_a - plot_b
```

A signed structure does not imply that its members are also signed. The signedness of its members is decided by each of its member declaration.

If all member types of a structure are 2-state, the structure is treated as a 2-state type, else it is treated as 4-state type.

3.2 Unions

A union type is similar to a structure type, except that there is storage allocated for only one member, and all members of a union type share the same storage. This allows for manipulating various types of data in a single area of storage. The one member is stored with different interpretations. Each such interpretation may be of a different type. An example of a union is:

```
union {
  int i;
  int unsigned u;
} p_data;
```

Variable *p_data* is declared to be of an *anonymous union* type. It can hold values of type *int* or unsigned *int*. Note that there is only one storage with data. To store an *int* value, simply assign it to *p_data*.

```
p_data.i = 29;
```

and to read:

```
a = p_data.i;
```

It is important that a value be read back from the union in the same type that it was written to, else it is possible to get indeterminate results.

```
p_data.i = -17;

a2 = p_data.u;
  // May show different values on different simulators.
```

Here is an example of *typed union* (union defined as a typedef).

```
typedef union {
  int int_val;
  bit [7:0] vec_val;
} t_val;

t_val nibble_msb, nibble_lsb;
```

Type *t_val* is a union type and has two members. However, storage is allocated for the largest type and both members share the same storage area. See Figure 3-2.

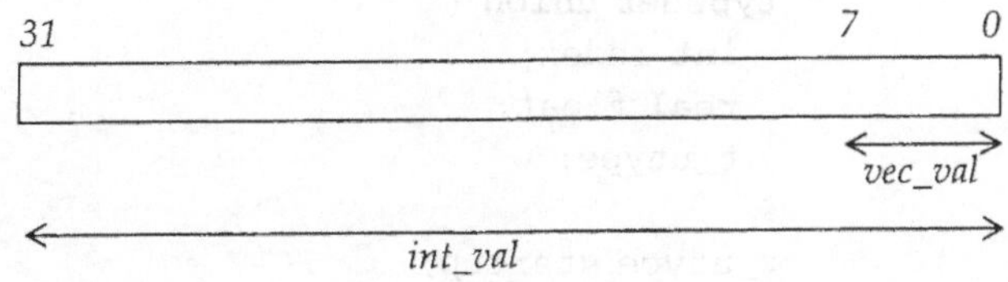

Figure 3-2 Storage is for only one member in a union.

Any member can be assigned a value consistent with its type; it goes into the same storage area and any member can be read; it is read from the same storage area. Members of a union can be accessed similar to structure member access.

```
union_variable . member_name
```

Here are examples of union members read and write.

```
nibble_msb.int_val = 23;
a = nibble_msb.vec_val[2] & nibble_msb.vec_val[0];
nibble_msb.int_val = 2 + nibble_msb.vec_val[7:3];
```

Here is another example of a typed union.

```
typedef union {       // Typed union.
  int i;
  int unsigned u;
} t_memdata;           // t_memdata is a union type.

t_memdata mac, mp;
  // mac, mp are variables of type t_memdata.
t_memdata fq_page [1:30];   // Unpacked array of unions.

t = mac.u;            // Read value of member.
mp.u = 55;            // Write to member; note that both
                   // members represent the same storage space.
```

The same operations that are permissible for structures are also allowed for unions, including passing as arguments in a function, task or a port. A union can contain fixed sized packed arrays.

```
typedef union {
  int index;
  real float;
} t_utype;

t_utype startup;

initial
  begin
    startup.index = 27;         // Assign integer value.
    $display ("index=%d", startup.index);
    startup.float = 3.14;       // Assign a real value.
    $display ("float=%f", startup.float);
  end
```

Note that a structure is different from a union in that a structure represents multiple member types while a union represents only one storage but for multiple types.

3.2.1 Packed Union

A packed union contains members that are packed structures, packed arrays or integer data types, which are all of the same size.

```
typedef union packed {
  bit [7:0] opcode;
  bit [7:0] a_reg;
} t_up;

t_up ir_bk;
```

Type *t_up* is a packed union type that contains only packed arrays.

In a packed union, the number of bits of each union member must be the same. A packed union cannot contain real, shortreal, unpacked structures, unpacked unions and unpacked arrays. All members must be of the same size. Here is another example, the storage area of which is shown in Figure 3-3.

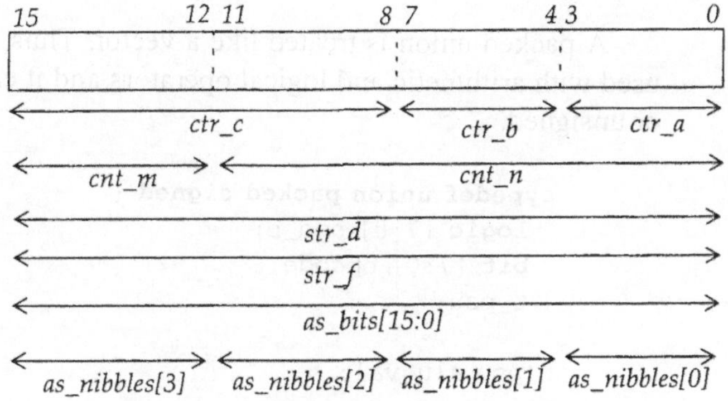

Figure 3-3 Packed union of structures.

```
typedef struct packed {
  logic [3:0] ctr_a;
  logic [3:0] ctr_b;
  logic [7:0] ctr_c;
} t_ctr;

typedef struct packed {
  logic [11:0] cnt_n;
  logic [3:0] cnt_m;
} t_cnt;

typedef union packed {
  t_ctr str_d;
  t_cnt str_f;
  bit [15:0] as_bits;
  bit [3:0][3:0] as_nibbles;
} t_rtc;

t_rtc rtc;

rtc.str_d.ctr_a = 3;
rtc.as_bits[15:12] = 3;
rtc.as_nibbles[3] = 3;
// All three assignments above are equivalent.
```

A packed union concatenates multiple layouts for accessing the same data. Thus, a packed union is represented by a fixed number of bits and data written in one type can be read back in another type without any type conflicts.

A packed union is treated like a vector. Thus, a packed union can be used with arithmetic and logical operators and it can be marked as signed or unsigned.

```
typedef union packed signed {
  logic [7:0] opd_b;
  bit [7:0] opcode;
} t_psu;

t_psu alu_val;
```

The leftmost bit of the equivalent vector is assumed to be the most significant bit and the vector range is (N - 1) to 0. Elements of a packed union can be selected just like vectors.

```
ir_b[0] = ir_b[2] & ir_b[3] | ir_b[5];
```

If a packed union contains all 2-state values, then the union is a 2-state type, else it is 4-state. Type *t_up* is a 2-state packed union since it contains only 2-state values. Type *t_psu* is a 4-state type.

An unpacked union can contain any type including real, unpacked structures and unpacked arrays.

3.2.2 Tagged Union

A *tagged union* is a type-checked union. An untagged union can be updated using one member and read as the value of another member, which may be problematic in some cases. A tagged union stores the member value plus a tag - the tag (using a number of bits) represents the current member name. The tag and value can only be updated together, thus ensuring that any update or read is consistent with the current tag value.

Here is an example of a tagged union.

```
typedef union tagged {
  int int_val;
  byte vec_val [3:0];
} t_ut;

t_ut lctr, mctr;
```

Variables *lctr* and *mctr* are of a tagged union type. An additional bit is used in storage to keep track of which member was assigned, say 0 for *int_val* and 1 for *vec_val*.

```
mctr = tagged int_val 56;
```

The right hand side is called a *tagged union expression*. It is of the form:

```
tagged member_name expression
```

The value 56 is stored in the member *int_val* with a tag value of 0.

A member of a tagged union can be read and assigned using the dot notation. However, strong type checking is done at runtime to ensure that the read and write are consistent with the current tag value. A runtime error occurs if the strong type checking fails.

3.3 Classes

A class is a composite type, similar to a structure, that not only includes members of different types but also the functions and tasks that can operate on these members. The members are referred to as *class properties* and the functions and tasks are referred to as *class methods*.

```
class t_queue;
  bit [3:0] qbuf [128];
  int head;
  int tail;

  task push (bit [3:0] val); . . . endtask
  function bit [3:0] pop; . . . endfunction
endclass
```

The *t_queue* is a class type. It has three properties and two methods that are allowed to operate on these properties. Here is another example of a class type declaration.

```
class t_intarray;
  int buffer [256];

  function int size; . . . endfunction
  task sort; . . . endtask
  function int min; . . . endfunction
  function int max; . . . endfunction
endclass
```

The type *t_intarray* is a class type that has only one property and has four methods that can operate on it. Here is another example of a class type.

```
class t_memory;
  bit [7:0] mem [0:1023];

  task write (bit [7:0] data, bit [9:0] addr);
    mem[addr] = data;
  endtask
  function bit [7:0] read (bit [9:0] addr);
    return mem[addr];
  endfunction
endclass
```

The class *t_memory* has one property *mem* and two methods, *write* and *read.* Here is another example of a class type declaration.

```
class t_matrix;
  union {
    struct {
      byte a1, a2, a3;
      byte b1, b2, b3;
      byte c1, c2, c3;
    } as_names;
    byte as_bytes [1:3][1:3];
  } bon;
```

```
    function byte get_byte (int row, int col);
      return bon.as_bytes[row][col];
    endfunction
    task set_byte (int row, int col, byte bval);
      bon.as_bytes[row][col] = bval;
    endtask
    function void display();
      $display (this.to_string());
    endfunction
    function string to_string; . . . endfunction
  endclass
```

A class provides a means for encapsulating data and functionality into a single scope.

3.3.1 Class Objects

To use a class, an object is created by instantiating the class and then calling the object's methods.

```
t_intarray req;
  // Declares a pointer to an object of class t_intarray.

t_queue qz;
t_memory mem_a, mem_b;
t_matrix mat_p;

req = new; // Allocates a new object of class t_intarray.
```

The handle (pointer) to the object of class *t_intarray* is in *req*. Uninitialized object handles are set to a default value of **null**. Properties of a class can be accessed using the "." (dot notation).

```
req.buffer[2] = 2;          // Assign to a class property.
elem = req.buffer[100];     // Read from a class property.

num = req.size();           // Calling a class method.
t = mat_p.get_byte(rval, cval);
mat_p.display();
mat_p.set_byte(rval, cval, 'h0B);
```

It is possible to initialize a class variable when it is declared.

```
t_intarray ack = new;
```

The function *new* is called a *class constructor*. Every class has a default *new* constructor that is called if there is no explicit *new* function described in the class type.

The *new* function can have arguments.

```
t_intarray req_a = new (2, 5, 6);
```

In such a case, the function *new* has to be explicitly defined in the class type. Such a function cannot have a return type. Here is an example.

```
class t_int3arr;
  int buffer [1:3];

  function new (int f1=0, f2=0, f3=0);
    buffer[1] = f1;
    buffer[2] = f2;
    buffer[3] = f3;
  endfunction
endclass

t_int3arr ta1, ta2;  // ta1 and ta2 are null by default.
ta1 = new;           // Creates a class object and
                     // ta1 points to it.
ta2 = new (23, 15, 6);
ta2 = ta1;         // Only the pointer is passed. ta2 and
                   // ta1 both point to the same object.

ta2 = new ta1;
  // A new object with same contents as ta1 is created.
```

In the last assignment, there is a minor exception. If any of the property is a pointer, then only the pointer is copied, not the contents of the pointer. This is referred to as a *shallow copy.* To do a full copy, write an explicit method to do this that would recursively traverse down all pointers and create separate copies of such objects.

3.3.2 Static Properties

Consider the following declaration.

```
t_intarray ip, ir;
```

In this case, each object *ip* and *ir* have their own copy of the properties, that is, *ip* and *ir* each have a separate 256 element *buffer* array. It is possible to declare a property to be static. This allows the property to have only one copy and be shared by all objects of the same class type.

Consider the following example.

```
class t_q;
  int head;
  int tail;

  static int que[128];
endclass

t_q tcm, qam;
```

In this case, class variables *tcm* and *qam* each have a copy of all properties, *head* and *tail*, except for property *que* that is shared by both the objects *tcm* and *qam*. That is, there is only one copy of *que* that is visible to both class variables *tcm* and *qam*.

3.3.3 Static Methods

A method in a class can be declared as static. Such a method can only access other static methods and static properties of a class; it cannot access non-static properties. Furthermore, a static method can be called just like any function or task call, without any class instantiation.

```
class t_pipe;
  int ptr;
  static int pipe [128];
```

```
    static function void sort ();
      . . .
      // ok to access pipe but not ptr.
    endfunction
  endclass

  t_pipe strobe_a, strobe_b;
```

The method *sort* has been declared to be static. It can only access the static property of the class, *pipe* in this case. The static method can be called using either of the following mechanisms:

```
strobe_a.sort()     // Using class instantiation.
sort()              // Without a class instantiation.
```

By default, class methods have automatic lifetime for variables declared in the method, that is, they are created and die as and when call from functions or tasks occur. A function can be declared to have static variable lifetime as shown in next example. However, such a function cannot be a class method.

```
// It is illegal for this function to be a class method
// since it has a static variable lifetime:
function static qsort();
  . . .
  // Variables declared in function have static
  // lifetimes, that is, they retain their values
  // through multiple invocations of the function.
endfunction
```

Note the distinction of where the **static** keyword appears. In a *static method*, it is the first keyword. When it is used after the **function** or **task** keyword, it refers to the lifetime of the arguments and variables within the task or function.

3.3.4 Keyword this

The **this** keyword refers to the current instance class. That is, it denotes a predefined object handle that refers to the object that was used to invoke the task or function. This qualifier is useful in methods to uniquely identify a property.

```
class t_hit;
  int hit_cnt;

  function void max ();
    int hit_cnt;
    this.hit_cnt = hit_cnt + 2;
  endfunction
endclass

t_hit hit_class;

hit_class.max()           // this in the function refers
  // to the hit_class pointer for this function call.
```

In the function *max*, **this** refers to the class that called the function, which uniquely identifies the property *hit_cnt* of the class as being assigned a value (and not the variable *hit_cnt* declared within the function).

3.3.5 Inheritance

A class can be created that inherits the members of another class. Such a new class is derived from an existing class and inherits its characteristics. The class that it is being inherited from is called the *base class*. The new class is referred to as a *derived class* and is a more specialized version of the base class.

```
class t_sub_ia extends t_intarray;
  // t_intarray is the base class and
  // t_sub_ia is the derived class.
  int test;

  task uniquify ();
    . . .
  endtask
endclass
```

The class *t_sub_ia* is derived from the class *t_intarray*. It inherits all the properties and methods of the base class *t_intarray*. In addition, it has a new property called *test*, and a new method called *uniquify*. All methods and properties of *t_intarray* are also part of class *t_sub_ia*.

Here is another example.

```
class check;
  int amount;
  bit [3:0] pincode;
endclass

class my_check extends check;
  string acct_name;
endclass

class child_check extends my_check;
  int myspace;
endclass
```

Class *my_check* is derived from class *check*. All characteristics of class *check* are also in class *my_check*. An object of class *my_check* contains the members *acct_name*, *amount* and *pincode*. Class *child_check* is a derived class of another derived class *my_check*.

Given a class, all of its extensions are also referred to as its *subclasses*. All of the classes from which a class is derived are also referred to as its *superclasses*. In the above example, *my_check* and *child_check* are subclasses of the class *check*; classes *check* and *my_check* are superclasses of class *child_check*. A superclass is also referred to as a *parent class*.

A pointer (handle) of a subclass can be assigned to a superclass variable. However, a superclass variable can be assigned to a subclass variable only using a type cast. A method in a subclass can override a method in the superclass.

The **super** keyword can be used within a derived class to refer to members of the base class. This is especially useful if there is a conflict in a property or a method that has the same name in the base class and in the derived class.

```
class t_sub_ib extends t_intarray; // Derived class.
  int buffer [16];

  task sort ();
    . . .
```

```
      super.sort();
        // Refers to the sort task in the base class.
      t = super.buffer[2] + buffer[4];
    endtask;
  endclass
```

When a *new* of a derived class is called, the *new* of its superclass is invoked up the inheritance hierarchy until the base class. Consider the following derived classes. Class *t_sub2_ia* is a derived class of *t_sub_ia* and class *t_sub3_ia* is a derived class of *t_sub2_ia*.

```
  class t_sub2_ia extends t_sub_ia;
    . . .
  endclass

  class t_sub3_ia extends t_sub2_ia;
    . . .
  endclass
```

If the class method *new* for *t_sub3_ia* is invoked, this causes as a first step for it to call the *new* of its superclass *t_sub2_ia* that in turn calls the *new* of its superclass *t_sub_ia* that in turn calls the *new* of the base class *t_intarray.*

In some cases, it may be useful to hide methods and properties from being available outside of a class. A property marked as **local** is visible only within the class and not to its subclasses.

```
  class t_card_list;
    local int count;  // In superclass - not
                      // visible to derived classes.
  endclass
```

In the definition on class *t_memory*, it would be useful to declare the property *mem* as both static and local, static indicating that there is only one copy of the memory for various objects of the same class and local indicating that only the class methods can access the memory. Here is such an example.

```
  class t_memory_a;
    typedef bit [7:0] t_data;
```

```
  typedef bit [9:0] t_addr;

  static local t_data mem [0:1023];

  task write (t_data data, t_addr addr);
    mem[addr] = data;
  endtask
  function t_data read (t_addr addr);
    return mem[addr];
  endfunction
endclass
```

A property or a method marked as **protected** is similar to **local** except that it can be inherited and therefore is visible to its subclasses.

```
class t_card_list;
  protected int count;
endclass
```

This technique of hiding and protecting members is also referred to as *data hiding* and *encapsulation*.

Inheritance provides a means for reusing existing code. A new class can be created by inheritance that extends the functionality of another class, thus allowing reuse of code from the base class.

3.3.6 Constant Properties

A class property that is read-only can be marked as a **const** just like a constant declaration. However in a class, there are two such kinds:

- *Global constant*: Can only be assigned a value in its declaration. These can be declared static, if necessary, if it is the same value for all instances.
- *Instance constant*: It is not assigned a value in its declaration, but is assigned once at runtime, in the class constructor. These cannot be declared as static.

```
class t_card_list;
  const int MAX_CNT = 52;
  // Global constant; cannot be assigned again;
  // could be marked as static.

  const int MAX_DEAL;
    // Instance constant; can only be assigned once at
    // runtime; cannot be static.
endclass
```

3.3.7 Abstract Class

A base class that is not instantiated (can occur if there are only derived classes of this base type) can be marked as an abstract class by using the keyword **virtual**.

```
virtual class t_expand;
  . . .
endclass
```

3.3.8 Virtual Method

An abstract class can have virtual methods (using keyword **virtual**). A virtual method provides a way of specifying the method template, that is, its name and its set of arguments. This allows objects through inheritance to have different behaviors for the same operation. However in the subclass, the virtual method must be overridden by providing a complete method body.

```
// Abstract class:
virtual class t_frame;
  virtual task make_unique (int arg [2:0]);
    . . .
  endtask
endclass

// Subclass:
class t_subframe_q extends t_frame;
  task make_unique (int arg [2:0]);
    . . . // Body here.
```

```
    endtask
  endclass

  // Subclass:
  class t_subframe_p extends t_frame;
    task make_unique (int arg [2:0]);
    . . . // Body here - may have behavior different
          // from that defined in t_subframe_q.
    endtask
    static task reverse; . . . endtask
  endclass
```

The virtual function *make_unique* is implemented differently in each of the subclasses. The base class *t_frame* defines the properties of the class and the methods that are possible, and the derived classes can modify the behavior of these methods.

Virtual functions are used to support polymorphism where multiple classes can be used interchangeably, each with different behaviors.

3.3.9 Scope Resolution Operator

The scope resolution operator (::) can be used to refer to a static property or a static method in a class without instantiating the class.

```
t_pipe::pipe[2]
  // Refers to static property pipe in class t_pipe.

t_subframe_p::reverse
  // Refers to static method reverse in
  // subclass t_subframe_p.

t_memory_a::t_data
  // Type t_data defined in class t_memory_a can be
  // referred outside of the class.
```

The scope resolution operator allows to uniquely identify properties and methods of a particular class, especially where properties and methods can have same names. In addition, this operator is useful in accessing static methods and properties from outside of the class. Also any types or subtypes within a class can be accessed from outside the class using the scope resolution operator.

3.3.10 Method Prototypes

It is possible to declare the complete body of a method outside of a class. In such a case, the class contains the *method prototype* specified using the keyword **extern**.

```
class t_stack;
  bit [1023:0] [15:0] stk;
  int top;

  // Two method prototypes:
  extern function bit is_empty();
  extern task push (bit [15:0] element);
endclass
```

The complete body of the method prototypes appears outside of the class. However, the method name must be qualified by the class name using the scope resolution operator.

```
// Full method declarations (also referred to
// as out-of-block method declarations):
function bit t_stack::is_empty ();
  return (top == 0 ? 1'b1 : 1'b0);
endfunction

task t_stack::push (bit [15:0] element);
  stk[top++] = element;
endtask
```

The full method declarations must be present in the same scope as the class declaration.

3.3.11 Parameterized Class

A parameterized class allows for generic programming, that is, defines a class that can be configured with different parameter values. The normal Verilog HDL syntax is used to describe a parameterized class.

```
typedef bit [3:0] t_4bit;
class t_abus #(int SOC = 1, t_4bit DMA = 'h4);
  . . .
endclass
```

Class *t_abus* is a parameterized class and it has two parameters, *SOC* and *DMA*, with their default values specified. Instances of a parameterized class with specific values for the parameters create *specializations*, that is, versions of the code with the parameters applied.

```
t_abus #(10, 'hA) p1;          // SOC is 10 and DMA is 'hA.
t_abus #(.SOC(2)) p0;          // DMA is 'h4.
typedef t_abus #(.DMA('h3), .SOC(6)) t_3_6_abus;
```

The above declarations create specializations of the parameterized class *t_abus*. The specializations are unique types. Note that a generic class is not a type by itself. Only a specialization - the combination of a generic class and the actual parameter values - comprise a type.

The above showed examples of *value parameters*. One could also define a *type parameter*. Type parameters allows type-independent code to be written such that the class can be used on a wide range of data types.

```
class t_min #(type MY_TYPE = int);
  . . .
  function MY_TYPE compute_min (MY_TYPE a, MY_TYPE b);
    . . .
  endfunction
endclass
```

The parameterized class *t_min* has a function *compute_min*. The function body could be written such that it is independent of the type of parameters to the function. Here are some examples of its specializations.

```
t_min #(bit[1:10]) s2;          // 10-bit vector type.
typedef real t_float;
t_min #(t_float) s3;            // t_float type.
```

A parameterized class supports reusability, and allows for writing of generic code, code that is independent of data type and size.

3.3.12 Forward Declaration

Sometimes it may be necessary to use a class type before it can be declared. In such cases, a forward declaration of the class can be made and later the complete declaration of the class may follow.

A forward declaration is accomplished using the typedef declaration. Here is an example.

```
typedef class t_linked_list;
  // Forward (incomplete) declaration.
. . .
< Can use class t_linked_list >
. . .
class t_linked_list;               // Complete declaration.
  . . .
endclass
```

❑

Chapter 4

Expressions

This chapter describes the extensions to SystemVerilog on operands and operations that can be used in expressions. Operands can be parameters, constants, variables or nets. New operators that are allowed in the language are described. Different kinds of casting supported are described as well.

4.1 Parameters

4.1.1 $ Parameter Value

A parameter can be specified a value of **$**. This represents an unbounded (or unspecified) value.

```
parameter MAX_BITS = $;
```

The **$** value can also be passed as parameter values. For example,

```
module add #(parameter SIZE = 16) . . .
// Parameter definition.
  . . .
endmodule

add #(.SIZE($)). . .
  // Parameter value assignment in module instance.
```

To check if a parameter is unbounded, SystemVerilog provides the system function **$isunbounded**. This function returns a 1 if the value is **$**, else it returns a 0.

4.1.2 Type Parameter Value

A parameter value can be a data type; such a parameter is called a *type parameter* (as opposed to a *value parameter* that accepts a constant expression). Here is an example of its use in a module.

```
module modem #(parameter type ptype = logic, . . .
     // Parameter type defined with a default type.
  ptype mod_req;              // The type can then be
                              // used to declare variables.
  . . .
endmodule
. . .
// Usage of type parameter:
modem #(.ptype(bit), . . .    // Change parameter type
                              // to bit in instantiation.
```

Having such parameters supports type-independent functions, tasks, and modules, thus enhancing reusability.

4.1.3 Port List

The keyword **parameter** is optional in SystemVerilog. One could simply write:

```
module pixel_blk
  #( int BITS = 5, TOT_BITS = BITS * 16,
     type MY_T = int, MY_T MARK = 0
  )
  . . .
```

The module *pixel_blk* has a total of four parameters, *BITS*, *TOT_BITS* and *MARK*, which are value parameters, and *MY_T*, which is a type parameter. Parameter *TOT_BITS* depends on the parameter *BITS*. And parameter *MARK* is of type *MY_T*, a type parameter declared earlier.

A parameter can be defined to depend on parameters declared earlier, as the previous example shows.

4.2 Constants

SystemVerilog provides the capability to declare a constant using the keyword **const**. A *const constant* is similar to a local parameter, except that a const constant is computed during simulation while a local parameter is evaluated at elaboration time.

```
const int TCM = 9;
const DBI = 6.2;        // Error - type must be specified.
const logic [7:0] URD = "000000";
const logic OPTION = ucore.ufss.RMA;
```

While parameters, specify parameters and local parameters get their value at elaboration time, const constants get their value after elaboration is complete. Thus they can be used in dynamic contexts such as in automatic tasks and functions, be assigned a net, or a variable, or be assigned a value that is defined elsewhere in the hierarchy. A const constant receives its value at runtime.

```
const t_states wst = RED;
  // RED is an enumeration value of type t_states.
```

The value of a const constant can only be set once via a declaration and cannot be changed subsequently. It is like a variable that cannot be written to.

A static const constant can be assigned any constant expression including hierarchical references. On the other hand, an automatic const constant can be any arbitrary expression, not necessarily limited to a constant.

4.3 Variables

4.3.1 Variable Declaration

A variable is declared by specifying its type.

```
int count;              // count is a variable of type int.
bit is_done;            // is_done is a variable of type bit.
enum int {S0, S1, S2, S3} nxt, prev;
logic [3:0] hsize;
```

A variable can optionally be declared using the keyword **var**.

```
var reg rtp;                // Variable of type reg.
var byte rxp;               // Variable of type byte.
```

When a variable is declared using the keyword **var** and the type of variable is not specified, then the default type is *logic*.

```
var ctl;               // Variable is of default type logic.
```

A variable can be initialized in its declaration.

```
var int irq = 5;
```

The assignment of 5 to *irq* occurs before any initial or always statements are executed before start of simulation. The initial value of a variable can be any non-constant arbitrary expression. For example,

```
var [7:0] urd = rd_data[7:0] & mask[15:8];
```

For a variable that does not have any initial value defined, here are the default values based upon the variable type:

- 4-state: **x**
- 2-state: 0
- real, shortreal: 0.0
- enumeration: base type default initial value
- string: " " (empty string)
- class: **null**
- event: new event can occur.

A variable can either be a 2-state type (e.g. *count*) or a 4-state type (e.g. *hsize*).

4.3.2 Variable Usage

In SystemVerilog, a variable can be assigned in a continuous assignment statement, receive a value from a module output, or be assigned a value from the new kind of procedural construct: *always_comb, always_ff*, or *always_latch*.

Here is an example of a variable assigned using a continuous assignment.

```
assign rtp = ^ qda;
```

However a variable cannot be assigned by more than one continuous assignment or by more than one procedural construct.

The advantage of relaxing these rules (as compared to Verilog HDL) is that one can use variables to describe an entire design without thinking about which are wires and which are flip-flops. However, SystemVerilog does not allow a variable to be assigned by multiple sources, that is, have multiple drivers. This is because there is no concept of a resolution function for variables.

Guideline: Use a variable if it has only one driver.

So a good guideline is that where multiple drivers are present, use nets instead of variables. One caveat is that to be backward compatible with

Verilog HDL, a variable is allowed to be assigned by multiple always statements. However, this is only an exception.

4.3.3 Static and Automatic Variables

A variable can be declared as automatic or static, using the keyword **automatic** or **static** in the variable declaration respectively. The keyword appears in the declaration of the variable.

```
var automatic logic [0:15] fmt;
static int error_count;
  // By default a variable is static if the
  // keyword automatic is not used.
```

Such declarations can occur within tasks, functions, sequential (begin-end) blocks and parallel (fork-join) blocks. Variables declared at the module level are always static (and cannot be declared as automatic).

An automatic variable can only be used within the block in which it is defined. This is as opposed to static variables that exist throughout the entire simulation and are global in nature. Static variables can be accessed using their qualified path names.

```
// Data declared outside of module is global and static.
int pixel_cnt = 10;
byte next_state;

module top;
  // Data declared inside module is static and
  // available to all inside module including
  // tasks and functions in that module.
  byte next_state;

  initial
    begin
      automatic int tk;
      // tk is automatic and local to the block.
      // Any reference to next_state refers to variable
      // declared inside module.
      // Reference to next_state defined outside of
      // module is done using $root.next_state.
```

```
            // pixel_cnt can be referred directly since it is
            // unique in scope.
            . . .
        end
    endmodule
```

All variables by default are static unless declared otherwise. If a function or task is declared as automatic, all local variables declared are also by default automatic unless explicitly declared as static.

4.3.4 Variable Initialization

Variables declared at the module level or in a task or a function can be assigned an initial value.

```
int rdt = 2;          // Declaration provides an initial
                      // value for the variable.
```

What is the difference between the above declaration and the following two statements?

```
int rdt;
initial rdt = 1;
```

The difference is that in the latter case, the assignment to *rdt* occurs after simulation starts at time 0, that is, it creates a simulation event and thus *rdt* gets the value at time 0, whereas in the former case, the initial value to the variable does not create any new event; simulation starts with a value of 2 for *rdt*.

For static variables, the initial value is assigned at one time, before start of simulation.

```
task test;
  static bit [31:0] cnt = 5;
  . . .
```

By default, a static variable is initialized at start of simulation and it never gets initialized upon subsequent task or function calls. For an automatic variable, the initial value is set every time the variable is created (every time the task or function is called).

```
function void rotate;
  var automatic logic [3:0] cnt = -6;
  . . .
```

Every time function *rotate* is called, variable *cnt* is initialized to -6.

```
function automatic create_clk;
  var logic [0:3] drd_cnt = 2;
  . . .
```

The variable *drd_cnt* is inside an automatic function (arguments and variables have automatic lifetime) and is by default automatic and is therefore initialized to 2 on every call to the function.

SystemVerilog defines that all inline initial values are evaluated prior to any execution of events at start of simulation. This guarantees that when initial and always statements read variables with inline initialization, the initialized value is read.

```
integer grants = 5;        // Declare and initialize to 5.

initial
  j = grants;
    // Initial statement is executed after inline value
    // to grants is set.
```

Inline variable initialization does not cause any simulation events to occur. Note that this behavior is different from that of Verilog HDL where an inline initialization is treated like an initial statement. In Verilog HDL,

```
integer num_coins = 6;
```

is equivalent to,

```
integer num_coins;
initial num_coins = 6;
```

which means that *num_coins* gets the value of 6 only when the initial statement is executed. In SystemVerilog, a variable initialization causes the variable *num_coins* to get a value before any of the statements are executed.

SystemVerilog initialization ensures that inline initialization occurs first, then followed by the execution of the procedural constructs. This removes the non-deterministic behavior of such assignments in Verilog HDL and leads to a deterministic behavior in SystemVerilog.

4.4 Nets

Here are examples of net declarations. A net type keyword[1] must be explicitly specified.

```
trireg logic [1:0] txq;
wire logic pgen;
wor logic [7:0] ret;
typedef enum logic [2:0]
  {ST0, ST1, ST2, ST3, ST4, ST5} t_fsm_state;
wire t_fsm_state wen;
wire clr0;                        // Default type is logic.
```

If a net declaration has no type specified, then the default type is *logic*. A net type has to be a 4-state integral type (contrast this to a variable which can either be 2-state or a 4-state type).

```
wire bit [3:0] kdata; // Error - net must be 4-state type.
logic ready;          // This is a variable declaration -
                      // needs a net type keyword to be a net.
wand logic empty;              // This is a net declaration.
```

A structure can be explicitly declared to be a variable or a net; by default, it is a variable.

1. Is one of **wire, tri, wor, trior, wand, triand, trireg, tri1, tri0, supply0, supply1**.

```
wire struct {
  logic trace_clk;
  logic [7:0] trace_data;
} snr;                          // snr is a net.
struct { . . . } bpp;           // bpp is a variable.
```

If a structure is declared as a net kind, all members of the structure have to be 4-state types, for example, see net *snr* above.

One caveat in SystemVerilog is that the **reg** keyword cannot immediately follow the net type keyword.

```
wire reg hop_flag;          // Error.
```

4.5 Operators

4.5.1 Assignment Operators

SystemVerilog defines new assignment operators that are of the form:

```
LHS op = RHS
```

For example,

```
rme *= 2;
```

is equivalent to:

```
rme = rme * 2;
```

Here are the list of assignment operators. The result of the operation is assigned to the left hand side.

```
+=              // Adds RHS to LHS.
-=              // Subtracts RHS from LHS.
*=              // Multiply LHS by RHS.
/=              // Divide LHS by RHS.
&=              // Bitwise-and LHS and RHS.
|=              // Bitwise-or LHS and RHS.
^=              // Bitwise-xor LHS and RHS.
<<=             // Bitwise left-shift the LHS by RHS.
```

```
>>=           // Bitwise right-shift the LHS by RHS.
<<<=          // Arithmetic left-shift LHS by RHS.
>>>=          // Arithmetic right-shift LHS by RHS.
```

These assignment operators provide the capability to write a statement in a compressed form where both the operand and the result are the same. All assignments are treated as blocking assignments. Here are some more examples.

```
a += 3;                 // Equivalent to a = a + 3;
s &= mask;              // Equivalent to s = s & mask;
f <<= 3;                // Equivalent to f = f << 3;

function int bit_count (input unsigned [31:0] arg);
  // Counts the number of 1's in the argument.
  begin
    for (bit_count = 0; arg != 0; arg >>= 1)
      if (arg & 2'b01) bit_count += 1;
    return bit_count;
  end
endfunction
```

Precedence of the assignment operator is lower than all other operators except for concatenation that is lowest. The assignment operators are also sometimes referred to as accumulate operators.

Since the assignment operators are treated as blocking assignments, they should be used with care when trying to infer sequential logic. It is recommended that these operators be used only to model combinational logic, or in a context where the operand is not being read by another concurrent process.

4.5.2 Assignment in Expression

An expression can contain an assignment, including an assignment operator.

```
while ((bar = tpa || qsm))
  . . .
```

```
if ((tpa ^= bar))
    . . .

qsm = (tpa += 1);
qsm = (bar = tpa >> 2);
```

An extra set of parentheses is required on the blocking assignments to make the intent clear. The blocking assignments cannot have any timing controls.

Note that the following is an error.

```
if (bar = tpa) . . . // Requires extra set of parenthesis
                     // for an assignment in an expression.
```

and:

```
if ((tpa = bar)) . . .
```

is equivalent to:

```
tpa = bar;
if (tpa) . . .
```

4.5.3 Bump Operators

These are the increment and decrement operators. The increment operator ++ adds 1 to its operand, while the decrement operator -- subtracts 1. These operators can be used as prefix operators, such as in ++*n*, or as postfix operators, as in *n*++. In both cases, the effect is to increment *n*. But the expression ++*n* increments *n* before its value is used, while *n*++ increments *n* after its value has been used. This means that in a context where the value is being used, ++*n* and *n*++ are different.

```
j = i++; // Post-increment operator.
         // j is assigned the value of i and then i is
         // incremented by 1.

j = ++i; // Pre-increment operator.
         // i is incremented by 1 and then assigned to j.
```

```
j = i--; // Post-decrement operator.
         // i is assigned to j and then the value
         // of i is decremented.

j = --i; // Pre-decrement operator.
         // i is decremented before assigning to j.
```

Here are some examples.

```
trm = map++;             // If map is 5, it sets trm to 5 and
                         // then increments map to 6.
trm = ++map;         // If map is 10, it increments map to
                     // 11 first and then assigns 11 to trm.

bar = bdd + trm++; // The current value of trm is used to
  // compute the right-hand side expression whose value
  // is assigned to bar. trm is then incremented by 1.

--i                      // Decrement i before using it.

if (--crt > 17) crt = 0;
    // Decrement crt first and then compare.
```

The increment and decrement operators can only be applied to variables, not to expressions. Also these operators behave like blocking assignments. For example,

```
i++
```

is equivalent to:

```
i = i + 1;
```

Guideline: Do not use multiple bump operators on same variable in a single expression.

Consequently, use these operators to model combinational logic only. Another guideline is not to use multiple bump operators on the same variable in one expression as the results may be non-deterministic. For example,

```
j = ++i + --i; // An implementation may choose to evaluate
  // either the left operand or the right operand first.
```

Here is another example.

```
i = 4;
while (i--) . . . // Test i, and then decrement i.
                  // Loop is executed 4 times.

i = 4;
while (--i) . . . // Decrement i and then test i.
                  // Loop is executed 3 times.
```

The precedence of the bump operators is the same as the + and – arithmetic operators.

4.5.4 Comparison Operators

SystemVerilog adds two additional comparison operators.

```
==?          // Wildcard equality operator.
!=?          // Wildcard inequality operator.
```

These operators do bitwise comparison of bits between left hand side and right hand side expressions. Any **x** or **z** values in the right hand side expression are treated as don't-cares (not the ones in the left hand side expression) and the don't-care bits are masked for comparison purposes. The operators return a value 1 if the comparison is successful, else it evaluates to a 0. It could also evaluate to an **x** if the result is unknown - for example, when the left hand side has an **x** and there are no wildcard in the right hand side expression. Assume:

```
dpp = 4'b00z0, doe = 4'bxx11
```

then:

```
dpp ==? doe                // is 0.
dpp !=? doe                // is 1.
  // z in dpp is ignored, x's in doe are treated
  // as don't-care.
```

Assume:

```
dpp = 4'b1110, doe = 4'b1x1z
```

then:

```
dpp ==? doe                 // is 1.
dpp !=? doe                 // is 0.
```

The **x** and **z** values in the left hand side expression are not treated as don't-cares.

```
if (instr ==? 4'b0???) . . .
```

If *instr* has the value 4'bx011, then the **x** value in *instr* is not treated as a don't-care, and the result of the comparison would be an **x**.

If the operands are not the same sizes, then the operands are expanded to the same size before doing the comparison as shown in the next example. Assume:

```
bsr = 3'b100, ssf = 5'b0010x
```

then:

```
bsr ==? ssf                 // is 1.
bsr !=? ssf                 // is 0.
   // bsr is expanded to 00100 before
   // doing the comparison.
```

The precedence of these operators is the same as for the comparison operators.

4.5.5 Logical Operators

SystemVerilog adds two additional logical operators.

```
->              // Logical implication operator.
<->             // Logical equivalence operator.
```

An expression with a logical implication operator such as:

```
expr1 -> expr2
```

is equivalent to:

```
!expr1 || expr2
```

An expression with a logical equivalence operator such as:

```
expr1 <-> expr2
```

is equivalent to:

```
(expr1 -> expr2) && (expr2 -> expr1)
```

Given:

```
par = 0, bar = 1
```

then:

```
par -> bar      // is a 1.
par <-> bar     // is a 0.
```

4.5.6 Set Membership Operator

SystemVerilog defines an operator **inside** that can be used to check if the value of an expression is present in a set of values. The operator returns a 1 if the value is in the set, else it returns a 0. This operator is used in the form:

```
expression inside { set_of_comma_separated_values }
```

The values in the set are scanned left to right until a match occurs with the value of the expression. The values in the set need not be unique. The following expression:

```
phy0 inside {2, 5, 6, 7, 8}
```

checks if *phy0* is one of the values specified and returns 1 if true. The expression:

```
adt inside {exp1, exp2, exp3}
```

is same as:

```
(adt ==? exp1) || (adt ==? exp2) || (adt ==? exp3)
```

Here are some examples.

```
if (ppo inside {31, 26, 93}) . . .

while (ypt inside {YELLOW, RED, BLUE}) . . .

logic [3:0] awt = 4'b1??0;
logic [3:0] rma = 4'b110x;
assign rtr = 4'b0011 inside {awt, rma};

if (ppm inside {4'b1?01}) . . .
  //The value ? can be 0, 1, x or z.
```

If no match is found and if any one of the comparison results in an **x**, then the inside operator returns an **x**. Set values can be specified as non-decreasing ranges.

```
bar inside {[16:22], 5, 6}
```

The set of values being checked could include constants, variables or arrays. The **z** (**?**) or **x** value can be used to represent don't-care values in the set. Any **x** or **z** value in the left hand side operand is not treated as a don't-care. The wildcard equality operator is used for comparison if the values in a set contain **x** or **z** values. Here are some more examples.

```
adt inside {[0:3], [12:15]}     // Set values can be
  // specified as non-decreasing ranges.
rma inside {4'b0x1z}
  // Compares with 0010, 0011, 0110, 0111; x and z are
  // treated as don't-care.
adt inside {bdx, ccb, ddg}
  // Set values are variables.
```

```
logic [3:0] fifo [2:0]= {4'b1000, 4'b0010, 4'b1111};
rma inside {fifo} // Set values are values in fifo array.

if (i inside {10, 20, 30, 40}) . . .

logic [0:3] count;
if (count inside {4'b0001, 4'b0010, 4'b0100, 4'b1000})
   . . .

if (5 inside {count})
  $display ("count is 0101");
```

The inside operator can also be used in a case statement.

```
case (pub) inside
  3'b0x1          : . . .
  3'b000, cpp     : . . .
  drm, elf, 3'bz10  : . . .
endcase
```

This is very similar to the casex statement except that only **x** and **z** in the case values are treated as don't-care (not the ones in the case expression *pub*).

4.5.7 Static Cast Operator

Type Casting

The cast operator (') allows for casting of a value from one type to another type. It can be used to change or qualify the type of data. It is of the form:

```
type_name ' ( expression )
```

and the expression is converted to the named type. The ' is the cast operator, and the type preceding that is the cast type, and the expression has to be enclosed within parenthesis. For example,

```
int'(2.0)
```

is a value of type *int* (with value 2). The type can be any user-defined type as well.

```
t_myint'(2.2 * PI)
```

Explicit type conversion can be forced in any expression by using the cast operator. The precise meaning of a cast operator is as if the expression is assigned to a variable of the specified type. Using this operator, a variable of one type can be cast to a variable of another type.

```
int i;
real f = 3.16;
i = int'(f * 0.5);
int'(2 * 26.1)
shortint'(8'hFA)
```

Size Casting

If a positive decimal number is used instead of a type with a cast operator, size casting can be performed. The size specifies the number of bits in the result of the expression.

```
size ' ( expression )
```

Here are a couple of examples.

```
10'(2 + 5)  // Result of expression is stored in 10 bits.
32'(15)   // Integer 15 is represented as a 32-bit value.
17'(gcnt - 2)   // 17-bit value.
```

Signed Casting

An expression can be cast as a signed or an unsigned expression using the cast operator.

```
signed | unsigned '( expression )
```

For example,

```
signed'(2 + 5)
```

specifies that the result of the expression is a signed value. Here are some more examples.

```
bit [3:0] bdr;
signed'(bdr)

byte unsigned uns_byte;
signed'(uns_byte)

logic signed [7:0] sum, a, b;
logic co, ci;
assign {co, sum} = a + b + signed'({1'b0, ci});
  // Signed 8-bit adder.
```

Since a bit-select or part-select of an array is always unsigned, this can be converted to signed using signed casting.

```
assign add4bit = signed'(a[3:0]) + signed'(b[3:0]);
```

Bit-streams

Type casting can be performed between composite types. The mechanism used to perform the type conversion is through bit-streaming, that is, by first converting to a vector form. A composite type value on a right hand side is converted into a bit-stream and then the same bit-stream is composed to the left hand side type. A composite type could be an array, structure, class or a dynamic array.

Assuming that *acx* and *bmx* are composite types, and *bmx* is of type *t_pkt*:

```
bmx = t_pkt'(acx);
```

causes value of *acx* to be converted to a stream of bits. The same stream of bits is recomposed into *bmx*'s type. Data is placed into the destination type in a left to right order. The assignment is made left to right, leftmost bits of the source vector are assigned to the first element of *bmx*.

```
typedef struct {
  bit [4:0]  arb;
  byte       bmp [1:2];
  reg        cnt;
} t_d1;

typedef struct {
  byte       acp;
  bit [2:0]  brb;
  bit [10:0] cnn;
} t_d2;

t_d1 d1_var;
t_d2 d2_var;

typedef logic [21:0] t_logic22;
t_logic22 a_var;

d2_var = t_d2'(d1_var);
a_var = t_logic22'(d1_var);
d1_var = t_d1'(d2_var);
```

Only a bit-stream type can be converted to a stream of bits. Such a type is:

- any integral (that represents a basic integer data type) type, packed type (array, structure or union) or a string type (treated as a unbounded array of bytes).
- unpacked arrays, structures or classes of above.
- dynamically sized arrays of above types.

Bit-stream type casting is only allowed between bit-stream types. Furthermore, bit-stream type casting is allowed on only same size data.

4.5.8 Dynamic Cast Operator

The static cast operator does not provide any error or warning if the value of the expression does not belong to the type being cast. In a static cast, the expression is converted at compile time and thus no check is made to ensure that the resulting value is legal or not.

Consider:

```
t_states'(state + 1)
```

The expression value may not correspond to any value of the enumeration type *t_states* and no check is done. So it is possible that the resulting value does not belong to that type.

Dynamic casting allows for stronger type checking, where dynamic runtime checking is required. This is performed using the **$cast** method which can be used as a task or as a function. It is of the form:

```
$cast ( dest_var , source_expression );
```

If the assignment result is invalid for the target type, a runtime error is reported and the destination variable is left unchanged. Casting a *real* to an *int* where the real number is too large to be represented is not an invalid cast; casting wrong enumeration values are examples of invalid casts. Here are some examples.

```
$cast(cpp, arg * 9);
$cast(col_a, 2);

typedef enum
  {RED, BLUE, GREEN, YELLOW, VIOLET} t_colors;
t_colors col_b;
$cast(col_b, 2 + 3);
```

The **$cast** method can be called as a task or as a function. When used as a function, it returns a status of 0 or 1 depending upon whether the cast was successful (1) or not (0). If the cast is unsuccessful, the value of the target variable does not change. When used as a function, no runtime error is reported. However the status value returned can be used to perform any necessary actions.

```
status = $cast(bnn, 3.14 * cst);
if (status) . . .
```

The source expression cannot change in a cast expression; thus operators, such as ++ and --, cannot be used in a dynamic cast.

4.5.9 Type Operator

The *type operator* returns the data type of the expression. It is of the form:

```
type ( expression )
```

And it can be used wherever a type can be used. Here are a couple of examples.

```
var type(rec) cst;
tsc = type(ggo + 1)'(vol_15);
typedef type(slv) t_eval;
```

In the first example, the variable *cst* is declared to be the same type as the variable *rec*. In the second example, the value of *vol_15* is cast to the type of the "*ggo*+1" expression. In the third example, the type operator is used to define a new type *t_eval* which is the type of *slv*.

When a type operator is used to declare a variable or a net, the **variable** keyword or the net kind keyword is required (that is, it is not optional).

4.5.10 Concatenation

SystemVerilog allows concatenation of values of type string. For example,

```
string test = "xyz";
string sma = {"abc", " def ", test};
```

produces the following string in the variable *sma*.

```
"abc def xyz"
```

The replication operator can also be used with objects of type string. For example,

```
string str_a;
str_a = {3{"I do "}};
```

produces the string:

```
"I do I do I do "
```

One point to note is that the result of a string concatenation expands the left hand side string to accommodate the new size; it does not truncate the right hand side to match the left hand side size.

4.5.11 Streaming Operators

The streaming operators are:

- >> : This operator causes the data to be streamed out left to right.
- << : This operator causes the data to be streamed out right to left.

These operators, when used on the right hand side, perform packing of a bit-stream type into a sequence of bits in a user-specified order. The stream of bits can be of any arbitrary length and can be created from almost any collection of expressions including unpacked arrays, structures and class objects. The resultant stream of bits can be assigned to a target variable.

When these operators are used on the left hand side, they unpack the bit-stream into one or more variables.

These operators behave differently from bit-stream casting in that the ordering of the bit-stream is user-specified. The format of using these operators is:

```
{ stream_operator slice_size list_of_expr_concat }
```

The slice size specifies how the bit-stream is to be broken up into slices - each slice being the specified number of bits. The default slice size, if not explicitly specified, is 1 bit.

```
byte jpp = 8'b1100_0001;
bit [7:0] asm;
bit [3:0] dds;
```

```
bit a, b, c, d;
bit [3:0] e;
bit [7:0] f;
bit [7:0] g;

// Packing operator usage:
asm = {<< {jpp}};          // Bit reverse: stores 1000_0011.
asm = {>> 2{jpp}};         // Assigns same, 11_00_00_01.
  // Packed results can be assigned to
  // bit-stream type variable.

g = {>> {a, b, c, d, e}};    // Assembles a bunch of bits
  // using left to right streaming. If a and c are 0,
  // b and d are 1 and e is "1101", then g is "0101_1101".

g = {<< {f}};    // Reverses a vector using right to left
         // streaming with a default slice size of 1 bit.
         // If f is "1100_0101", then g is "1010_0011".

g = {<< 4{f}};          // Reverses a vector using right to
           // left streaming using a slice size of 4.
           // If f is "1100_0110", then g is "0110_1100".

dds = {>> 4 {jpp}};          // Error; right hand side is
                             // larger than left hand side.

// Unpacking operator examples:
{>> {a, b, c}} = asm;
  // Right hand side is larger than left hand side -
  // this is ok - bits are filled left to right in target.
  // If asm is "1010_0011", then a is 1, b is 0 and c
  // is a 1.
  // It is an error if the left hand side is larger
  // than the right hand side.

{>> {a, b, c, d, e}} = "1100_1100";
  // a and b are 1, c and d are 0, and e is "1100".
```

The streaming operators operate on only bit-stream types.

4.6 Operator Overloading

Operators can be overloaded to operate on types that are normally not allowed. This is performed using the bind construct. The bind construct links an operator to a function prototype (declaration). Here is an example.

```
bind + function t_complex
  add_complex (t_complex opd1, opd2);
```

overloads the "+" operator to operate on two operands of type *t_complex* and returns a value of type *t_complex.*

```
t_complex cma, cmb, cmc;

function t_complex add_complex (t_complex opd1, opd2);
  . . .
endfunction

assign cma = cmb + cmc;
```

The "+" operator can be used on *t_complex* types. This is equivalent to calling the function *add_complex.*

```
cma = add_complex(cmb, cmc);
```

Either form can be used. Note that the overloaded function can perform any task, not necessarily the meaning of the operator that is being overloaded. But typically, it should perform an equivalent task of the operator, else the code may be confusing.

Only arithmetic operators, relational operators and assignment operators can be overloaded.

4.7 Expression Templates

A *let construct* defines an expression template. A let declaration is of the form:

```
let let_name [ ( formal_argument_list ) ] = expression ;
```

The formal argument list specifies the list of variables used to customize the expression. Here are examples of let declarations.

```
let sum(a, b) = a + b;           // Has two arguments.
let parity = a ^ b ^ c ^ d;      // Has no argument.

let masked_result(mpo) = mpo && mask_vector;
  // One argument. Not all variables in expression
  // need to be in the argument list.
  // Only mpo is to be customized.

let fft(m1, m2 = 32, m3 = dbus ) = m2 * (m1 + m3);
  // Two arguments have default values. A default
  // value need not be a constant.
```

The *let* can be used in any expression by using the *let* name with its list of actual arguments, if any. A *let expression* is of the form:

```
let_name [ ( actual_argument_list ) ]
```

Here are some examples of *lets* used in expressions.

```
sum(opd1, opd2) * 6
if (parity == 1) . . .
pdata[7:0] || masked_result(haddr)

fft(filter_coeff[0]) - BASE_MARGIN
  // It is not necessary to specify actual arguments
  // for those that have default values.
```

The semantics of a let expression is such that the let declaration gets replaced with the list of actual arguments, if any, and the result of the substitution is enclosed within parentheses. So for the above examples, here are the equivalent expressions.

```
(opd1 + opd2) * 6
if ((a ^ b ^ c ^ d) == 1) . . .
pdata[7:0] || (haddr && mask_vector)
(32 * (filter_coeff[0] + dbus)) - BASE_WIDTH
```

A let construct is much like a text macro. However, it has the advantage that it has a local scope; it is declared and available for use in its scope. A text macro, in contrast, is global in nature and is visible to the entire compilation unit scope.

The let construct is useful is defining assertions, though it can be used in any other general expression context.

❑

Chapter 5

Behavioral Modeling

This chapter describes the additional behavioral modeling constructs that are part of the SystemVerilog language. This includes, amongst others, new kinds of procedural constructs, enhancements to if statements, case statements and loop statements.

5.1 Procedural Constructs

SystemVerilog adds three additional kinds of always statements.

i. always_comb statement.

ii. always_latch statement.

iii. always_ff statement.

These statements execute as infinite loops, just like an always statement. However, the semantic intent is captured using the different kinds of statements.

5.1.1 Combinational Procedural Construct

The *always_comb statement* is used to model combinational logic. The syntax for the always_comb statement is:

```
always_comb
  procedural_statement
```

No timing control (also sometimes referred to as a sensitivity list) is required. This is because the timing control is automatically inferred to be a list of all the signals[1] read inside the procedural statement. What this means semantically is that if any of the signals that are read in the procedural statement has an event, the procedural statement executes - exactly like a combinational logic block. Here is an example.

```
always_comb
  if (sel)
    yout = in0;
  else
    yout = in1;
```

The implicit timing control is "*sel* **or** *in0* **or** *in1*". So any time an event occurs on *sel*, *in0* or *in1*, the if statement executes.

Local variables that are declared within the procedural statement are not included in the implicit timing control. Here is another example.

```
always_comb
  begin
    var int temp1;

    temp1 = app + bwp;
    tyo = temp1 * cty;
  end
```

The variable *temp1* is not included in the implicit timing control, which in this example is "*app* **or** *bwp* **or** *cty*".

1. A *signal* is either a variable or a net. We use the general term *signal* to refer to either of these in this text.

The always_comb statement executes any time there is a change of value in any of the signals that are read, which causes the outputs to be updated with their possibly new values. Also an always_comb statement is evaluated once at time 0 irrespective of any change of signals in its implicit timing control but after all initial and always statements are executed at time 0. This automatic evaluation ensures that the outputs of the procedural statement (that represents combinational logic) are consistent with its input values at time 0.

Note that an always statement also executes at time 0 but can get suspended due to a timing control. In contrast, an always_comb statement always executes completely once at time 0. Here is another example of an always_comb statement.

```
always_comb
  case (op_code[1:0])
    2'b10     : y = a;
    2'b11     : y = b;
    default   : y = 1'b0;
endcase
```

The default case, if not specified, will cause it not to infer combinational logic and a warning may be reported. Here is another example that may generate a warning since combinational logic is not inferred.

```
always_comb
  if (is_zero)
    rx_done = 0;
  else
    begin
      rx_done = check_flag;
      tx_start = go_tx;
    end
```

Note that a latch is inferred for *tx_start*.

A variable assigned in an always_comb statement cannot be assigned a value in any other statements. Furthermore, an always_comb statement is also sensitive to signals that are read inside any functions called from the procedural statement.

An always_comb statement is preferred over an always statement since the always_comb statement captures the complete sensitivity list including signals that are read within a function. The "**always @***" does not account for signals that are read by functions that are called within the procedural statement. To correctly handle signals read in a task call, write it as a void function so that the correct sensitivity list is inferred for the always_comb statement.

```
task arbiter;
  . . .
endtask

// Rewrite as:
function void arbiter;
  . . .
endfunction
```

The always_comb statement also handles arrays with variable index in sensitivity list correctly. In this example,

```
always_comb
  rd_data = memory_a[cpu_addr];
```

cpu_addr is part of the implicit timing control.

To summarize, an always_comb statement is similar to the always statement except for the following:

i. Timing control is inferred.

ii. Variables assigned values cannot be assigned in any other statements.

iii. Statement is executed once after all initial and always statements are executed. This ensures that the outputs are consistent before simulation starts.

iv. Have no statements that block, that is, have no blocking timing and event controls or a parallel block (fork-join) statement.

v. A warning is generated if the always_comb statement does not model combinational logic.

vi. Signals read in functions that are called in the procedural statement are considered part of the timing control.

5.1.2 Latched Procedural Construct

SystemVerilog provides the *always_latch statement* for modeling latched logic behavior. The syntax is:

```
always_latch
  procedural_statement
```

Here is an example.

```
always_latch
  if (mclk)
    q <= drp;
```

Similar to the always_comb statement, the timing control is inferred to be the list of signals that are read within the procedural statement. In the above example, the implicit timing control is "*mclk* **or** *drp*", that is, any time an event occurs on *mclk* or *drp*, the if statement is executed. A variable assigned in an always_latch statement cannot be assigned a value in any other statement. Also, the always_latch statement executes once at time 0 to make sure that the outputs are consistent with its inputs. Here is another example.

```
always_latch
  case (op_code[1:0])
    2'b10: arg = opd_a;
    2'b11: arg = opd_b;
  endcase
```

Execution semantics is similar to the always_comb statement. A warning may be issued by a tool if the logic does not represent latched logic behavior.

5.1.3 Sequential Logic Procedural Construct

SystemVerilog provides the *always_ff statement* to model sequential logic behavior. The syntax is:

```
always_ff
  timing_control procedural_statement
```

A timing control must be an edge-triggered event control form, that is, every signal in the timing control must be qualified with a **posedge** or a **negedge** keyword. The timing control includes the synchronous (such as clock) and asynchronous (such as set, reset) signals.

Here is an example.

```
always_ff
  @(posedge clock or negedge reset)
    if (!reset)
      q <= 1'b0;
    else
      q <= d;
```

The structure and semantics of an always_ff statement shall conform to the synthesizable sequential logic form (see IEEE 1364.1[1]). Basically, the timing control is an edge-triggered event control, which is a list of edge events, one of them is for a clock and the rest are for asynchronous set and reset signals. The procedural statement shall contain one if statement with zero or more *else-if*'s and the last *else* implicitly referring to the clock edge. Also no blocking statements are allowed. Here is another example.

```
logic clk, soft_reset;
logic [7:0] counter;

always_ff
  @(posedge clk)
    if (!soft_reset)
      counter <= '0;
```

---

1. IEEE Std 1364.1-2002: IEEE Standard for Verilog Register Transfer Level Synthesis.

```
else
  counter <= counter + 1'b1;
```

A tool may issue a warning if the behavior of the always_ff statement does not model or represent sequential logic.

5.2 Loop Statement

5.2.1 For-Loop Statement

In SystemVerilog, the for-loop variable can be declared local to the loop. Such a variable is treated as an automatic variable.

```
for (int index = 1; . . . ) . . .
  // index is local to the for-loop and
  // is an automatic variable.
```

In addition, SystemVerilog allows multiple initial assignments and multiple step assignments.

```
for (int j = 1, byte k = 0; i < 128; i++, j++) . . .

for (int i = 0, j = 2, k = 3; cnt < 100; j++, k++, i--) . . .
```

Guideline: Declare the for-loop variable local to the loop.

Note that automatic variables are temporary and thus cannot be referred hierarchically or dumped in a VCD file. Here are some more examples.

```
factorial = 1;
for (int number = 2; number < N; number++)
  factorial *= number;

always_ff
  @(posedge clk)
    for (int k = 0; k < MAX_COUNT; k++)
      mac_cnt += incr_by[k];
      // k is local only to for-loop.
```

Where possible, always declare the for-loop variable in the for-loop. This avoids any conflict or collisions with any such variable declared outside the for-loop.

5.2.2 Do-while-loop Statement

SystemVerilog introduces the additional *do-while-loop statement.* It is of the form:

```
do
  procedural_statement
while ( condition ) ;
```

This loop statement executes the procedural statement first and then checks the value of the condition. If it is true, the procedural statement executes again. If false, the loop exits to the next statement following the loop statement. Here is an example.

```
do
  begin
    @(posedge clk);
    count++;
    $display ("The value of count is %d", count);
  end
while (count < 10);

j = 0; sum = 10;
do
  begin
    sum += 2;
    j += 3;
  end
while (j < 20);
```

5.2.3 Foreach-loop Statement

SystemVerilog introduces the *foreach-loop statement.* This loop statement is of the form:

```
foreach ( array_argument )
  procedural_statement
```

The foreach-loop statement can be used to iterate over the elements of a single or a multi-dimensional array without having to specify the dimensions. The argument must be an array with a list of loop variables. These loop variables are automatic by default and are local to the for-loop.

```
bit word [0:7] [0:1023];
. . .
foreach (word[i, j])
  word[i][j] = i * j;
```

The loop variables, *i* and *j*, are implicitly defined and are local to the for-loop. The iteration occurs from left to right. For each *i*, iterate over all values of *j*. In the next example, with three indices in the array argument like:

```
logic matrix [1:3][5:8][15:0];
. . .
foreach (matrix[i, j, k]) . . .
```

the first iteration is over the range of *k* (15 downto 0), then over the range of *j* (5 through 8) and then over the range of *i* (1 through 3). The innermost loop variable is *k* and the outermost loop variable is *i*. Here are additional examples.

```
logic [31:0] read_parity;
logic [31:0] [7:0] rdata;
foreach (read_parity[i])
  read_parity[i] = ^rdata[i];

int sum [15:0] [31:0];
foreach (sum[i, j])
  sum[i][j] += i * j;
```

The for-loop variables, *i* and *j*, are local variables and need not be declared; they are automatic and read-only and local to the loop and the type is implicitly that of the index type.

5.2.4 Jump Statement

It is sometimes convenient to be able to exit a loop from the middle of a loop statement. SystemVerilog adds the following three kinds of jump statements, the first two forms can be used in a loop statement and the third form can be used in a task or a function.

i. Break statement
ii. Continue statement
iii. Return statement

The *break statement* causes the execution of the loop statement to terminate and exit. The next statement executed is the one following the loop statement. In a for-loop, a break causes the innermost loop to be exited.

```
while (i <= 63)
  begin
    . . .
    break; // Causes execution of while loop to terminate
           // and execution continues with the next
           // statement following the while-loop statement.
    . . .
  end
. . .      // <<-- This statement is executed after break.
```

```
sum = 1; j = 0;
forever
  begin
    j += 21;
    sum *= 10;
    if (sum > 100) break;
  end
. . .      // <<-- This statement is executed after break.
```

The *continue statement* is related to the break statement, but is less often used. It causes the next iteration of the enclosing for-loop, while-loop, or do-loop to begin. In the while-loop and the do-loop, it means that the test part is executed; in the for-loop, control passes to the next increment step and the next loop iteration starts. The continue statement causes the execution to jump to the end of the loop, that is, it exits the current iteration.

```
for (int i = 0; i < 10; i++)
  begin
    . . .
    continue; // Causes to go to end and continue
    // with next iteration of for-loop. The following
    // statements until keyword end are skipped.
    . . .
  end

do
  . . .
  if (ready) continue; // Causes to go to end and
  // check for condition of loop. The following
  // statements until keyword while are skipped.
  . . .
while (sum < 25);

for (int j = 10; j >= 5; j--, k++)
  if (sum < TOTAL_SUM)
    sum += 2;
  else if (sum == TOTAL_SUM)
    continue;               // Do next iteration of for-loop.
```

The continue statement is often used when the part of the loop that follows is complicated so that reversing a test and indenting another level would nest the model too deeply.

```
int n = 0;
forever
  begin
    n++;
    if (n % 3 == 0)
      continue;
    if (n == 32)
      break;
  end
```

A *return statement* can be used in a task or a function to exit the task or function respectively.

```
function int test (. . .);
  . . .
  if (a < b)
    return (a + b);
  else
    return (a - b);
  . . .
endfunction
```

The return statement may optionally specify an expression, in which case, it can only be used in a function and the return expression must match the return type.

5.3 Block and Statement Labels

SystemVerilog optionally allows block labels to be added at the end of a named block.

```
begin : block_label          // Named block.
  . . .
end [ : block_label ]        // Enhanced in SystemVerilog.
```

Guideline: Specify the block label at the end of a named block to improve readability.

The block label used at the beginning and at the end must match.

SystemVerilog supports adding a statement label to any procedural statement. It is of the form:

```
statement_label : statement

lbl_incr: sum += 1;           // lbl_incr is a label.
```

A sequential (begin-end) or a parallel (fork-join) block can have either a block label or a statement label, but not both.

```
lbl_a: begin
  // lbl_a is a statement label for the sequential block.
  . . .
end
```

When a label is used in a sequential block or a parallel block, the label may be used at the end as a block label.

```
lbl_b: fork
  . . .
join_any: lbl_b
```

The disable statement can be used to stop the execution of a statement with a label.

5.4 Case Statement

SystemVerilog provides three keywords, **unique, unique0** and **priority**, that can be used with any case statement. Using these keywords allows a tool to perform certain violation checks and to report the violations, if any.

5.4.1 Unique and Unique0 Case

A *unique case statement* specifies that the case expression evaluates to only one of the case values. Thus the order in which the case values are specified is not important and the selection can occur in parallel.

```
bit [1:0] opcode;

unique case (opcode)
  2'b00 : . . .
  2'b01 : . . .
  2'b10 : . . .
  2'b11 : . . .
endcase
```

In a unique case statement, all case items must be non-overlapping and each case can be evaluated in parallel. Furthermore, it is illegal to have more than one case item matching the case expression. A violation report is generated if either more than one case item matches the case expression or if no case item matches. If the keyword **unique0** is used, then no violation report is generated if no case item matches.

Here are some examples.

```
unique case (hit_cnt)
  0, 2, 5   : . . .
  3, 4      : . . .
  8         : . . .
endcase          // Any other value of hit_cnt will cause
                 // a violation report to be issued.

unique0 case (current_state)
  3'b101 : . . .
  3'b110 : . . .
endcase          // No violation is reported if
  // current_state does not match either of the
  // two values specified.
```

The **unique** and **unique0** keywords can be applied to a casex or a casez statement as well.

5.4.2 Priority Case

A *priority case statement* specifies that at least one case item value must match the case expression value and that if more than one match occurs, then the first matching branch is executed. Thus this option implies that it is ok for the case expression to match more than one branch case value and that the order of the case branches specified is important.

```
priority case (1'b1)
  ireg0 : . . .
  ireg1 : . . .
  ireg2 : . . .
endcase
```

The branch that first matches is executed. A violation report is generated if the case expression value does not match any case item value.

The **priority** keyword can be used with casex and casez statements as well. Here is an example.

```
priority casez (sms)
  3'b0?0    : $display ("sms is 0 or 2");
  3'b11?    : $display ("sms is 6 or 7");
  default   : $display ("sms is 1, 3, 4 or 5");
endcase
```

5.4.3 Case Inside

The *case inside statement* (case statement with **inside** operator) can be used to check for set membership. The case expression is compared with each of the case item value. The inside operation performs wildcard matching.

```
priority case (guard_exp) inside
  [0:31] : $display ("guard_exp is between 0 and 31");
  [64:70],
  [82:92]: $display (
    "guard_exp is between 64 and 70 or between 82 and 92"
    );
endcase

case (fstate) inside
  4'b00??: $display ("fstate is 0, 1, 2, or 3");
  4'b1000,
  4'b1001: $display ("fstate is 8 or 9");
  4'b1x10: $display ("fstate is 10 or 14");
endcase
```

The case inside statement only considers the **x** and **z** (**?**) values in the case items as don't-cares and hence only these particular bits are masked. Any **x** or **z** (**?**) in the case expression is not considered as a don't-care.

5.5 *If Statement*

SystemVerilog supports the use of the **unique, unique0** and **priority** keywords with an if statement as well. This allows a tool to perform certain violation checks and to report the violations, if any.

5.5.1 Unique and Unique0 If

The **unique** modifier indicates that the order of condition evaluation is not important. The *unique if statement* assumes that all conditions in a series of if-else-if statement are mutually exclusive and can be evaluated in parallel. The inferred priority of an if statement thus is not honored.

```
unique if (num_errors == 1)
  $display ("num_errors is 1");
else if ((num_errors >= 2) && (num_errors <= 5))
  $display ("num_errors is 2, 3, 4, or 5");
else if ((num_errors > 5) && (num_errors <= 10))
  $display ("num_errors is 6, 7, 8, 9 or 10");
else
  $display ("num_errors is greater than 10");
```

In a unique if statement, the condition in all branches have to be unique and must be mutually exclusive so that execution can occur in parallel. In addition, at least one branch must be executed. This implies that at least one condition must be satisfied; the *else* branch can be used as a catch-all.

It is illegal for more than one condition to be true in such an if statement. Also, if no condition is true, then it is an error. In such cases, a violation report is generated.

In the above example, all if conditions are mutually exclusive and only one of them is true or the last *else* branch is executed. Here is one more example.

```
logic [2:0] mode;
always_comb
  unique if (mode == 3'b001)
    y = a;
  else if (mode == 3'b010)
    y = b;
  else if (mode == 3'b100)
    y = c;
  else
    y = 'b0;
```

No violation is reported for this example as all conditions are mutually exclusive and an *else* branch has been specified.

If the keyword **unique0** is used and if no condition matches, then no violation report is generated. Here is an example of a *unique0 if statement.*

```
unique0 if (cnt == 16)
  high_bits = 3'b001;
else if (cnt == 32)
  high_bits == 3'b010;
else if (cnt == 64)
  high_bits = 3'b100;
```

If *cnt* has a value that causes none of the conditions to match, no violation is reported.

5.5.2 Priority If

The **priority** modifier indicates that the order of the conditions in an if-else-if statement is important, which is the same as a normal if statement semantics. The *priority if statement* evaluates the conditions in the order listed and the first branch with the true condition is evaluated. It is an error if no condition is true, and therefore the last *else* condition is required.

```
priority if (arg1 == arg2)
  . . .
else if (arg1 > arg2)
  . . .
else                              // arg1 < arg2.
  . . .
```

As with the unique if statement, at least one branch must be executed in the priority if statement. Here is another example.

```
priority if (lock[3:0] == 'b0)
  $display ("Lower 4 bits are 0");
else if (lock[2:0] == 'b0)
  $display ("Lower 3 bits are 0");
else if (lock[1:0] == 'b0)
```

```
    $display ("Lower 2 bits are 0");
  else
    $display ("None of the lock conditions are true");
```

The **$display** call that corresponds to the first condition that is true is executed.

5.6 Final Statement

The final statement is like an initial statement. This statement executes at the end of simulation in zero time.

```
final
  procedural_statement
```

The final statement can be used to print statistics of simulation, for example. The statements allowed inside a final statement are same as that of a function call; this is because a final statement needs to execute in zero time. However, unlike an initial statement, it is not a separate process and is more like a function call.

```
final
  begin
    $display ("Number of tests passed: %d", num_passed);
    $display ("Number of tests failed: %d", num_failed);
  end

final
  $display ("All done - simulation ends at time: %t",
            $time);
```

5.7 Disable Statement

SystemVerilog allows a disable statement to exit a task that does not contain a disable statement.

```
task timeout;

  . . .
endtask
```

```
p1:
always
  begin
    . . .
    t1: timeout();
    . . . // <<- Execution continues after disable task.
  end

p2:
always
  begin
    . . .
    disable u1.p1.t1;          // u1 is the module instance
                      // that contains the p1 always statement.

    . . .
  end
```

This causes the task to end immediately and control to jump to the next statement following the task call.

5.8 Event Control

5.8.1 If Conditional Event

SystemVerilog adds the **iff** qualifier (if and only if) to the @ event control. The event expression triggers only if the condition is true.

```
always @(wclk iff enable == 1)
  . . .
```

The iff expression is evaluated only when *wclk* has an event (not when *enable* has an event). Here is another example.

```
always @(posedge sysclk iff !reset)
    q <= d;

always @(d iff enable)
    q <= d;
```

5.8.2 Sequence Event

Sequences are described in Chapter 9. A sequence represents a series of actions and has a label.

```
@ sequence_label procedural_statement
```

The procedural statement is executed only after the named sequence with the label has reached its end point, that is, it has completed the set of events in sequence. The end of sequence causes the procedural statement to be executed.

5.8.3 Level-sensitive Sequence Control

This is accomplished using the wait statement with the *triggered* sequence method. The triggered method is true if the sequence has reached its end in the current time step. Such a wait statement causes the execution of sequential statements to suspend until the specified action becomes true.

```
wait (sequence_label.triggered);
```

5.9 Edge Event

In addition to the posedge and negedge events, SystemVerilog defines the *edge* event. An edge event occurs whenever a posedge or a negedge event occurs and it can be used to form event expressions, just like posedge and negedge events.

```
always @(edge fclk)
  count_all_edges += 1;
```

5.10 Continuous Assignments

SystemVerilog allows continuous assignments on variables of any data type. While nets can be driven by multiple continuous assignments, a variable can only be driven by one continuous assignment or one procedural block.

```
var int timer_addr;
assign timer_addr = cpu_addr * 2;     // timer_addr is a
        // variable assigned using a continuous assignment.

bit wdog_intr;
assign wdog_intr = wdog_cnt > 12 ? 'b1: 'b0;
```

5.11 Parallel Block

SystemVerilog enhances the parallel block construct to support fork-join-any and fork-join-none forms.

The *fork-join-any* form blocks until any one of the processes spawned by the fork completes.

```
fork
  process1
  process2
  process3
join_any
. . .         // <<- Continue execution with this statement
              // after any one of the processes complete.
```

The parallel block exits if any of the processes completes. Here is an example.

```
initial
  begin
    #5ns;
    fork
      begin: p1
        #10ns;
      end
      begin: p2
        #7ns;
      end
      begin: p3
        #25ns;
      end
    join_any
    $display ("It is now %t", $time);
  end
```

At 5ns, all three processes *p1*, *p2* and *p3* are spawned in parallel. Process *p2* is the first one to complete after 7ns and thus the fork-join-any block exits at time 12ns.

The *fork-join-none* form causes the parent process to continue executing concurrently with all the new processes spawned by the fork. The spawned processes from the fork do not start execution until the parent process blocks.

```
. . .
fork
  process1
  process2
  process3
join_none
. . .
#5;      // All fork processes start execution at this
         // point because parent gets blocked and all three
         // processes execute in parallel with the
         // parent process.
```

Here is another example.

```
initial
  begin
    #5ns;
    fork
      begin: p1
        #10ns;
      end
      begin: p2
        #7ns;
      end
      begin: p3
        #25ns;
      end
    join_none
    $display ("It is now %t", $time);
    #50ns;
    $display ("Ends at time %t", $time);
  end
```

In this example, all the three processes are spawned at 5ns. However, the parent process is not yet suspended and it continues execution. So the first display statement prints a time of 5ns. The following statement causes the parent process to suspend that in turn triggers all the three processes to start. The parent process and processes *p1*, *p2* and *p3* all execute in parallel. Process *p2* completes at 13ns, process *p1* completes at 15ns, and process *p3* completes at 30ns. However the parent process is still in the process of timing out and gets to the second display statement at 55ns.

Note that if the above example was a normal fork-join (parent process blocks until all spawned processes complete), the first display statement would be executed at time 30ns and the second display statement would be executed at 80ns.

5.12 Process Control

SystemVerilog provides constructs to suspend a process and to wait for completion of other processes. The wait-fork statement waits for completion of other processes while the disable-fork statement stops the execution of a process.

The *wait-fork statement* ensures that all child processes of a parent process have completed their execution. The syntax of the wait-fork statement is:

```
wait fork ;
```

Here is an example.

```
initial
  begin
    #5ns;
    fork
      begin: p1
        #10ns;
      end
      begin: p2
        #7ns;
      end
      begin: p3
```

```
        #25ns;
      end
    join_none
    $display ("It is now %t", $time);
    wait fork;
    $display ("Ends at time %t", $time);
  end
```

The wait-fork statement causes the parent process to suspend at 5ns and wait for all spawned processes *p1*, *p2* and *p3* to complete - they complete at 30ns. The second display statement, consequently, prints a time of 30ns.

The *disable-fork statement* terminates all child processes of the parent process. The statement is of the form:

```
disable fork ;
```

Here is an example.

```
initial
  begin
    #5ns;
    fork
      begin: p1
        #10ns;
      end
      begin: p2
        #7ns;
      end
      begin: p3
        #25ns;
      end
    join_none
    $display ("It is now %t", $time);
    #20ns;
    disable fork;
    $display ("Ends at time %t", $time);
  end
```

Processes *p1*, *p2*, *p3* are spawned at 5ns. The parent process issues the disable fork at 25ns. This causes process *p3* to terminate. Note that by then processes *p1* and *p2* have completed.

5.13 Fine-grain Process Control

SystemVerilog provides the capability to allow one process to access and control another process once it has started. This is accomplished using the **process** built-in class. Its implicit declaration is of the form:

```
class process;
  typedef enum
    {FINISHED, RUNNING, WAITING, SUSPENDED, KILLED}
    state;

  // Returns a handle to the process making the call:
  static function process self(); . . . endfunction

  // Returns the process status:
  function state status(); . . . endfunction

  // Terminates the process and all its subprocesses:
  function void kill(); . . . endfunction

  // Allows one process to wait for the
  // completion of another process:
  task await(); . . . endtask

  // Allows a process to suspend its own execution
  // or that of another process:
  function void suspend(); . . . endfunction

  // Resumes a previously suspended process:
  task resume(); . . . endtask
endclass
```

Every time a process is created, an object of the above class is automatically created for that process. Objects can be created of type *process* explicitly, if required.

```
process prc_ptr [7:0];
  // Variable to store process handles.

prc_ptr[2] = process::self();  // Get a process handle.

prc_ptr[2].suspend();          // Suspend the process.

if (prc_ptr[2].status == process::KILLED)
  // Check status of process.
  . . .
```

❑

Chapter 6

Structural Modeling

This chapter describes the enhancements made to module declarations in SystemVerilog. This includes the new kinds of named port connections. The new concept of interfaces is also described. The advantages of using interfaces are presented with detailed examples.

6.1 Module

6.1.1 Module Prototype

SystemVerilog allows the specification of a declaration of a module (that is, without its body). This is done using the **extern** keyword. That is, an *extern module declaration* defines the name of the module and its ports without defining the module behavior. This allows compilation of modules in separate files with stronger type checking.

Here is an example of a module prototype.

```
extern module alu
  #( int NUM_BITS = 8
  ) (
    input bit mclk,
    input bit [NUM_BITS-1:0] arg1, arg2,
    output bit [NUM_BITS-1:0] result
  );
```

The module prototype can be declared inside of any module or outside of a module. If a module prototype is declared outside of another module, then any module in that compilation unit can instantiate the prototype module.

```
// File: check.sv
. . .
extern module fpp . . .;
. . .
module arm9 . . .
  . . .
  fpp u_fpp . . .                    // Instance in module arm9.
  . . .
endmodule
. . .
module arm7 . . .
  . . .
  fpp u_fpp . . .                    // Instance in module arm7.
  . . .
endmodule
. . .
// End of file.
```

The file *check.sv* is one compilation unit (strictly speaking, a compilation unit is a set of files all of which are compiled together). An extern declaration for module *fpp* is present outside of the module definitions. Thus, it can be instantiated in both modules *arm9* and *arm7* that are in the same compilation unit as the extern declaration. It is not necessary for the extern declaration to occur prior to its instantiation.

Note that declaring a module prototype is not a requirement for instantiating a module. However it does help in simplifying the compilation process and helps in documenting the external interface of the module being instantiated.

One advantage of using a module prototype is that it is no longer necessary to repeat the port declaration in the actual module declaration. Instead the ".*" can be used in place of the port list to indicate that it is the same as that specified in the module prototype.

```
extern module super_nand
  #( int NUM_BITS = 16
  ) (
    input logic [NUM_BITS-1:0] a0, a1,
    output logic [NUM_BITS-1:0] y
  );
. . .
module super_nand (.*);
  . . .
endmodule
```

The ".*" infers both the parameter list and the port list of the module prototype.

6.1.2 Named Module

An optional module name can be specified at the end of the module declaration. This name, if specified, must match the name of the module.

```
module module_name . . .
  . . .
endmodule: module_name      // Both names should match.
```

6.1.3 Nested Modules

SystemVerilog allows a module to be declared within another module. This provides for avoiding potential conflicts with other modules with the same name.

```
module dma . . .
  logic swait;
  . . .
  usb u_usb . . .
  . . .
  module usb . . .                        // Nested module.
    logic sclk;
    . . .
  endmodule: usb
endmodule: dma
```

Nested modules are not visible outside of the hierarchy scope in which they are declared. Module *usb* can only be used inside module *dma* and is not visible outside of module *dma*.

A nested module has visibility to all signals of its parent, that is, all signals declared in the parent can be used inside the nested module. For example in module *usb*, variable *swait* can be used inside module *usb*. However, signals declared inside the nested module are not visible to its parent. For example, variable *sclk* declared in module *usb* is not visible in module *dma*.

Since a common practice is to write each module in a separate file, the **`include** directive can be used to nest the modules.

```
// File: top.sv
module top . . .
  `include timer.sv
  `include gpio.sv
  timer u_timer . . .
  gpio u_gpio . . .
endmodule: top

// File: timer.sv
module timer . . .
  . . .
endmodule: timer

// File: gpio.sv
module gpio . . .
  . . .
endmodule: gpio
```

Nested modules allow for the same module name to be used in different parts of the design without creating any conflict. An alternate way to handle this is by using configurations.

6.1.4 Module Ports

If no port type or direction is specified for the first port, then all port types and directions should be declared in the body of the module, not in the port list.

```
module adder (a, b, cin, sum, cout);
  input a, b, cin;
  output sum, cout;
  // Type and direction are specified in
  // the body of the module.
  . . .
endmodule: adder
```

If the type or kind (variable or net) of the first port is specified, but no direction is specified, it is assumed to be an inout port by default.

```
extern module cnt4 (logic sclk, . . .);
// Port sclk has inout direction.
```

Also in a port list, any subsequent port with no port direction defaults to the direction of the previous port.

```
extern module test_flop
  (logic bypass, output logic q, logic qbar);
```

Port *bypass* is an inout port since no direction is specified and port *qbar* is an output port - same as that of the previous port *q*.

Guideline: Explicitly specify the direction and type of all ports in the port list.

If the direction of the first port is specified, but no kind or type is specified, it is assumed to be a wire of type *logic*.

```
extern module ahb_matrix
  ( input hclk, pclk,
    input logic [31:0] din,
    output logic [31:0] dout
  );
// Port hclk is a wire by default of type logic.
```

For subsequent ports in a port list, they get the kind, type and direction from the preceding port. In the above example, all ports are wires by default and *pclk* is also an input port of type *logic*.

6.1.5 Port Kind

SystemVerilog allows a port to be a variable instead of a net. Note that a variable can have only one driver while a net can have multiple drivers. So if a port has only one driver, it is preferred to use a variable as it provides for automatic multi-driver checking.

```
extern module cpu11 #(int WIDTH = 8)
  (output var [WIDTH-1:0] hwdata; . . .);
```

Use a net kind port only if it has multiple drivers, such as for a bidirectional port.

```
extern module ahb_bridge #(int WIDTH = 16)
  (inout wire [WIDTH-1:0] data_bus; . . .);
```

6.1.6 Implicit .name Named Port Connection

In many cases of port connections in module instantiations, the port name and the signal name are the same. SystemVerilog simplifies this by allowing the port to be specified without specifying any signal name; the signal name is implicit and is identical to the port name. So instead of using:

```
.arm_clk(arm_clk)
```

in a named port connection, one can simply use:

```
.arm_clk
```

and the signal *arm_clk* is implicitly assumed to be connected to the port *arm_clk*. Since the signal name is implicit, it has to be explicitly declared. Here is another example.

```
logic carry_in, carry_out;
logic a, b, sum;     // Signals explicitly declared, but
    // implicitly connected to ports of equivalent names.
adder u_adder
    (.a, .b, .cin(carry_in), .sum, .cout(carry_out));
```

The explicit signal connections for ports *cin* and *cout* are required since the signal name differs from the port name. A named port connection is also required if a port is not connected, for example, as in:

```
.cout()
```

Similarly, a named port connection is required if only part of a bus is used to connect to a port, for example, as in:

```
.haddr(haddr[15:0])
```

No positional association can be used in this connection scheme. Here is another example.

```
extern module dff
  ( input [7:0] d,
    input clk, nrst,
    output [7:0] q
  );
. . .
logic clk, nrst;
logic [7:0] q, d;
logic [15:0] dbus;
logic [3:0] resetn;
. . .
dff u1_dff (.q, .nrst, .d, .clk);
dff u2_dff
  (.d(dbus[7:0]), .q(), .nrst(resetn[2]), .clk);
```

In instance *u1_dff*, the signals implicitly connected to the ports *q*, *nrst*, *d* and *clk*, are explicitly declared. Furthermore, the listing of the port order is not important. In instance *u2_dff*, only part of the bus connects to port *d*, so the port has to be explicitly connected to the bus part-select. Only a bit of a bus connects to port *nrst*; so this connection also has to be explicitly specified. Since port *q* is not connected, the parentheses are required to indicate that no signal is connected to this port.

6.1.7 Implicit .* Named Port Connection

SystemVerilog provides a shorthand notation (using ".*") for connecting ports of modules that have a large number of ports. The ".*" indicates that all ports and signals of the same name should automatically be connected together for that module instance. Any connection that cannot be inferred by ".*" must be explicitly connected.

```
extern module super_flop (ck, d, reset, q, qbar);
. . .
logic ck, d, reset, q, qbar, data_in, scan_out;
. . .
super_flop u1_super_flop (.*);
  // Connects ports of module instance u1_super_flop
  // to signals with same name.

super_flop u2_super_flop (.*, .d(data_in), .qbar());
  // All ports of instance u2_super_flop are implicitly
  // connected to signals with same name except for
  // port d which is connected to data_in and
  // port qbar which is open.
```

An explicit named association is required where the signal name differs from the port name, where the port is not connected, and in the case where a bit-select or a part-select connects to the port, such as in:

```
.acc(acc[15:0])
```

The signals that connect to the ports have to be explicitly declared. Furthermore, positional association cannot be used with this scheme.

It is recommended to use the implicit ".*" connection to catch all size mismatches and unconnected ports. Here are some more examples.

```
dff u3_dff (.*);        // Connected to implicit nets that
                        // have been declared explicitly.
```

```
dff u4_dff (.*, .q());              // q is not connected.
dff u5_dff (.*, .nrst(resetn[2]), .d(dbus[15:8]));
                          // Bit-select of resetn connected.
                          // Part-select of dbus connected.
```

6.1.8 Port Types

SystemVerilog allows arrays, including unpacked arrays, to be passed through ports. The port also must be an array. Values are passed just like an assignment.

SystemVerilog also allows any type of port including real values, any packed or unpacked array, structures or unions. However a variable type can have only one source. Unpacked types must be assignment-compatible.

In SystemVerilog, variables can be used to connect to ports as well.

```
var bit clk200;                        // Variable declaration.
. . .
dff u_dff (.clk(clk200), . . .);       // Module instance.
```

6.1.9 Reference Ports

SystemVerilog adds a fourth port direction called a **ref** port (the other three directions being **in**, **out**, and **inout**). A *ref port* passes a hierarchical reference to a signal through a port instead of passing its value. The name of the ref port is essentially an alias to the hierarchical reference. Any change to either the signal connected to the port or to the port within the module is immediate and visible at both the higher-level and within the module.

```
module ssi (. . . , ref log);
  . . .
  log = 2;
  . . .
endmodule: ssi
```

```
module top;
  . . .
  tlg = 2;
  . . .
  ssi u_ssi(. . ., .log(tlg));
  . . .
  tlg = 1;
  . . .
endmodule: top
```

The port *log* is a ref port and is connected to the signal *tlg*. So any changes to *tlg* are seen by *log* within module *ssi* and any changes to *log* are seen as changes to *tlg* in module *top*.

If a ref port is a variable (as opposed to a net), then effectively this creates a shared variable as the variable can be assigned values across multiple modules. However, there are no resolution functions with such variables. Variables simply store the value that they are assigned. Thus if a ref port is a variable, the value of the variable is the last value written, which could come from any module that shares the variable.

6.1.10 Parameterized Types

In SystemVerilog, the net and variables types in a module or those in the module ports can be parameterized. A parameterized type is declared using the **parameter type** keywords.

```
extern module payload
  #( parameter type VAR_TYPE = int
  ) (
  input VAR_TYPE grants, expected, . . .
  );
```

The type used by ports *grants* and *expected* is *VAR_TYPE* and they are by default of type *int*. In a module instantiation, the parameter type can be changed to any other type.

```
payload #(.VAR_TYPE(byte)) u_payload . . .
```

6.2 Interface

SystemVerilog introduces the new *interface construct.* The interface construct offers a new paradigm for modeling abstraction. It can simplify the task of modeling and verifying large complex designs.

6.2.1 What is an Interface?

An interface encapsulates the connectivity between two or more modules. It allows a number of signals to be grouped together and be represented as a single port. Each module then uses the single interface port instead of many signal ports. Here is an example of an interface declaration.

```
interface i_ahb_bus;
  logic [31:0] hwdata;
  logic [11:0] haddr;
  logic hwrite;
  // And other common set of signals that are
  // shared between modules.
  . . .
endinterface: i_ahb_bus
```

The advantage of encapsulating the signals in an interface is that it eliminates the redundant declarations of these signals within each module.

```
module top;
  i_ahb_bus ahb ();          // Instance of an interface.
  dma u_dma (.ahb_port(ahb), . . .);    // Interface
                                        // connection.
  usb u_usb (.ahb_port(ahb), . . .);    // Interface
                                        // connection.
endmodule: top

module dma (i_ahb_bus ahb_port);
  . . .
endmodule: dma

module usb (i_ahb_bus ahb_port);
  . . .
endmodule: usb
```

The top level module and all modules that make up the blocks do not have to repetitively declare the common signals declared within an interface. Instead these modules simply use the interface as the connection. See Figure 6-1. The interface contains all the signals used between modules *usb* and *dma*. An interface can also describe how the data is sent and received - we shall see this in a later section.

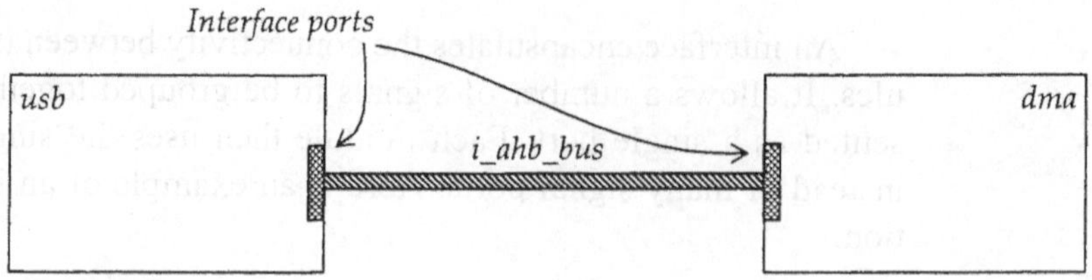

Figure 6-1 Interface describes connectivity between modules.

Here is an example that shows the advantage of using interfaces. Consider two blocks, *timer* and *uart*, that talk to each other through their ports. First we show the model without using interfaces.

```
module timer (
  input logic clk,
  input logic reset,
  input logic sel,
  input logic write,
  output logic [31:0] rdata,
  input logic [31:0] wdata);
  . . .
endmodule: timer

module uart (
  input logic clk,
  input logic reset,
  input logic sel,
  input logic write,
  output logic [31:0] rdata,
  input logic [31:0] wdata);
  . . .
endmodule: uart
```

```
module core_top;
  . . .
  timer u_timer (sysclk, preset, sel_timer, rw,
                prdata_timer, pwdata);
  uart u_uart (sysclk, preset, sel_uart, rw,
                prdata_uart, pwdata);
endmodule: core_top
```

Notice that modules *timer* and *uart* are tied intrinsically in the module *core_top* and it is not possible to test the *timer* module without developing the *uart* module as well. In addition, any time the communication protocol between the two module changes, either by addition or by deletion of a signal, the block module and the top module have to change simultaneously to reflect that. There is no way to abstract the interface between the two modules independent of the modules themselves. An interface helps achieve this. Using an interface, the above design can be modeled as follows.

```
interface i_pbus;
  logic clk, reset, sel, write;
  logic [31:0] rdata, wdata;
endinterface: i_pbus

module timer
  ( input logic sel,
    output logic [31:0] rdata,
    i_pbus intf1                    // Interface port.
  );
  . . .
endmodule: timer

module uart
  ( input logic sel,
    output logic [31:0] rdata,
    i_pbus intf2                    // Interface port.
  );
  . . .
endmodule: uart
```

```
module core_top;
  . . .
  i_pbus pbus ();              // Interface instantiation.

  timer u_timer (.sel(sel_timer), .rdata(prdata_timer),
                 .intf1(pbus));
  uart u_uart (.sel(sel_uart), .rdata(prdata_uart),
               .intf2(pbus));
endmodule: core_top
```

The common signals that connect the two modules have been grouped into an interface.

An interface is basically a *bundle of signals*, that is, it is a higher level of abstraction than a signal. An interface can be instantiated to create the bundle and then connected to various module ports.

An interface allows for structuring the information flow between modules. It helps to keep the code maintainable. If a new signal needs to be added between modules *timer* and *uart*, only the interface *i_pbus* declaration needs to be changed; there is no need to edit many files just to insert one signal.

Using an interface creates more compact code and leads to fewer wiring mistakes. An interface is not just for encapsulation of signals into a bundle but the interface can also describe how the data is sent and received.

Most bugs occur between modules. The key is to encapsulate the connections at a higher level of abstraction instead of wires. See Figure 6-2. An interface can be used to reduce the complexity by combining wires into buses. It captures the interconnect and communication of the *bundle*, and separates the communication from functionality. Wires are a simple choice of how to communicate between blocks in a physical world. An interface allows to focus on the information being communicated at a higher level than at a wire-level detail. This abstraction helps eliminate *wiring* errors. Furthermore, interface objects can be reused.

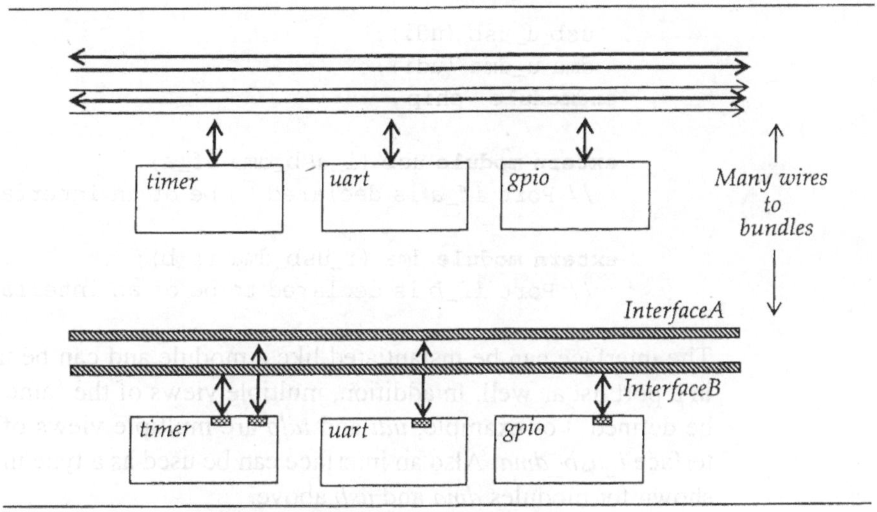

Figure 6-2 Abstracting wires to bundles.

6.2.2 Interface Declaration

An interface is defined just like a module declaration, except that it cannot contain module declarations and module instances. Here is the syntax of an interface declaration.

```
interface interface_name ;
  // Same constructs as a module except no
  // module instantiations and module declarations.
endinterface [ : interface_name ]
```

Here is another example of an interface declaration, its instantiation and its usage.

```
interface i_usb_dma;
  bit mclk, usb_clk;
  logic [31:0] wbus, rbus;
  logic ready, read_write;
endinterface: i_usb_dma

module chip;
  i_usb_dma udi ();     // Instantiates the interfaces.
  i_usb_dma udo ();
```

```
    usb u_usb (udi);
    dma u_dma (udi);
endmodule: chip

extern module usb (i_usb_dma if_a);
  // Port if_a is declared to be of an interface type.

extern module dma (i_usb_dma if_b);
  // Port if_b is declared to be of an interface type.
```

The interface can be instantiated like a module and can be used as a type in a port list as well. In addition, multiple views of the same interface can be defined. For example, *udi* and *udo* are multiple views of the same interface *i_usb_dma*. Also an interface can be used as a type in a port list, as shown for modules *dma* and *usb* above.

An interface declaration can contain anything that can be in a module declaration except for other module definitions or instances. An interface, further, can contain more than just wires. It can contain, in addition, communication protocols for the interface, protocol checkers, type declarations, tasks, functions, process blocks, program blocks and assertions. An interface cannot contain any design hierarchy, that is, instances of modules or primitives, but it can contain other interface instances.

6.2.3 Instantiating an Interface

An interface instantiation is similar to a module instantiation.

```
i_usb_dma d_if ();
i_usb_dma u_if ();
```

d_if is an instantiation of the interface *i_usb_dma* and the instantiation includes all the signals defined in the interface. The signals in this interface can be referenced using the hierarchy separator, like:

```
d_if.ready
```

u_if is another instantiation of the same interface and this creates a second set of signals, which are not related to the first. *u_if.ready* is a distinct signal from *d_if.ready*. An array of instances is also permitted.

```
i_usb_dma m_if [0:3] ();
```

Interface instances can appear after their use, that is, they need not be instantiated before use. Once an interface is instantiated, its individual signals can be referenced individually as shown above. In addition, the interface instance can be used to connect module ports that are of interface type. We saw this example before. Here is the same module declaration repeated.

```
extern module usb (i_usb_dma udi);
  // Port is an interface.
```

The interface instance can be used to connect to port *udi*, for example. It is illegal to have an interface port unconnected.

Interface declarations can be either local to a module or it can be in the compilation-unit scope. If it is local to a module, only the containing module can instantiate the locally declared interface. If it is declared outside of a module, it can be instantiated and used to connect to a port anywhere in the design hierarchy.

6.2.4 Interface Methods

An interface not only captures the connectivity, but also captures the communication between two or more modules. Tasks and functions can be defined within an interface. Such tasks and functions are referred to as *interface methods.* The advantage of any interface method is that the details of the communication between modules is moved to the interface which is shared by all modules. Thus an interface can not only be used to capture common data, but also the communication protocols between modules.

Here is an example of an interface declaration with interface methods.

```
interface i_hbus;
  wire hclk;
  wire hresetn;
  wire hsel;
  wire hwrite;
  wire [15:0] haddr;
```

```
    wire [31:0] hrdata;
    wire [31:0] hwdata;

    // Interface methods can access all signals
    // defined within the interface.
    task bus_read (. . .);
      . . .
    endtask: bus_read
    task bus_write (. . .);
      . . .
    endtask: bus_write
    function bus_status (. . .);
      . . .
    endfunction: bus_status
  endinterface: i_hbus

  module cpu (i_hbus hbus_a);
    . . .
    hbus_a.bus_write();     // Access an interface method.
  . . .
  endmodule: cpu

  extern module int_ctrl (i_hbus hbus_a);

  module esoc (. . .);
    . . .
    // Instantiate two interfaces:
    i_hbus hbus_q (), hbus_p ();
    . . .
    hbus_p.bus_read();     // Call to task in interface.
    stat = hbus_q.bus_status();
    . . .
    // Connect the modules using the interfaces:
    cpu u_cpu (hbus_q);
    int_ctrl u_int_ctrl (hbus_q);
    . . .
  endmodule: esoc
```

A task or a function defined inside an interface declaration is same as how they would get defined inside a module. However, a task or a function defined in an interface can be called from anywhere it is visible in scope.

To call a method in an interface, use the hierarchical form:

interface_instance . method_name

hbus_p.bus_read is an example of calling a task defined in an interface directly.

An interface can also contain initial and always statements.

6.2.5 Ports of an Interface

An interface declaration can have a port list. If a signal needs to be shared across one or more interfaces, it could be defined as a port of the interface. Ports in different instances of such an interface can be connected to different signals.

An interface port is similar to a module port. It has a direction: input, output or inout. And the signal that is connected to the port in the interface instantiation can be referred using its hierarchical name.

```
interface i_qbus (input bit qclk, qresetn);
  wire qsel, qwrite, qready;
  wire [15:0] qaddr;
  wire [31:0] qrdata, qwdata;
  . . .
endinterface: i_qbus

module cpu (i_qbus cpu_qbus);
  . . .
  if (cpu_qbus.qwrite) . . .
  always @(posedge cpu_qbus.qclk) . . .    // Input port
            // of interface accessed using hierarchical name.
  . . .
endmodule: cpu

module int_ctrl (i_qbus int_ctrl_qbus);
  . . .
  @(int_ctrl_qbus.qresetn);  // Input port of interface
                   // accessed using its hierarchical name.
  . . .
endmodule: int_ctrl
```

```
module esoc (. . .);
  wire sclk, mclk, mresetn, sresetn;
  . . .
  // Two instances of same interface:
  i_qbus qbus_a (mclk, mresetn),
         qbus_b (sclk, sresetn);

  // Connect the modules using the interface:
  cpu u_cpu (.cpu_qbus(qbus_a));
  int_ctrl u_int_ctrl (.int_ctrl_qbus(qbus_a));
endmodule: esoc
```

Interface *i_qbus* includes the signals connected to its port *qclk* and *qresetn* to its bundle of signals. So the interface instance *qbus_a* includes *mclk* and *mresetn* in its bundle, and instance *qbus_b* includes *sclk* and *sresetn* in its bundle.

An interface port can be shared across multiple instantiations of the same interface. An interface port is also useful when one or more external signals need to be brought into an interface. Figure 6-3 shows an example. Here is the description of the top module.

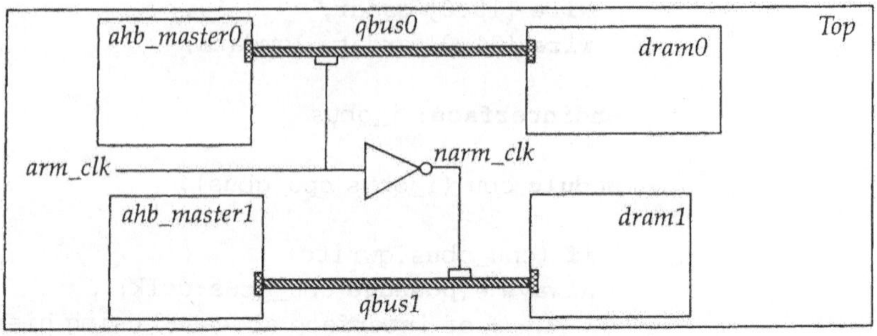

Figure 6-3 Ports of an interface can be shared.

```
extern module dram (i_qbus dram_qbus);

module top;
  wire arm_clk, narm_clk, reset0, reset1;

  assign narm_clk = !arm_clk;
```

```
        i_qbus qbus0 (arm_clk, reset0);
        i_qbus qbus1 (narm_clk, reset1);

        dram u_dram0 (.dram_qbus(qbus0));
        ahb_master0 u_ahb_master0 (.cpu_qbus(qbus0));
        dram u_dram1 (.dram_qbus(qbus1));
        ahb_master1 u_ahb_master1 (.cpu_qbus(qbus1));
    endmodule: top
```

There may be a slight confusion in terminology when someone refers to an interface port: whether it refers to a port of an interface or to a module port of type interface. Hopefully the context will help clarify what port is being referred to. In this text, *interface port* refers to the port of an interface.

6.2.6 Modport

A module connected to an interface may use a slightly different view of the interface, such as one of the signals being an input or an output or inout. Such a difference is specified in an interface declaration using the *modport* declaration. For one module, an interface signal could be an input and for another module, the same signal could be an output. For example, in the above *i_qbus*, signals *qwrite* and *qaddr* are outputs of module *cpu* while these are inputs to module *dram*. Similarly, signal *qready* is an output of module *dram*, but an input to module *cpu*. The direction of the signals in an interface that are specific to each module is specified using a modport.

A modport configures the directions of various signals used in an interface for a specific module. A modport declaration is of the form:

```
modport modport_name
  ( list_of_signals_and_their_directions ) ;
   // No type information is specified for the signals,
   // only direction.
```

Once a modport is declared, it can be used to qualify the interface when it is attached to a port of a module. This is of the form:

```
interface_name . modport_name   module_port_name
```

Here is the declaration of two modports in interface *i_qbus*.

```
interface i_qbus (input bit qclk, qresetn);
  wire qsel, qwrite, qready;
  wire [15:0] qaddr;
  wire [31:0] qrdata,qwdata;
  modport mp_master
    (output qsel, qwrite, qaddr, qwdata,
     input qready, qrdata);
  modport mp_slave
    (output qready, qrdata,
     input qsel, qwrite, qaddr, qwdata);
endinterface: i_qbus
```

The modports can then be used in the module declarations.

```
module dram
  (i_qbus.mp_slave dram_bus);         // Modport attached.
  . . . dram_bus.qwrite . . .
  always @(posedge dram_bus.qclk)
endmodule: dram

module cpu
  (i_qbus.mp_master cpu_bus);         // Modport attached.
  . . . cpu_bus.qsel . . .
  @(cpu_bus.qclk) . . .
endmodule: cpu
```

An interface can have any number of modport declarations, each one describing how one or more modules see the signals in the interface. Each modport provides a view. To specify which modport is used, one can explicitly specify it as:

```
interface_instance_name . modport_name
```

as a connection to a port of a module, such as in:

```
cpu u_cpu0 (.cpu_qbus(qbus_c.mp_master));
```

Alternately, the modport can be specified directly as part of a module port declaration interface, such as in:

```
extern module cpu (i_qbus.mp_master cpu_bus);
```

By default, all signals in an interface are assumed to be inout. Figure 6-4 shows how modports connect the modules to the interface.

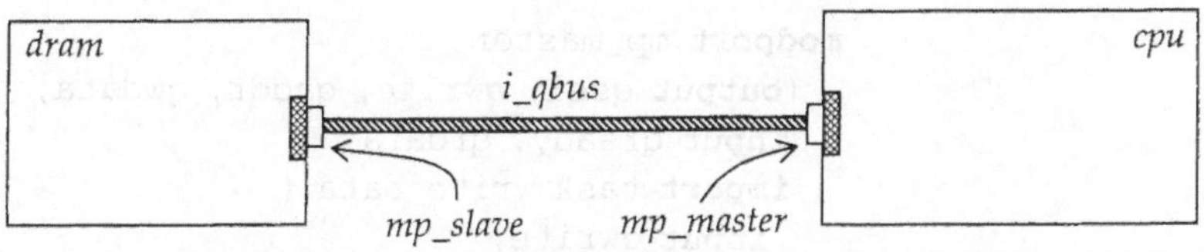

Figure 6-4 Modports connect module to interface.

A method can be passed as an argument to a modport using the **import** keyword. A module can then access the task through its modport. Here is an example.

```
interface i_qbus (input bit qclk, qresetn);
  wire qsel, qwrite, qready;
  wire [15:0] qaddr;
  wire [31:0] qrdata, qwdata;
  modport mp_master
    (output qsel, qwrite, qaddr, qwdata,
     input qready, qrdata,
     import write_data); // Import the task into modport.
  modport mp_slave
    (output qready, qrdata,
     input qsel, qwrite, qaddr, qwdata);
  task write_data (                // Task definition.
    input qwrite,
    input [15:0] qaddr,
    input [31:0] qwdata);
  . . .
  endtask
  . . .
endinterface: i_qbus
```

Having imported the task through the modport, module *cpu* can access the task without any qualification.

```
module cpu (i_qbus.mp_master cpu_bus);
  . . . cpu_bus.qsel . . .
  @(cpu_bus.qclk) . . .
  write_data( . . .);                // Task call.
endmodule
```

An alternate way of specifying a function or a task in a modport declaration is by specifying its full prototype, as shown in this example.

```
modport mp_master
  (output qsel, qwrite, qaddr, qwdata,
   input qready, qrdata,
   import task write_data (
    input qwrite,
    input [15:0] qaddr,
    input [31:0] qwdata)
  );
```

SystemVerilog allows a task or a function in one module to be exported to other modules via its interface. Thus is done using the **export** keyword.

```
interface i_qbus (input bit qclk, qresetn);
  wire qsel, qwrite, qready;
  wire [15:0] qaddr;
  wire [31:0] qrdata;
  wire [31:0] qwdata;

  modport mp_master
    (output qsel, qwrite, qaddr, qwdata,
     input qready, qrdata,
     import write_data);              // Import task.

  modport mp_slave
    (output qready, qrdata,
     input qsel, qwrite, qaddr, qwdata,
     export is_ready);                // Export function.

  . . .
endinterface: i_qbus
```

```
module dram
  (i_qbus.mp_slave dram_bus);        // Modport attached.
  . . . dram_bus.qwrite . . .

  always @(posedge dram_bus.qclk)
    . . .

  function bit is_ready ( . . .);
    . . . // Body of function here.
  endfunction
endmodule: dram
```

The modport *mp_slave* exports the function *is_ready* defined in module *dram*. The function can then be used in other modules that share the same interface. For example:

```
module cpu (i_qbus.mp_master cpu_bus);
  . . . cpu_bus.qsel . . .
  @(cpu_bus.qclk) . . .

  if (cpu_bus.is_ready()) . . .
  . . .
endmodule: cpu
```

Importing a task or a function through a modport gives the module access to that task or function by prepending the interface port name with the task or function name.

Note that it is also possible to import a task or a function without associating it with a modport by using the **extern** keyword in the interface declaration.

```
interface i_ram;
  . . .
  // Task definition is somewhere else (this
  // is a task prototype):
  extern task check_parity (input logic [31:0] data);

  modport . . .
endinterface: i_ram;
```

```
module mem_a (i_ram ram_bus);
  // Complete task definition here:
  task check_parity (input logic [31:0] data);
    . . .
  endtask
  . . .
endmodule: mem_a

module mem_b (i_ram ram_bus);
  // Task can be used in this module as well.
  ram_bus.check_bus(read_data);
  . . .
endmodule: mem_b
```

6.2.7 Generic Interface

It is possible to define a *generic* interface port using the **interface** keyword, such as:

```
extern module usb (interface udi);
  // Port udi is a generic interface.
```

The advantage of the generic interface port is that such a module port can connect to any interface, since the interface type is not specified explicitly.

6.2.8 Parameterized Interface

An interface can be parameterized so that it can be used with a variety of modules. The syntax for parameterizing an interface is very similar to that of a module. Here is an example of a parameterized interface.

```
interface i_mbus
  #( parameter DWIDTH = 32, AWIDTH = 16
  ) ( input bit qclk, qresetn
  );

  wire qsel, qwrite, qready;
  wire [AWIDTH-1:0] qaddr;
  wire [DWIDTH-1:0] qrdata;
  wire [DWIDTH-1:0] qwdata;
```

```
      modport mp_master
        (output qsel, qwrite, qaddr, qwdata,
        input qready, qrdata);
      modport mp_slave
        (output qready, qrdata,
        input qsel, qwrite, qaddr, qwdata);
      . . .
    endinterface: i_mbus
```

The interface *i_mbus* is parameterized on the *DWIDTH* and *AWIDTH* parameters whose default values are 32 and 16 respectively. So when an interface is instantiated, the default value of *DWIDTH* is 32 and for *AWIDTH* is 16. However, these values can be overridden in the instantiation by providing different values for the parameters. This is shown in the next example.

```
    module top;
      . . .
      i_mbus cpu_mbus ();  // Has default width of 32 and 16.
      i_mbus #(.DWIDTH(16)) dram_mbus ();
        // DWIDTH of 16 and AWIDTH of 16.

      i_mbus #(64, 24) dma_mbus ();
        // DWIDTH of 64 and AWIDTH of 24.
      . . .
    endmodule: top
```

Even a type can be parameterized in an interface to make the interface customizable for different types.

```
    interface i_tbus
      #(parameter type T_OTP = int);
      T_OTP pkt_status;          // Parameterized type signal.
    endinterface: i_tbus

    module test;
      i_tbus int_tbus ();
        // Interface instance uses the default int type.

      i_tbus #(.T_OTP(logic [31:0])) v32_bus ();
        // Overrides parameter type to "logic [31:0]".
    endmodule: test
```

6.2.9 Structure vs Interface

An interface encapsulates communication like a structure encapsulates data. Here is an example of declaration of two data objects:

```
int index;
logic [7:0] mask;
```

And here they are encapsulated in a structure type:

```
typedef struct {
  int index;
  logic [7:0] mask;
  } t_mask_rec;
```

And here they are encapsulated into an interface:

```
interface i_mask_bus;
  int index;
  logic [7:0] mask;
endinterface: i_mask_bus
```

In both cases, signals are grouped to create a larger composite object. A signal can be thought of as a standard built-in interface. Both a signal and an interface is connected to the module ports in this example:

```
wire wma;
i_mask_bus ifm ();

moda u_moda (wma, ifm);
```

So it may appear that a structure can also do what an interface does. However, an interface can contain many other declarations that define connectivity and communication between modules, such as:

i. Interface allows initial and always statements, which can be used to create stimuli for signals in an interface.

ii. An interface can have tasks and functions, which can be called from outside the interface, providing a mechanism to modify the signals in the interface through high-level commands.

iii. An interface can define the direction of a signal for each module in a separate modport. Thus a signal can be an input in one modport and an output in another modport.

6.2.10 Interfaces Improve Verification

Interfaces provide a mechanism to improve the verification flow. Many system bugs occur in interfaces between blocks. Let us look at a conventional verification strategy shown in Figure 6-5. Each testbench is separate and cannot be reused. And each block is tested in isolation.

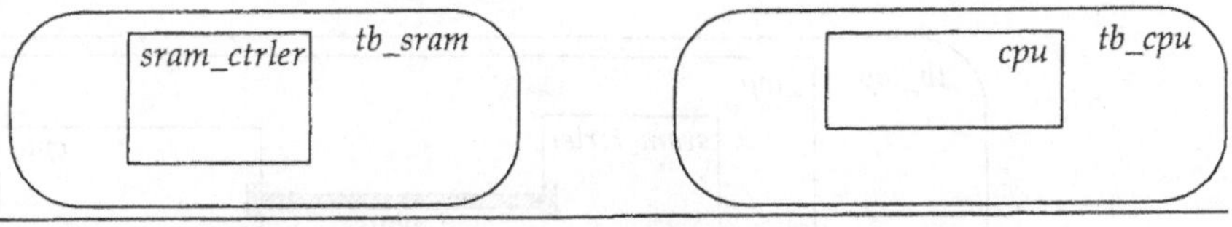

Figure 6-5 Conventional verification strategy.

When the blocks are then hooked up, only the interconnect needs to be verified, for example, to check for twisted buses. However, the interconnect in some cases is complex and it is hard to create tests to check all combinations of signal connectivity. Furthermore, it may take a long time just to run simulation on the entire design, see Figure 6-6, even though only the interconnect needs to be verified.

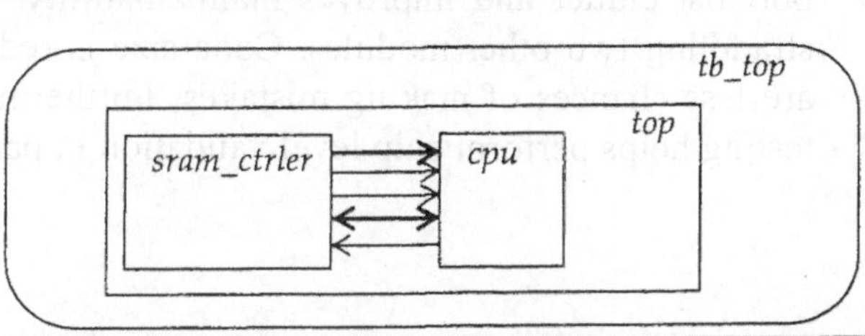

Figure 6-6 Running top-level simulation to verify interconnect is inefficient.

Let us now consider the scenario where interfaces are used. Interfaces allow the communication of blocks to be captured, designed and verified at the block level. Figure 6-7 shows the components that are tested in isolation. The interface is written and tested as part of each block.

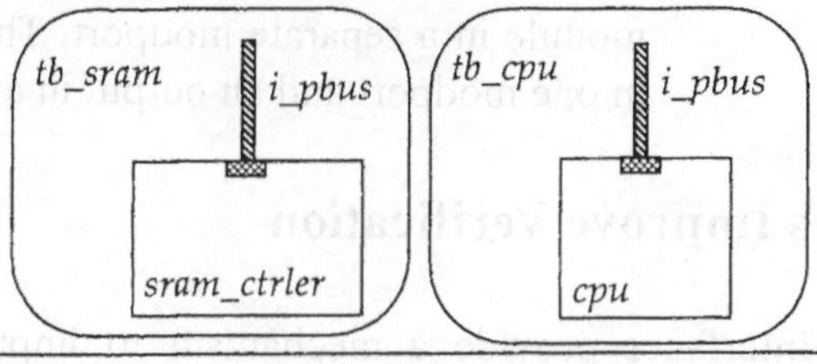

Figure 6-7 Each block is tested with its interface.

Now when the top-level is tested, see Figure 6-8, the protocol bugs have already been flushed out.

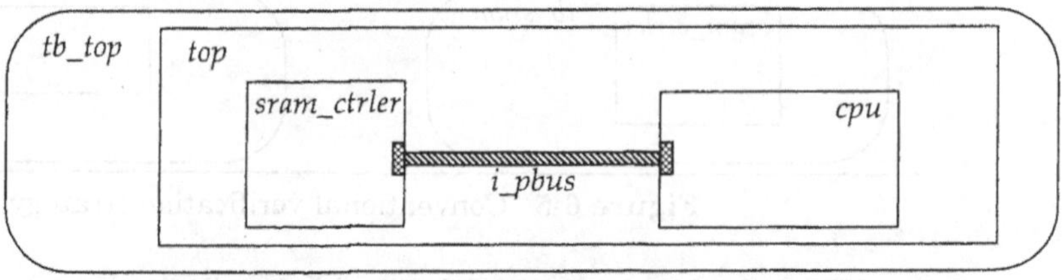

Figure 6-8 Top-level verification with interface.

The interface is an executable specification and can contain protocol checkers and coverage counters. It encapsulates connectivity as a bundle of wires. Wiring up an interface is simple and less error-prone. An interface can be instantiated and passed through module ports. It thus reduces port list clutter and improves maintainability. It is similar to a module straddling two other modules. Code size is reduced, implying that there are less chances of making mistakes. Furthermore, block level interface testing helps perform chip level validation in parallel.

❑

Chapter 7

Other Topics

This chapter describes packages and compilation units. It also describes enhancements made to subroutines in SystemVerilog. Tasks and functions are the two forms of subroutines.

7.1 Packages

A package allows for user-defined definitions, such as parameters, data types, tasks, functions, properties and sequences, to be shared across multiple modules and interfaces.

A package declaration is of the form:

```
package package_name ;
    // Parameter and local parameter declarations.
    // Constant declarations.
    // Type declarations.
    // Task and function declarations.
    // Import other packages.
    // Variable declarations.
    // Net declarations.
```

```
  . . .
endpackage [: package_name]
```

A package can be in a separate compilation unit, that is, it is not part of a module and can be written in a separate file and compiled by itself. It is at the same scope as a module. Here is an example of a package.

```
package p_misc;
  typedef enum {MAY, JUNE, JULY, AUG, SEP} t_summer;
  parameter time PIN2PIN_DELAY = 125ns;
  typedef logic [15:0] t_logic16;
  function t_logic16 encode (int arg);
    . . .
  endfunction
endpackage: p_misc
```

A parameter declaration in a package behaves just like a localparam declaration in the sense that its value cannot be modified in a module.

Elements of a package can be *directly referenced* by using the scope resolution operator (::). For example,

```
input p_misc::t_summer day;
```

directly references the type *t_summer* from the package *p_misc*. Here is another example of direct referencing.

```
result = p_arith_blks::mul(opda, opdb);
  // Calls the function mul from package p_arith_blks.
```

To import the elements of a package into a module or into another different declaration space, use the *import statement*. The import statement makes the items in a package visible in current scope, and the items can be referenced directly without specifying the package name.

```
// Import only the function encode from package p_misc:
import p_misc::encode;

// Import only the type t_logic_16 from package p_misc:
import p_misc::t_logic16;
```

```
// Wildcard import - imports all elements in package:
import p_misc::*;
```

One caveat of importing or referencing an enumeration type is that only the type name gets imported, not the enumeration literals.

```
import p_misc::t_summer;          // Imports only the
        // enumeration type definition t_summer, not the
        // enumeration literals, for example, AUG.

import p_misc::MAY;  // Imports the enumeration literal.

import p_misc::*;
  // Imports all items, including enumeration literals.
```

Wildcard importing from multiple packages can cause name collisions. Here is an example.

```
package pkg_a;
  parameter SIZE = 8;
endpackage: pkg_a

package pkg_b;
  parameter SIZE = 16;
endpackage: pkg_b

module mod_c;
  import pkg_a::*;                    // Wildcard import.
  import pkg_b::*;                    // Wildcard import.

  logic [SIZE-1:0] reg_file;
    // Which SIZE is being referred?
endmodule: mod_c
```

This can be avoided by importing items from a package selectively and by not wildcard importing both packages. Another option is to directly reference the item using the scope resolution operator.

```
logic [pkg_a::SIZE-1:0] reg_file;
```

A package cannot contain any module prototype declarations or procedural blocks. Net declarations with continuous assignments are also not allowed. Furthermore, no hierarchical references are allowed within a package declaration.

SystemVerilog provides a built-in package, called *std*, that contains system types, variables, tasks and functions. This package is implicitly wildcard imported into every compilation unit.

It is recommended not to refer items in a package via hierarchical references but to use the scope resolution operator to refer to items in a package.

7.2 Compilation Unit

A compilation unit is a list of all source files that are compiled at the same time.

```
shell_prompt> sv_compile1 f1.sv f2.sv f3.sv f4.sv

shell_prompt> sv_compile f5.sv f6.sv

shell_prompt> sv_compile f7.sv
```

Files *f1.sv*, *f2.sv*, *f3.sv* and *f4.sv* form one compilation unit. Also files *f5.sv* and *f6.sv* form another compilation unit. The third compilation unit contains file *f7.sv* by itself.

A source file can contain:

```
Time unit and time precision declarations.
Module declarations.
UDP declarations.
Interface declarations.
Program declarations.
Package declarations.
Bind directives.
Config declarations.
External declarations.
```

1. The command used to compile SystemVerilog source files.

Declarations that are valid within a package can also be specified as external declarations, which include amongst others, variable and net declarations, type declarations, function and task declarations. Note that these declarations are outside of a design unit (a *design unit* is a module, primitive, interface, program, package, or a config declaration, each of which can be compiled separately). The declarations are said to be in the *compilation-unit scope*, that is, in general, all declarations in a compilation unit that are not in any other scope are in the compilation-unit scope.

Declarations in the compilation-unit scope are visible to all design units in that compilation unit. However, a package cannot refer to items declared in the compilation-unit scope.

```
// File: common.sv

/* External declarations (in the
   compilation-unit scope)*/
// Time unit, time precision declarations.
// Variable declarations.
// Net declarations.
// Constant declarations.
// User-defined data types.
// Function and task declarations.

module rx_mac . . .
  // Can access any of the external declarations.
  . . .
endmodule: rx_mac

module tx_mac . . .
  // Can access any of the external declarations.
  . . .
endmodule: tx_mac
// End of file.
```

Even if all the external declarations are in a separate file, for example, in file *f1.sv*, and module *rx_mac* is in file *f2.sv* and module *tx_mac* is in *f3.sv*, as long as they are compiled together (*f1.sv*, *f2.sv*, *f3.sv*), the external declarations are still visible to the modules in *f2.sv* and *f3.sv*.

Items in a compilation-unit scope cannot be accessed from outside the compilation unit. Modules, primitives, programs, interfaces and packages are visible to all compilation units. Compiler directives affect only one compilation unit.

Guideline: Use a package to share declarations across modules.

It is recommended that packages be used when sharing declarations across modules as it makes it compile-independent.

A package can be imported into a module by specifying it in its compilation-unit scope, such as:

```
/* Compilation-unit scope */
import p_types::t_logic32;
  // Import only the type t_logic32.
import p_constants::*;  // Import all items in package.

module pop_fifo . . .
  . . .
endmodule: pop_fifo
```

Again here, there is an option to keep all the imports in one file and the module in another file, and then compile both files at one time, or keep the imports and the module in one file. It is recommended that the external declarations and the modules that use the external declarations be kept in one file to improve readability.

Note that it is illegal to import a package item more than once into a compilation unit. If the same package is used in multiple files, then there is a possibility that someone may compile all the files together. To handle such a case, check and set a define flag at the beginning of each file (like in C) so that the package is not imported more than once.

Guideline: Do not use .sv extension for a file that is not to be compiled by itself.

```
// File: pack2.pkg

// Do not use the .sv extension as this file is not to
// be compiled by itself.
`ifndef PACK2_LOADED                // If not loaded already.
  `define PACK2_LOADED              // Define only once.

  package pack2;
    . . .
  endpackage: pack2
```

```
    import pack2::*;              // Import all contents.
  `endif
```

and then add this to every file with:

```
  `include "pack2.pkg"
```

If there are variable declarations and static tasks and static functions, then this mechanism does not work. If a variable is defined in a package and shared in the same compilation unit, then it acts like a shared variable. However, if the modules are compiled separately with a package, then each variable is a separate instance of the variable. The same is true for static tasks and static functions. Here is an example that has three files.

```
// File: pack_c.pkg
`ifndef PACK_C_LOADED
  `define PACK_C_LOADED
  package pack_c;
    var int count;
    static function bin2hex . . .
      . . .
    endfunction
  endpackage: pack_c
  import pack_c::.*
`endif

// File: gpu.sv
`include "pack_c.pkg"
module gpu;
  . . .
endmodule: gpu

// File mpu.sv
`include "pack_c.pkg"
module mpu;
  . . .
endmodule: mpu
```

If files *gpu.sv* and *mpu.sv* are compiled as one compilation unit, then variable *count* is a shared variable that can be read and updated by either of the module *gpu* or *mpu*. If the file *gpu.sv* is compiled separately from *mpu.sv*, then there are two instances of variable *count*, each one local to the module.

The same define flag mechanism can be used to ensure that all external declarations are read only once in a compilation unit.

```
// File: gen_clock.sv
// At beginning of file, put following line:
`ifndef GEN_CLOCK_SV
  // External declarations.
  // Module declarations.
  // At end of file, put the following two lines:
  `define GEN_CLOCK_SV
`endif
```

This ensures that the external declarations and all the design units are read only once in a compilation unit.

7.2.1 $unit

$unit is a special name for the current compilation-unit scope and can be used to access items explicitly within the current compilation unit using the scope resolution operator (::).

```
success = $unit::count_3s(sin);
  // Use the function count_3s declared in the current
  // compilation-unit scope.
```

$unit is a declaration space that is visible to all design units that are compiled together. Any user-defined types, tasks, functions, parameters or variable declarations that are not inside a module, interface, program or a package are automatically placed in a **$unit**. The **$unit** can be thought of as a package that is automatically imported into all design units being compiled.

All declarations in **$unit** are directly accessible in various design units. However, they can also be explicitly referenced using the scope resolution operator, such as in:

```
typedef enum logic [2:0]
  {WAIT, READY, FIX, HOLD, SETUP} t_states;
```

```
module send_frame;
  $unit::t_states fsm_state;
  . . .
endmodule: send_frame
```

It is recommended to use a package for shared declarations instead of using **$unit**. This will ensure that the declarations have their own name space and any name conflicts with other packages can be resolved using the scope resolution operator.

What if each file has external declarations and both files are compiled at once? In this case, all external declarations are part of a single **$unit**.

```
// File: send_frame.sv
// External declarations. Example:
typedef logic signed [31:0] t_slogic32;

module send_frame;
  $unit::t_slogic32 result;
  logic [$unit::AWIDTH-1:0] haddr;
  . . .
endmodule: send_frame
// End of file.

// File: receive_frame.sv
// External declarations. Example:
parameter int AWIDTH = 12;

module receive_frame;
  $unit::t_slogic32 pwdata;
  . . .
endmodule: receive_frame
// End of file.
```

If *send_frame.sv* and *receive_frame.sv* are in one compilation unit, then the external declarations from both files are part of a single **$unit**. Notice that the parameter *AWIDTH* can be accessed in module *send_frame* as well. Compiling these two files separately will not work. This style of coding should be avoided as the behavior is dependent on how the files are compiled.

Name conflicts may also occur and compiling each file separately may cause different behavior from compiling multiple files at once. To avoid such behavior, it is recommended to use packages to share declarations across files. If a **$unit** is needed, then it is preferred to put all external declarations of one compilation unit into a separate file. Then this file can be compiled with the other files in the compilation unit without causing any conflicts.

It is possible that an implementation may restrict each file to be a separate compilation unit.

7.2.2 $root

The top level instance of a hierarchy can be explicitly identified using **$root**.

```
$root.u_mpu.u_arith.u_sff
```

7.3 Tasks and Functions

7.3.1 Top-level Sequential Block

SystemVerilog does not require the top-level begin-end keywords in a task or a function; this is implied. That is, the top-level sequential block in a task or a function can be specified without the begin-end keywords. Here is an example of a task.

```
task arith_unit
  ( input int a, b,
    input t_op opcode,
    output int y,
    output bit ycomp);
  // begin-end keywords are optional.
  case (opcode)
    ADD : y = a + b;
    SUB : y = a - b;
    LT : ycomp = a < b;
    GT : ycomp = a > b;
    EQ : ycomp = a == b;
```

```
    endcase
  endtask
```

A sequential block is implied inside the task at the top-level.

7.3.2 Labels

A label can be specified at the end of a function or task. If specified, it must match the name of the task or function.

Guideline: Use end labels for readability.

```
task rotate_right;
  . . .
endtask: rotate_right

function smallest;
  . . .
endfunction: smallest
```

7.3.3 Empty Body

A function or a task can be empty, that is, have no statements.

```
function super_and (logic m0, m1);
endfunction: super_and

task load (input a, b, c, output d, e);
endtask: load
```

7.3.4 Arguments

A function can have input, output and inout arguments. This allows functions to return values via function names or through its output and inout arguments. A void function can return values through its output and inout arguments.

A function with output and inout arguments cannot be called from an event expression, an expression within a procedural continuous assignment and an expression that is not within a procedural statement.

Guideline: Pass values only through arguments. Do not use global variables inside subroutines.

If no direction is specified for a formal argument, then the argument is assumed to be input by default.

```
task compute (bit a, b, output bit y1, y2);
  . . .
endtask: compute
```

The input arguments are *a* and *b*, and the output arguments are *y1* and *y2*. Unpacked arrays, packed and unpacked structures can be passed via arguments. Here is an example.

```
typedef struct {
  logic [23:0] paddr;
  logic [7:0] pdata;
  byte crc;
} t_packet;

function void make_packet (
    input logic [7:0] din,
    output t_packet pkt);
  pkt.pdata = din;
endfunction: make_packet
```

However, passing large data via such arguments may be undesirable; argument passing by reference is better in such a case.

7.3.5 Passing by Reference

When a task or a function is called, the input values are typically copied over and used as values in the task or function. SystemVerilog allows the capability to pass values by reference instead of by copy. The keyword **ref** is specified for the argument direction in such a case. Only automatic functions and tasks can have a reference argument by name.

```
function automatic int random (ref int seed);
  . . .
endfunction: random
  . . .
new_val = random(svar);
```

The name of the reference becomes an alias within the task or function. Changing the value within the task or function automatically changes the value at the calling level as it refers to the same variable. The reverse is also true, which is, any changes to the variable at the calling task level is immediately reflected in the reference variable within a task (note that this cannot happen in a function since a function never suspends). In the above example, *seed* is an alias for *svar*, so essentially they are the same variable. Any update to *seed* within the function is immediately reflected in *svar*.

If there is a reference argument that is read-only in a task or a function, then the argument can be specified as a **const** ref argument. This provides the protection that such a variable will not be modified within the task or function.

```
function automatic int largest (const ref int start,
    stop);
  . . .
  // start and stop cannot be changed within
  // the function.
endfunction: largest
```

This protects arguments passed by reference from being modified by the task or function, that is, the argument is a read-only reference inside the task or function.

Note that for arguments that are passed by reference, their values are always the most current value (not just the value when the task or function is called) and any update to a reference argument is seen in the calling scope immediately. In short, a reference argument is simply an alias for the variable passed in and any read or write is always immediate.

Since a function with reference arguments can modify values outside its scope, it cannot be called in an event expression, an expression in a continuous assignment, an expression within a procedural continuous assignment and an expression that is not within a procedural assignment.

Only variables can be passed by reference, not nets.

7.3.6 Passing Values by Name

SystemVerilog allows argument values to be passed by name, rather than by position. Arguments can be passed by using explicit named association.

```
mp_max = largest(.stop(stp), .start(stt));
```

When passed by name, the order of the arguments is not important in the call. It is ok to mix positional and named association but the positional associations have to occur before any of the named associations occur.

7.3.7 Default Argument Values

Formal arguments can have optional default values.

```
function bit is_done (int count = 0, step = 1);
  . . .
endfunction: is_done
```

When such a default value is present in an argument, it is not necessary to pass a value in its call. In such a case, the default value is used for the argument.

```
check1 = is_done(.step(20));    // count is 0 by default.
check2 = is_done(.count(5));    // step is 1 by default.

check3 = is_done();
  // count is 0 and step is 1 by default.

check4 = is_done(15, 18); // count is 15 and step is 18.
check5 = is_done(.step(2), .count(5));
  // count is 5 and step is 2.
```

Guideline: Specify arguments with default values at the end of the argument list for easier use of the subroutine.

SystemVerilog allows the parentheses ("( )") in an empty argument list in a task call or a function call to be omitted in certain cases. These are for void functions and class function methods that have no arguments. In addition, tasks, void functions and class function methods that require arguments but have default values specified for all their arguments can also omit the parentheses. Assignment to *check3* above requires parentheses for the argument list since it is not a void function.

```
task print_leader (int num = 16);
  $display (".......");
endtask: print_leader

function void readline;
  . . .
endfunction

// Parentheses are optional in these calls:
print_leader;           // Argument with default value.
readline;               // Void function.
```

7.3.8 Tasks

In a task, the argument direction is optional and the default is an input. Also following arguments with no direction have the same direction as the argument preceding it. The default argument type is *logic*.

```
task compare (int a, b, output lt, eq, gt);
  lt = a < b;
  eq = a == b;
  gt = a > b;
endtask: compare
```

The input arguments are *a* and *b*. The output arguments are *lt*, *eq* and *gt*. Here is another example.

```
parameter int DWIDTH = 8;

task rotate_left
  ( input [DWIDTH-1:0] din,
    input [31:0] rot_by,
    output [DWIDTH-1:0] dout
  );
  logic [DWIDTH-1:0] tmp;

  {dout, tmp} = {din, din} << rot_by;
endtask: rotate_left
```

SystemVerilog allows formal arguments and local variables in a task to be declared as automatic in a static task. And it allows formal arguments and local variables to be declared as static in an automatic task.

```
// Static task:
task rotate (logic [31:0] arr, int start, stop, by);
  automatic int fill;
  logic done;
  // Since the task is a static task, all variables
  // are by default static, e.g. done. However fill
  // has been explicitly declared to be an automatic.
  . . .
endtask: rotate

// Automatic task:
task automatic alu_blk (int a, b, opcode, output y);
  static int pstate;
  logic flag;
  // Since task is automatic, all variables declared
  // in task are automatic by default, except that
  // pstate is static since it has been explicitly
  // declared to be static. flag is automatic.
  . . .
endtask: alu_blk
```

Return Statement

A return statement can be used to exit a task. Its syntax is of the form:

```
return;
```

Here is an example.

```
task memload (. . .);
  . . .
  if (done)
    return;                 // Task will exit here.
  . . .
  // Task can exit here as well.
endtask: memload
```

7.3.9 Functions

In a function, each argument can have a direction of input, output, ref or inout. For an input argument, the value is copied at the beginning of the function call. For an output argument, the value is copied at the end of the function call. A reference argument is an alias for the variable that is passed in. And for an inout argument, the value is copied into the argument at the beginning of the function call and again copied from the argument to the calling variable at the end of the function call.

The direction of an argument that is not explicitly specified is same as that of the preceding argument. Else, the default direction is input.

```
function my_and (m0, m1, output y0, y1);
  my_and = m0 & m1;
endfunction: my_and
```

Arguments *m0* and *m1* are inputs. Argument *y1* is an output because *y0* is an output. And the default type is *logic.*

A function with a value being written out (using output, inout or ref argument) cannot be used in an event expression, or in a procedural continuous assignment. A const ref argument is however allowed in such a context.

Avoid writing a function that operates on global variables (those defined outside the function and not passed in through its argument list). Use of global variables in a function can cause hidden side-effects. Consider the following function in which *carry_in* is a global variable and is not passed in through its argument list.

```
function xor3bit (a, b);
  return (a ^ b ^ carry_in);
  // carry_in is a global variable.
endfunction: xor3bit

assign parity3 = xor3bit(opd[0], opd[1]);
```

In the continuous assignment, if there is a change to *carry_in*, *parity3* does not get updated; this is because the assignment statement is sensitive to changes only on *opd*[0] and *opd*[1]. To infer any change on *carry_in* correctly, an always_comb statement could have been used.

```
always_comb
    parity3 = xor3bit(opd1, opd2);
```

In this case, based on the semantics of the always_comb statement, any change in *carry_in* causes the always_comb statement to get executed and *parity3* to get updated. However, such side behaviors should be avoided as these are sometimes hard to debug and whoever is reading the code is not obvious of the hidden behavior as well. The best style is to pass all variables used in a function through its argument list.

Void Function

A function can be declared to be of type **void**; such a function does not return any value. In other words, the void type can be used as a return type for functions indicating that it has no value to be returned.

```
function void print_dots (int num);
  for (int i = 0; i < num; i++)
    $write (".");

  $write ("\n");
endfunction: print_dots

print_dots(5);                    // Function call.
```

Such a function call behaves like a statement and appears like a task call. Here are some more examples.

```
function void half_adder (input a, b, output s, c);
  s = a ^ b;
  c = a & b;
endfunction: half_adder
. . .
half_adder(a1, a2, o1, c1);
```

```
parameter int N = 8;
. . .
function void compute_parity
  ( input [N-1:0] din, output parity);
  bit tpar = 0;

  for (int i = 0; i < N, i++)
    tpar = tpar ^ din[i];

  parity = tpar;
endfunction: compute_parity
. . .
compute_parity(dbus, pval);          // Function call.
```

Return Statement

A function can optionally return a value by using the return statement. The syntax is:

```
return expression ;
```

The return statement is optional. The function name can also be assigned a value. Either mechanism can be used. The function name can also be returned using the return statement.

```
function int max;
  . . .
  max = . . .;              // Can write to function name.

  if (max > 10)
    return max;             // Return the function name value.
  . . .
endfunction: max
```

A return statement can be used to exit a function at any point in the function. The above example shows the function exits when the condition "*max > 10*" is true.

A return statement must have an expression. However, if the return value is of no use, then it can be ignored by casting the function call to the void type.

```
function int send (. . .);
  . . .
  return 1;
  . . .
endfunction: send

void '(send(. . .));          // Disregard the return value.
```

Here is another example. A value can be returned from a function via the function name or using the return statement.

```
function automatic int exp (input int a = 2, b);
  exp = 2;
  return a ** b;
    // return overrides the value assigned to exp.
endfunction: exp

always_comb
  result = exp(.a(6), .b(arg1)); // Named association.
```

7.3.10 Import and Export

Functions and tasks can be exported out of the SystemVerilog context or into a SystemVerilog context using the import and export declarations. For example, C functions can be imported into SystemVerilog using the import declaration. SystemVerilog functions and tasks can be exported to the C environment using the export declaration. Further details are beyond the scope of this book.

7.4 System Tasks and Functions

7.4.1 $bits Function

This function returns the number of bits that are represented in the expression.

```
$bits ( expression )
```

Here is an example.

```
logic [7:0] addr;
byte byte_lane;

$bits(addr)                  // returns 8.
$bits(byte_lane)             // returns 8.
$bits(addr > byte_lane)      // returns 1.
$bits(addr + byte_lane)      // returns 8.
```

Other system functions and system tasks defined in SystemVerilog are described in the appropriate chapters.

7.5 Alias Statement

An *alias statement* can be used to declare an alternate name for a net. It models a bidirectional short circuit connection.

```
wire logic [15:0] data_word;
wire logic [7:0] data_bus;
wire logic [0:3] status;
wire logic reset, rx_ready;

alias data_bus = data_word[15:8];
alias status = data_word[3:0];
alias reset = data_word[4];
alias rx_ready = data_word[5];
```

The alias statement can also be specified in the reverse form and the meaning is identical.

```
alias data_word[5] = rx_ready;
```

Any changes to *data_word[5]* appears on *rx_ready* without any delay and any changes on *rx_ready* appears on *data_word[5]*. The alias is not a different object, but just an alternate name for the right hand side. Multiple aliases can be declared in a single declaration, such as:

```
wire [2:0] op_code, status, sign;
  // Type logic is implicit.
wire [15:0] rdata;
```

```
alias op_code = status = sign = rdata[2:0];
```

implies *op_code*, *status* and *sign* all refer to the same object *rdata[2:0]*.

Note that the alias statement is not an executable statement. It is only a declaration indicating that the left hand side and the right hand side both refer to the same net. One could have written in reverse order with absolutely no change in its meaning.

```
alias sign = rdata[2:0] = op_code = status;
```

All three are aliases of the same 3-bit net.

Only nets can be aliased, not variables. The type of the objects that are aliased must be same. Bit-selects and part-selects can be aliased as long as the size of the right hand side and left hand side match.

```
wire [63:0] mem_word;
wire [15:0][3:0] rf_word;
wire [0:7] rdata;
wire [3:0] cmd;

alias mem_word = rf_word;
alias rdata = mem_word[7:0];
alias cmd = rf_word[6][3:0];
```

The alias statement and the named port connection capability (.*) can be used to simplify writing of module instantiations.

```
extern module vip
  ( input reset, clock,
    output [31:0] rdata,
    output ready);

extern module cpu
  ( output rst, clk,
    input [31:0] rdata,
    output rdy);

wire reset, clock, rst, clk, rdy, ready;
wire [31:0] rdata;
```

```
alias reset = rst;
alias clock = clk;
alias rdy = ready;

vip u_vip (.*);
cpu m_cpu (.*);
```

Even though different (implicit) net names are connected to different module instances, the alias statements make them the same nets.

7.6 Local and Global Variables

Global variables are those that are declared outside of a module, interface, package, program, task or a function. Global variables have a static lifetime, that is, they exist for the entire elaboration and simulation time. Data types, tasks, functions and class definitions can also be in global scope. Global variables can be accessed explicitly using **$root**.

Local declarations are accessible in the scope in which they are defined and are by default static. However, they can be made automatic, using the keyword **automatic**. Static local variables can be accessed by their hierarchical path names, if possible.

```
// File: local_global.sv
int store0;                    // Static global variable.

function tube ();              // Static global function.
  . . .
endfunction: tube

module check;
  int store0;                  // Static, local to module.

  initial
    begin
      int store1;              // Static, local to initial.
      static int store2;       // Static, local to initial.
      automatic int auto1;
        // Automatic, local to initial.
    end
```

```
    task automatic top ();     // Local task to module.
      int auto2;               // Automatic, local to task.
      static int trp;          // Static, local to task.
      automatic int auto3;     // Automatic, local to task.

      $root.store0 = store0;   // Left hand side refers
        // to global store0 while right hand side
        // refers to local variable declared within module.
    endtask: top
  endmodule: check
  // End of file.
```

Data declared outside of a module is static and global. Data declared inside of a module is static and available to all tasks and functions in that module.

One recommendation is to avoid using static variables in a task or a function, especially when the task or function resides in a **$unit**, or in a package or in an interface. Also declare such functions or tasks as static.

SystemVerilog allows variables to be declared in unnamed blocks.

```
always @(posedge clk)
  begin                        // Unnamed block.
    int i;                     // Local variables.
    real r;
    . . .
  end
```

Such variables (either static or automatic) cannot be referenced hierarchically.

❑

Chapter 8

Advanced Verification Topics

This chapter describes advanced verification topics such as program blocks, clocking blocks, semaphores, mailboxes and events, that are useful for verification. Random constraint generation techniques are also described.

Programs along with modules, interfaces, packages, primitives, configurations and checkers form the basic building blocks used in describing a design and its verification environment. These are also referred to as *design elements* in SystemVerilog.

8.1 Clocking Block

A *clocking block* describes the timing and synchronization requirements of the signals in a module. It describes the relationship of signals with respect to clock edges. In particular, it separates the timing aspect of the design into a clocking block, as opposed to the functional aspects of the design that can be defined structurally or at a procedural level. Here is the syntax of a clocking block.

```
clocking clocking_block_name @ ( clock_event ) ;
  clocking_items
endclocking [ : clocking_block_name]
```

The body of the clocking block is used to describe synchronous events, the input sampling and the synchronous output drives. All the events described within a clocking block are with reference to the clock event specified on the first line. Here is an example of a clocking block.

```
clocking cb_modem @(posedge clk_125);
  default input #4ns output #3ns;
  input rstn, sync;
  output ena;
endclocking: cb_modem
```

The name of the clocking block is *cb_modem*. The clock associated with this block is *clk_125* and the clock event is a rising edge on *clk_125*. The *default* declaration specifies that all inputs have a default skew of 4ns and all outputs of the block has a default skew of 3ns. The input and output declarations specify the list of signals associated with the clock event and whose skew is described in this clocking block. Since these signals are already defined elsewhere, there is no need to specify the width and the type of the signals in the clocking block.

So what is a skew? For inputs and inouts, it specifies the delay before the clock event as the point where the input is sampled. For outputs and inouts, it specifies the delay after the clock event when output becomes available. See Figure 8-1.

So in our example, inputs *rstn* and *sync* are sampled 4ns before the rising edge of *clk_125* and the output *ena* is driven 3ns after the rising edge of *clk_125*.

A clocking block can only occur inside of a module, interface or a program block. In addition, there can be more than one clocking block. Also, there can be multiple clocking blocks for the same clock.

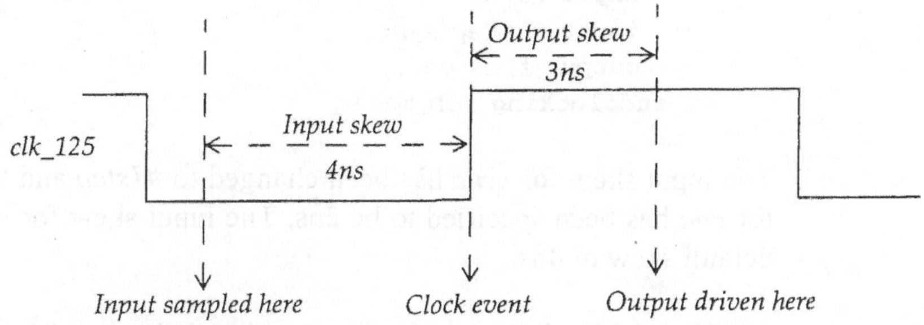

Figure 8-1 Clock skew for inputs and outputs.

It is possible to refer to a hierarchical signal inside the clocking block. For example,

```
input reset = tb.top.rst;
```

The skew specification for *reset* applies to the hierarchical signal *tb.top.rst*.

For sampling signals in the current time step, but before the clock event occurs, a new form of delay called *#1step* can be used. Here is another example of a clocking block.

```
clocking cb_macreg @(posedge clk_12);
  input lock, grant;
  output request;
endclocking: cb_macreg
```

Since the default statement is missing in this clocking block, when are the inputs sampled and outputs driven? In this case, the default input skew is *#1step* and the default output skew is 0.

Even when a default statement is present in a clocking block, the input and output skew can be overridden by explicit input and output declarations.

```
clocking cb_mailq @(posedge clk_125);
  default input #4ns output #3ns;
  input rstn;
  input #1step sync;
  output #2ns ena;
endclocking: cb_mailq
```

The input skew for *sync* has been changed to *#1step* and the output skew for *ena* has been specified to be 2ns. The input skew for *rstn* stays as the default skew of 4ns.

What is the difference between an input skew of *#1step* and an input skew of 0? An input skew of *#1step* will sample the data before the start of the current event (same as end of previous event), while an input skew of #0 will cause the input to be sampled at the same time the clock event occurs.[1] An output skew of #0 indicates that outputs will be driven at the same time that the clock event occurs.

Skew values can be parameterized in a clocking block.

```
parameter INPUT_SKEW = 4ns;
parameter OUTPUT_SKEW = 3ns;

clocking cb_mp @(posedge clk_125);
  default input #INPUT_SKEW output #OUTPUT_SKEW;
  input rstn;
  input #1step sync;
  output #2ns ena;
endclocking: cb_mp
```

If a module has multiple clocks, then multiple clocking blocks can be declared.

```
module top
  ( input bit sclk, mclk,
    input logic reset, ctrl,
    output [3:0] usb_out, ser_out
  );
```

1. This is a simplified explanation without going into the details of what comprises a time step.

```
clocking cb_sclk @(posedge sclk);
  input reset;
  output usb_out;
endclocking: cb_sclk

clocking cb_mclka @(negedge mclk);
  input #2ns ctrl;
endclocking: cb_mclka

clocking cb_mclkb @(posedge mclk);
  output #0ns ser_out;
endclocking: cb_mclkb
. . .
endmodule: top
```

To specify a delay in terms of number of clock cycles, the *cycle delay operator* (##) can be used:

```
##3;        // Wait for three clock cycles.
```

One question at this point is what clock cycle are we referring to? This is specified using a clocking block; one of the clocking blocks is identified as the *default clocking block*. So any reference to the cycle delay refers to the cycles specified by the default clocking block.

```
module top
  ( input bit sclk, mclk,
    input logic reset, ctrl,
    output [3:0] usb_out, ser_out
  );
  default clocking cb_sclk @(posedge sclk);
    input reset;
    output usb_out;
  endclocking: cb_sclk

  clocking cb_mclka @(negedge mclk);
    input #2ns ctrl;
  endclocking: cb_mclka

  clocking cb_mclkb @(posedge mclk);
    output #0ns ser_out;
  endclocking: cb_mclkb
```

```
   . . .
   ##3;           // Refers to three clock cycles of sclk.
   . . .
endmodule: top
```

The default clock is *sclk*, specified by the default clocking block *cb_sclk*, in the module *top* and ##3 refers to three clock cycles of *sclk*.

It is possible to declare global clocking that is valid for an entire elaborated model. This is done using the *global clocking block*. Here is an example of such a block.

```
global clocking cb_gc
  @(posedge arm_clk or negedge pclk);
endclocking: cb_gc
```

Only one global clocking block is allowed in an entire elaborated model. The main purpose of the global clocking block is to specify which clock events in simulation correspond to the primary clocks in formal verification.

The system function **$global_clock** returns the clock event of the global clocking block. In our example, it would return "**posedge** *arm_clk* **or negedge** *pclk*". This system function can be used wherever a clocking event can be specified.

Notice that a clocking block only describes how the inputs are sampled and outputs are synchronized. It does not modify the behavior of any signals. The clocking block separates the clocking behavior of the design from the functional behavior. The clocking block is useful in a cycle-based methodology where it enables users to define testbenches at a higher level of time abstraction, which is in cycles.

8.2 Program Block

A *program block* is the basic building block for writing a testbench. While the old methods of writing a testbench in Verilog HDL are still valid, SystemVerilog goes one step further and defines a construct exclusively for describing testbenches (as opposed to modules describing a design). The advantage of this approach is that it provides a single entry point of execution for testbenches and it provides special execution semantics that ensure there is no race condition between the design and the testbench. One such example is when a testbench receives a response from the design, it is required to send back a new set of stimulus at the same time, which may or may not be possible without this new construct. Note that while a module is used to describe design hierarchy, the purpose of the testbench is only to send input stimulus to the design and to receive and verify the response from the design.

Here is the syntax for a program block.

```
program program_block_name ( port_list ) ;
  // Continuous assignments.
  // Module declarations.
  // Initial statements.
  // Final statements.
  // Concurrent assertion statements.
  // Timeunits declarations.
  // Loop generate statements.
  // Conditional generate statements.
endprogram [ : program_block_name ]
```

A program block is syntactically very much like a module, except that not all constructs are allowed within its list of statements. Here is an example of a program block.

```
program test_memory
  ( input clk, reset,
    input [7:0] rdata,
    output var [7:0] wdata
  );
  logic parity;
  initial
    begin
      parity = ^ rdata;
      wdata = 8'hFF;
      . . .
    end
  . . .
endprogram: test_memory
```

The program block serves as a clear separator between a design and its testbench. Together with clocking blocks, a program block provides for race-free interaction between a design and its testbench and enables cycle-level and transaction-level abstraction. Here is another example of a program block.

```
program test_mac
  ( input clk,
    t_state pstate,
    output var resetn, bus_ena
  );

  initial
    forever @(posedge clk)
      begin
        if ($time < 200ns)
          resetn <= 1'b0;
        else
          resetn <= 0'b0;

        case (pstate)
          S0: bus_ena <= 1'b1;
          S1: bus_ena <= 1'b0;
          S2: bus_ena <= 1'b1;
          default: bus_ena <= 1'bx;
        endcase
      end
endprogram: test_mac
```

The definition of a program block may be in a separate file, just like a module, and then instantiated within a module, or it can be defined within a module itself.

Guideline: Declare each program block in a separate file.

```
module top;
  . . .
  // Instantiate the program block.
  test_memory u_test_memory (mclk, rst, rbus, wbus);
  . . .
endmodule: top
```

```
// Alternate method of using programs within a module:
module top_a;
  bit sysclk;
  . . .
  // Define the program block within a module.
  program test_cpu (. . .);
    @(posedge sysclk) . . .
      . . .
  endprogram: test_cpu
  // A program block definition creates it
  // own implicit instantiation.
  . . .
  program test_rom (. . .);
    initial @(negedge sysclk) . . .
      . . .
  endprogram: test_rom
  // The definition and its implicit instantiation.
  . . .
endmodule: top_a
```

A module may contain one or more program blocks. Each definition of a program block creates an implicit instantiation, which has the same instance name as the declaration name (in above case, the instance names would be *test_cpu* and *test_rom*). In addition, signals declared within a module can be shared across the multiple program blocks.

Just like a module, a program block can have zero or more input, output or inout ports. It can contain zero or more initial statements, continuous assignments, final statements, generate statements and specparam statements, concurrent assertions and timeunit declarations. It can also contain type and data declarations, as well as functions and tasks.

However, the difference with a module is that a program block cannot contain an always statement, user-defined primitive (UDP) instance, module instance, interface or another program block. A program block is always at a leaf level of hierarchy. A program block can call a task or a function defined within a module, but a module cannot call a task or a function defined within a program block.

Signals declared in a program block are called *program signals*. Program signals cannot be referenced outside of its program block. Non-program signals are referred to as *design signals*.

```
program dbus_wave (output bit pclk);
  logic [7:0] dbus;                    // Program signal.

  initial
    begin
      dbus = 8'hFF;
      #10ns dbus = 8'hF0;
      #12ns dbus = 8'h01;
      #5ns dbus = 8'h5C;
    end

  assign #12ns pclk = ~pclk;

  initial
    begin
      wait ($time > 250ns);
      $exit;
    end
endprogram: dbus_wave
```

The biggest difference between a module and a program block is in the way a program block is scheduled. A program block execution is scheduled after all design events (events on design signals) have been processed within a time step[1]. Furthermore, clocking blocks can be used within a program to ensure that steady state values of the design signals are sampled. These capabilities ensure that the execution of statements within a program block occurs in a well-defined order, and therefore, race conditions are avoided between a design and its testbench.

```
program test_mac
  ( input clk,
    t_state pstate,
    output var resetn, bus_ena
  );
```

1. A simplified representation without going into specific details of what comprises a time step.

```
clocking cb_mac @(posedge clk);
  default input #1ns output #2ns;
  input pstate;
  output resetn, bus_ena;
endclocking
...
endprogram: test_mac
```

The **$exit** system task can be used in a program block to terminate all processes spawned by the program block and to exit. The program block subsequently is no longer active. Note that **$exit** does not terminate simulation, it only terminates activity from the program block in which it is specified. When there is no explicit **$exit** task call in a program, the program implicitly calls **$exit** after all initial statements in the program complete.

An *anonymous program block* can be defined in a package or in the compilation-unit scope. Such a program block can store data, tasks and functions that are available for all program blocks.

The syntax of an anonymous program block is:

```
program ;
  // Task declarations.
  // Function declarations.
  // Class declarations.
  // Covergroup declarations.
  // Class constructor declarations.
endprogram
```

8.3 Interprocess Communication and Synchronization

SystemVerilog has defined two new ways for interprocess communication and synchronization via semaphores and mailboxes. Furthermore, it has enhanced the event types. While events (using the @ and the -> operators) provide a static way (known at compile time or elaboration time) of providing communication and synchronization, semaphores and mailboxes allow interprocess communication to occur dynamically, that is, at runtime.

8.3.1 Semaphores

There can be multiple processes trying to attempt to utilize a scarce resource. In order to avoid race conditions and to provide a regulated way to access the scarce resource, a *semaphore* can be used. A scarce resource for example could be a variable or an array or any other data object, or a port through which data has to be sent.

When a resource contention arises, the access to the shared resource needs to be arbitrated. SystemVerilog provides this arbitration functionality through the use of semaphores. A semaphore need not have any connection to the resource that it is trying to arbitrate; that is up to the user to associate. See Figure 8-2. A semaphore is typically used for mutual exclusion, access control to shared resources, and for basic synchronization.

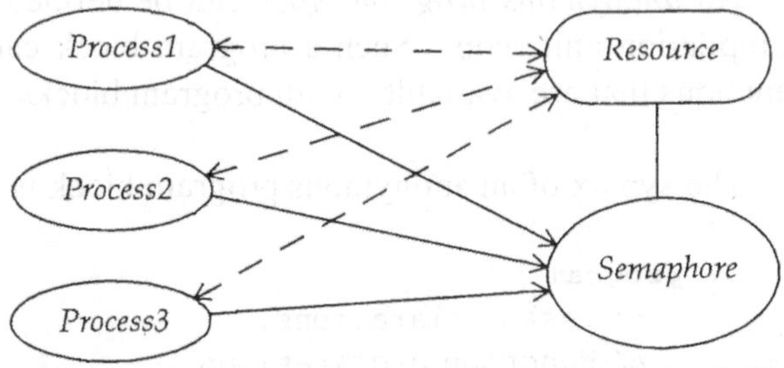

Figure 8-2 Semaphore allows race-free access to resource.

A semaphore is like a bucket that contains a fixed number of keys in it. A process that needs to access a resource must first get a fixed number of keys from the semaphore (bucket). If the required number of keys are available with the semaphore (in the bucket), the process can take the keys from the semaphore and can then access the resource until it no longer needs the resource, at which point, it returns the keys back to the semaphore (puts them back into bucket). If there are not enough keys available when a process requests it, the process may choose to wait. All other processes must wait until there are enough keys available with the semaphore. The association of number of keys required for a resource is done by the user (and not by the semaphore).

By enforcing a common set of rules to access a resource, a semaphore acts as a common gateway for all the processes that want that resource.

Any number of processes can request ownership of keys of a semaphore, but only a fixed number of requests can be granted at once; it need not be only one. Once a process has been granted access by the semaphore and is finished with the shared resource, it releases its ownership of the keys to the semaphore so that any new process request or any pending processes can acquire the keys from the semaphore.

The number of processes that can be granted access simultaneously to a resource is controlled by a key count. Each semaphore maintains a fixed set of keys and keeps track of all keys at all times. When a process requests access to the resource, it can ask for a specific number of keys. If the semaphore has the number of keys available, it grants access to the process and decrements the number of keys that it has. Once the process completes, it releases the keys and the semaphore updates its key count. If a process asks for a number of keys and the semaphore does not have that many keys available, the process either suspends waiting for access to the resource or does something else. In order for a semaphore to operate reliably, two rules have to be followed.

i. A process that is not granted access should not access the resource directly without checking with the semaphore.

ii. Once a process completes using the resource, it should return the keys back to the semaphore so that other processes can access the resource.

Here is the syntax for declaring a semaphore.

```
semaphore semaphore_name ;
```

A semaphore is a built-in class that allows only certain predefined methods on the keys by processes. These are:

i. **new**(*num_keys*) : Creates a semaphore with the specified number of keys.

ii. **get**(*num_keys*) : Obtains one or more keys from a semaphore and blocks until required number of keys are available.

iii. **try_get**(*num_keys*) : Obtains one or more keys from a semaphore without blocking, that is, if required number of keys are not available, it does not wait and continues execution.

iv. **put**(*num_keys*) : Returns specified keys to the semaphore.

The *new*() function returns a pointer to the semaphore with the specified number of keys. The default key count is 0.

```
semaphore sem_mem = new(4);
```

The semaphore *sem_mem* is created with four keys. The function *new* returns a null if the semaphore cannot be created. Note that the association of the semaphore to the resource (for example, a memory) is done by the user and is not described in the language.

The task *get*() gets the required number of keys, if available. The default number of keys is 1, if none specified. If the number of keys are not available, then the *get*() task blocks and waits until the required number of keys become available.

```
. . .
sem_mem.get(2);
. . .
```

In above case, if two keys are not available, the *get*() suspends and waits until two keys become available. All calls to *get*() are queued in a first-in first-out order and keys are delivered on a first-come first-serve basis.

The *try_get*() function tries to get the specified number of keys, but does not block if sufficient keys are not available with the semaphore. It returns a 1 if it is successful in acquiring the number of keys that it requested. But if it is not successful, it returns a 0 and does not block. The default key count for this function is a 1.

```
. . .
if (sem_mem.try_get(3))
  // Got the three keys - access the resource.
  . . .
else
  // Do something else.
. . .
```

Once a process has completed using the resource, it can return the keys to the semaphore by using the *put*() task. The number of keys is the argument and the default is 1.

```
. . .
sem_mem.get(3);
// Now can access the resource, do
// something with the resource.
. . .
// After done:
sem_mem.put(3);
. . .
```

The *put*() is a task because it is possible for the semaphore to be busy at that time and there could be a delay before it returns back. If a process that has been waiting now finds enough keys, it can acquire the keys and get access to the resource.

One problem with the *get*() task is that when the task is called, an attempt is immediately made to retrieve the required number of keys without first putting it on the first-in first-out queue. So the new request could succeed even when there are other processes waiting for it.

```
sem_mem.get(4);        // Say only 2 available - blocks.
. . .
// In another process:
sem_mem.get(2);        // Gets the 2 keys. Not fair.
```

This problem can be avoided by acquiring the keys one at a time (*get*(1)) when more than one key is required.

Since a semaphore is a built-in type class, it can be used as a base class to derive higher level classes. Here are two examples of using semaphores.

```
// Example 1:
program sem_example;
  semaphore sema = new(1);
  // Assume sema controls output port spi_out of design,
  // so only one process can write to it.
```

```
initial
  begin
    repeat (3)
      begin
        fork
          begin: process_a
            . . .
            sema.get(1);           // Wait for a key.
            // Do something with resource:
            spi_out <= parity;
            sema.put(1);           // Return the key.
            . . .
          end: process_a

          begin: process_b
            . . .
            sema.get(1);           // Wait for key.
            // Do something with resource:
            spi_out <= serial_data;
            sema.put(1);           // Return key.
            . . .
          end: process_b
        join
      end
  end
endprogram: sem_example

// Example 2:
program semex_two;
  semaphore semid = new(1);
  . . .
  task get_master (int id);
    // Wait for random number of clock cycles:
    repeat (4 + $random() % 64) @(posedge pclk);
    // Wait for address bus to be available:
    semid.get(1);
    // Use the address bus.
    $display ("Master %d has access to address bus.",
              id);
    // Model time to access address bus.
    repeat (10) @(posedge pclk);
    semid.put(1);          // Done, release the keys.
  endtask: get_master
```

```
initial
  fork
    get_master(id1);
    get_master(id2);
    get_master(id3);
  join
  . . .
endprogram: semex_two
```

8.3.2 Mailboxes

A *mailbox* provides another convenient way for interprocess communication. While semaphores provided such a feature indirectly, a mailbox provides this interprocess communication directly, that is, the processes work directly with the resource.

A mailbox is a first-in first-out storage array of any data type. One or more processes push data into the mailbox and one or more processes can read the data out of the mailbox. Figure 8-3 shows such a scenario. A process can suspend if the data is not available, that is, wait for another process to put data into the mailbox.

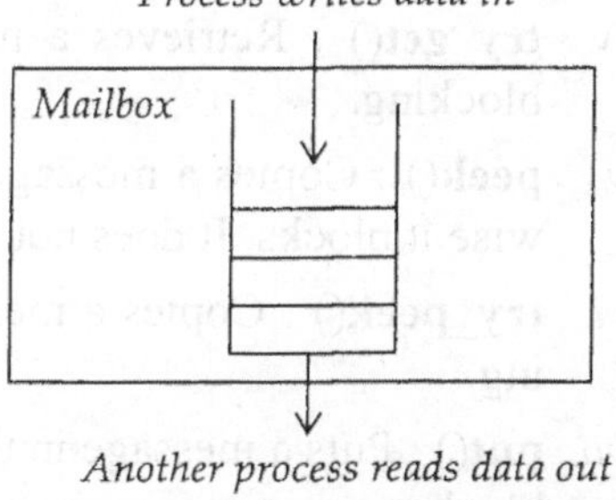

Figure 8-3 A mailbox is like a FIFO.

A mailbox acts as a synchronizer between one or more processes. While one or more processes are putting data into the mailbox, one or more processes are reading the data out of the mailbox, thus preventing race conditions between the processes that are writing to and reading from the mailbox. The writing and reading processes could be running at different speeds. If the writing process is faster than the reading process, the mailbox will start filling up and may become full, after which no process can no longer write to it. If the writing process is slower than the reading process, then the reading process will likely find an empty mailbox when it wants to read data and will have to wait until the writing process puts data into the mailbox, or the writing process can continue to do something else and check the mailbox later.

Here is the syntax of a mailbox declaration.

```
mailbox my_letters;
```

Just like a semaphore, a mailbox is a built-in class that has certain set of predefined methods that can operate upon it. Furthermore, a mailbox may be bounded (can become full), or unbounded (never becomes full).

Here are the predefined methods that can be used for accessing the messages in a mailbox. A message corresponds to a data value.

i. **new()** : Creates a mailbox with a capacity of the specified number of messages.

ii. **num()** : Returns the number of messages in the mailbox.

iii. **get()** : Retrieves a message from the mailbox, if available. If not available, it blocks.

iv. **try_get()** : Retrieves a message from the mailbox without blocking.

v. **peek()** : Copies a message from mailbox, if available, otherwise it blocks. It does not retrieve the message.

vi. **try_peek()** : Copies a message from mailbox without blocking.

vii. **put()** : Puts a message in the mailbox. If the mailbox is full, it blocks.

viii. **try_put()** : Attempts to put a message in mailbox and if mailbox is full, it does not block.

The function *new*() is the constructor method for the mailbox class. The argument is the bound (capacity) value. If the bound value is 0, then the mailbox in unbounded, that is, it can hold infinite number of messages.

```
mailbox mb_letters = new(200);
```

The mailbox *mb_letters* can store 200 messages. The default value of the bound value is 0.

The function *num*() returns the number of messages in the mailbox. And there is no argument to be specified.

```
if (mb_letters.num() > 195)
  $display ("About to be filled");
```

The task *put*() puts a message into the mailbox. It is a task because it can suspend, for example, when the mailbox is full, then the task call will block and wait until a slot becomes available.

```
mb_letter.put(6);
mb_letter.put("you got mail");
mb_letter.put(8'h3F);
```

An unbounded mailbox will never suspend on a *put*().

The function *try_put*() is similar to *put*() except that it does not block. If the mailbox is full, it simply returns back with a value of 0. If the put was successful, it returns back with a value of 1.

```
  . . .
if (mb_letters.try_put(23))
  // The data was put into the mailbox.
  . . .
else
  // Try later.
  . . .
```

The task *get*() gets a message from the mailbox. It blocks if there is no message left in the mailbox to retrieve. Also if the type of data being obtained does not match the target variable, a runtime error message is generated.

```
mb_letters.get(letter_val);
  // Type of letter_val must match value in mailbox.
```

The function *try_get*() is similar to *get*() except that it does not block. If a message is available, it will retrieve it. If not, it will return a 0. And if a wrong type of data is available, it returns a -1.

```
always          // Keep checking until data is available.
  begin
    flag = mb_letters.try_get(pval);

    if (flag == 1)
      $display ("Got the value %d from mailbox", pval);
    else if (flag == 0)
      $display ("Mailbox is empty");
    else if (flag == -1)
      $display ({"Type of value in mailbox does",
                 " not match type of pval"});
    else
      $display ("It should not reach this point");

    #10ns;
  end
```

The task *peek*() can be used to look at the data in the mailbox without actually removing it from the mailbox. If there is no message in the mailbox, the task blocks.

```
mb_letters.peek(var1);
```

The function *try_peek*() is similar to the *peek*() method, except that it does not block. It returns a 1 if a message of the correct type is present, 0 if mailbox is empty and -1 if the wrong type of data is present.

```
mb_letters.try_peek(var2);
```

Note that a mailbox can store any type of data. As long as what is put in matches what is being read out, there is no problem. However, if the requirement is for a mailbox to hold only one type of data, the mailbox can be parameterized by explicitly specifying the type of the data that will be stored in the mailbox.

```
mailbox #(int) mb_numbers = new(500);
```

The mailbox *mb_numbers* can only store integers. The advantage of parameterizing a mailbox in such a case is that it provides for additional checking at compile time to ensure that the correct type of data is being written or being read. It is recommended that all mailboxes be created of specific types so that additional type checking can be performed at compile time. Here is an example.

```
program pm_mailbox2;
  typedef logic [63:0] t_logic64;
  mailbox #(t_logic64) mb_logic64;
  parameter MAX_MESSAGES = 20;

  task get_data();
    t_logic64 from_mb;

    for (int k = 0; k < 10; k++)
      // Check if valid data exists in mailbox.
      if (mb_logic64.try_peek() == -1)
        $display ("Wrong data type present in mailbox");

        mb_logic64.get(from_mb);
          // Get data from mailbox and do something with it.
          // If not available, wait.
  endtask: get_data

  task put_data();
    t_logic64 to_mb;

    for (int k = 0; k < 10; k++)
      begin
        #10ns; // Get data into to_mb - this takes time.
        mb_logic64.put(to_mb);
        // If mailbox is full, wait until a slot is
        // available. Then put data into mailbox.
      end
  endtask: put_data
```

```
initial
  begin
    mb_logic64 = new(MAX_MESSAGES);

    if (!mb_logic64)
      $display ("Cannot allocate mailbox");

    fork
      put_data();
      get_data();
      #20ns;
    join_any

    #200ns;            // Wait until all data processed.
  end
endprogram: pm_mailbox2
```

Note that *put_data*() and *get_data*() have to be written as tasks and not as functions, since they can suspend due to either mailbox being full or being empty.

8.4 More on Events

8.4.1 Nonblocking Event Trigger

The nonblocking event operator "->>" is similar to the "->" event operator, except for the fact that while the "->" operator blocks execution of subsequent code, the "->>" operator allows execution of subsequent code without blocking and the event is scheduled to occur at the end of the time step.

```
event sync_flag;
. . .
always @(sync_flag)
  begin: ablk
    . . .
    arg = 2;
    . . .
  end
. . .
```

```
initial
  begin: iblk
    . . .
    ->> sync_flag;
    sum <= arg + brg;
    . . .
  end
```

The nonblocking event operator schedules an event on *sync_flag* to occur at the end of the time step, and execution continues with the next statement. To highlight the difference with the blocking event operator ("->"), consider the nonblocking event operator replaced with the blocking event operator. In this case, when the event operator is executed, the following assignment statement is blocked until the statements associated with the *sync_flag* event are executed, which in this case, includes an update to *arg*. So when execution returns back to the initial statement, the new value of *arg* is used in the computation for *sum*.

8.4.2 Property *triggered*

The wait on event statement can be used to wait for an event.

```
wait (sync_flag);
```

However what happens if the wait statement and the event on *sync_flag* occur at the same time? Does the wait statement see the event or does it wait for the next event on *sync_flag*? This race condition can be resolved by using the *triggered* property of an event. The *triggered* property is true for the entire time step that an event occurs, thus obviating the race condition.

```
wait (sync_flag.triggered);
. . .
event e_tx;
if (e_tx.triggered)
  $display ("Event occurred at time %t", $time);
```

8.4.3 Event Operations

SystemVerilog allows events to be assigned to each other, to be reset and to be compared to other events.

```
event parity, pkt_done, capture;
. . .
parity = pkt_done; // The two become merged, that is,
  // they are treated like aliases. Both point to the
  // same event. If there is an event on parity, it can
  // be seen on pkt_done and vice versa.
. . .
parity = null;          // Reclaim an event, that is, no
                        // events can occur on this.
. . .
if (pkt_done == null)
  . . .
if (parity != pkt_done)
  . . .
logic t1, t2;
t1 = (parity === capture);
t2 = (capture !== pkt_done);
. . .
if (capture)                        // 0 if null, 1 otherwise.
  $display ("Event is not null");
else
  $display ("Event is null");
```

8.4.4 Event Sequencing

The *wait_order statement* waits until all the events specified in the list occur in the specified order.

```
wait_order ( event1, event2, event3, . . . )
  [ [ statement1 ] else statement2 ] ;
```

If the events occur in the specified order, then the wait_order succeeds and *statement1* gets executed, else *statement2* is executed. Note that the wait_order statement suspends until all the specified events are triggered in the given order left to right. It does not consider time, only the specified order.

```
wait_order (parity, sync_flag, pkt_done);

wait_order (sync_a, sync_b, sync_c, sync_d)
else
  $display ({"The sync events did not occur",
            " in the right order."});

wait_order (fsm_in_S0, fsm_in_S3, fsm_in_S5)
  state_in_seq = TRUE;
else
  state_in_seq = FALSE;
```

The sequence has to be exact. A minor exception is that once an event occurs, the same event can occur again without causing it to fail. For the last example, the event sequence "*fsm_in_S0, fsm_in_S5*" is not valid (and hence will fail) since after the *fsm_in_S0* event, a *fsm_in_S3* event is expected before the *fsm_in_S5* event occurs.

8.5 Random Constraints Generation

SystemVerilog provides constructs to describe random constraints. These constraints can be processed by a tool (for example, a constraint solver) to generate the random values that meets the constraints. Such a capability is useful in random constraint-driven verification.

SystemVerilog uses the object-oriented paradigm for describing random constraints, which is, via a class. Objects in a class are identified as random variables and constraint declarations within a class determine the legal values that can be assigned to these random variables.

```
class t_mpu;

  // Random variable declarations:
  rand bit [3:0] opcode;
  randc bit [0:1] nxt_state;

  // Constraint declarations:
  constraint c_bit3_reserved {
    opcode[2] == 1'b0;
  }
```

```
  constraint c_low_limit {
    opcode >= 3;
    opcode < 10;
    nxt_state == 2;
  }
endclass
```

The class *t_mpu* has declared two variables *opcode* and *nxt_state* to be random variables. In addition, two constraints, *c_bit3_reserved* and *c_low_limit*, have been specified. The first constraint specifies that bit 2 of the *opcode* should always be 0. So when random values are generated for *opcode*, *opcode[2]* will always be a 0. The variable *nxt_state* is unconstrained. Therefore the random number shall be any number in its declared range, which is 0 through 3. In the second constraint, *opcode* can take values in the range 3 to 9 and *nxt_state* should have the value of 2.

The random numbers are generated using the *randomize*() method that is associated by default with every class. The *randomize*() method returns a 1 if it is successful in solving all the constraints and creating a random set of values, else it returns a 0.

```
t_mpu mpu_timer;
. . .
if (mpu_timer.randomize() == 1)
  $display (mpu_timer.opcode, mpu_timer.nxt_state);
```

Every time the *randomize*() method is called, a new set of random values that satisfy all the constraints are generated.

8.5.1 Random Variables

Properties in a class can be declared as random variables using the **rand** and **randc** modifiers.

```
class t_check;
  typedef enum {RED, GREEN, YELLOW} t_color;
  randc t_color ht_state;
  rand integer paddr;
  rand bit [4:0] pctrl;
  randc bit [1:0] pstate;
  randc bit [3:0] sys_state;
```

```
. . .
endclass
```

Only scalar variables of integer type, enumerated type, and bit variables of any size can be randomized. Associative and dynamic arrays of these types can also be declared as random variables.

Variables declared with the **rand** modifier are standard random variables. Their values are uniformly distributed over their range. The variable *pctrl* is a 5-bit unsigned integer in the range 0 to 31. If there are no constraints specified for this variable, then this variable can take any value from 0 through 31 with equal probability.

Variables declared with the **randc** modifier are random-cyclic variables that cycle through all the values in a random permutation of their range. That is, such a variable first generates a random permutation of all values in the range and then repeats with a different permutation of all values in the range, basically, no value is repeated within an iteration. Randc variables can only be of bit type or of an enumerated type. In the case of the randc variable *pstate*, the randomly generated permutations may be:

```
1st iteration     : 10 -> 11 -> 00 -> 01
2nd iteration     : 11 -> 01 -> 00 -> 10
3rd iteration     : 01 -> 10 -> 00 -> 11
. . .
```

In the case of randc variable *ht_state*, the randomly generated permutations may be:

```
1st iteration: RED     -> YELLOW -> GREEN
2nd iteration: YELLOW  -> RED    -> GREEN
3rd iteration: RED     -> GREEN  -> YELLOW
. . .
```

8.5.2 Other Randomization Methods

Constraint Mode

The *constraint_mode*() method can be used to check if a constraint is active or inactive. In addition, it can be used to set a constraint as active or as inactive. All constraints are initially active.

```
// Make constraint inactive:
mpu_timer.c_bit3_reserved.constraint_mode(0);

// Make constraint active:
mpu_timer.c_low_limit.constraint_mode(1);

if (mpu_timer.c_bit3_reserved.constraint_mode())
  // Returns 0 if inactive and 1 if active.
  . . .
```

Making a constraint inactive causes the randomizer to not use that constraint in future random generation.

Rand Mode

The *rand_mode*() method can be used to control whether a random variable is active or inactive. When a variable in marked as inactive, it is as if the variable is not a random variable; the variable is no longer randomized. All random variables are initially active.

```
t_check rtc;

rtc.pstate.rand_mode(0);
  // Makes the variable inactive.

rtc.pstate.rand_mode(1);
  // Makes the variable active.

if (rtc.pstate.rand_mode()) . . .
  // if expression is 0 if inactive, 1 if active.
```

Randomize With

This allows inline constraints at the point where the *randomize*() method is called. The format of the constraints is the same as that declared as constraints in a class and are in addition to the constraints in effect on the variable.

```
mpu_timer.randomize() with {paddr > 52 && paddr < 1100;}

mpu_timer.randomize() with {opcode[1] == 0;}
```

Pre_randomize and Post_randomize

The *pre_randomize*() and *post_randomize*() built-in methods of every class are automatically called by the *randomize*() method before and after it computes new random values.

When the *randomize*() method is called, it first invokes the *pre_randomize*() method on the object. This method can be overloaded by the user (function can be specified explicitly) to perform initialization and to set any pre-conditions before the variables are randomized.

Similarly, after the *randomize*() method generates the random values, it calls the *post_randomize*() method automatically. Such a method can also be overloaded (by specifying such a method explicitly) to perform any cleanup or print diagnostics after the variables are randomized.

```
class t_mbus;
  rand bit [15:0] pdata;
  rand bit [6:0] paddr;
  rand bit [3:0] pctrl;
  byte pxi;
  constraint c_large {pdata > 2000;};

  function void pre_randomize();
    $display ( "pdata=%d; pctrl=%d -- before random",
               " number generation.", pdata, pctrl);
  endfunction: pre_randomize
```

```
    function void post_randomize();
      $display ( "pdata=%d; pctrl=%d -- after random ",
                  "number generation.", pdata, pctrl);
    endfunction: post_randomize
  endclass
```

Random Variable Control

A variable that is not declared as a random variable in a class can be temporarily made a random variable by specifying it as an argument to the *randomize*() method. For example, in class *t_mbus*, the non-random variable *pxi* can temporarily be made into a random variable by specifying it as an argument to the *randomize*() method.

```
t_mbus pobj;

pobj.randomize(pxi)
  // pxi is used as a random variable and the randomize()
  // method generates a random number for pxi.
```

8.5.3 Constraint Declarations

The general syntax of a constraint declaration is:

```
constraint constraint_name { constraint_block } ;
```

The constraint block is a list of expressions that restrict the range of a variable or specifies relationships between variables. There are various forms of constraint blocks; these we look at next.

Set Membership

Set membership can be used to constrain a variable to be within a range of values (using the *inside* operator), or to exclude some values from the random values generated (using the ! and the *inside* operators).

```
// To include values and values in a range:
constraint c_inset {
  paddr inside {0, 2, 4, 6, 8, [64:127], [255:300]};
};
```

```
// To exclude certain values:
constraint c_outset {
  !(sys_state inside {4'h8, [4'h0:4'h3]});
};
```

Distribution

Values of a random variable can be given different weights so that some are generated more often or less often than others.

```
constraint c_pctrl {
  pctrl dist {
    4'b0000 := 10,     // Weight of 10/45.
    4'b1010 := 20,     // Weight of 20/45.
    4'b1101 := 15      // Weight os 15/45.
  };
};

constraint c_paddr {
  paddr dist {
    [0:31]     := 2,       // Weight of 2/71.
    [32:63]    := 5,       // Weight of 5/71.
    [64:127]   :/ 64  // Each element has weight of 1/71.
  };
};
```

The ":=" operator assigns the specified weight to the value, while the ":/" operator divides the weight and assigns it equally to all values in the range.

Implication

Constraints can be specified using the implication operator ("->") and using if-else.

```
constraint c_imply {
  ht_state == RED -> pctrl > 10;

  if (pstate == 2'b01) {
    paddr > 63;
    paddr < 255;
```

```
    } else if (pstate == 2'b10) {
      paddr > 10;
      paddr < 20;
    }
  }
```

The boolean equivalent of the implication operation *a->b* is *(!a || b)*. That is, if the expression is true, then the random numbers are constrained by the specified constraint, else the random numbers are unconstrained.

The if-else style constraint is equivalent to an implication. For example, in above:

```
pstate == 2'b10 -> paddr > 10;
pstate == 2'b01 -> paddr > 63;
```

The *else* is optional, and if present is always associated with the closest previous *if*.

Iterative

The iterative form of constraints allows elements of an array to be constrained using loop variables. Here is an example.

```
rand bit [7:0] bus_matrix [3:0];
...
constraint c_iterative {
  foreach (bus_matrix[k]) {
    bus_matrix[k] > 10;
    bus_matrix[k] < 100;
  }
}
```

The foreach statement iterates over each element of the array. The variable *k* is the loop variable. The loop variable is implicitly declared to be the same type as the array index and its scope is limited to the foreach statement. An array can have any number of dimensions, and multiple loop variables can be used in such a case, one loop variable for each dimension of array.

Variable Ordering

Variable ordering allows certain combinations to occur more frequently than others. This is accomplished using the solve-before construct.

```
rand bit [1:0] cnt_state;
rand bit [19:0] apb_addr;

constraint c_varorder {
  cnt_state == 2 -> apb_addr > 256;
  solve cnt_state before apb_addr;
  . . .
}
```

The effect of the constraint is that *cnt_state* will have value of 2 with a 25% probability and then *apb_addr* is chosen subject to the value of *cnt_state*. The solve-before construct makes the selection of *cnt_state* to be independent of *apb_addr*. Note that without the variable ordering, the probability of selecting *cnt_state* with a value of 2 is small since the randomizer has to give equal probability to all other values of *apb_addr*. Variable ordering can only be applied on rand variables (and not on randc variables).

Checking Constraints Inline

When the *randomize*() method is called with a value of **null**, no random numbers are generated but all the constraints are checked using the current values of the variables. The method returns a 1 if all constraints are satisfied, else it returns a 0.

```
all_cons_valid = mpu_timer.randomize(null);
```

8.5.4 Random Weighted Case Statement

The randcase statement is like a case statement and can be used to randomly select one of branches. The case branches are the weights that are assigned to each of the branches. The branch probability of selection is its weight divided by the total weight.

```
program pgm_rand;
  typedef enum {READY, PWAIT, GO, SLOW_DOWN} t_speed;
  t_speed sys_status;

  initial
    repeat (20)
      randcase
        1: sys_status <= READY;    // Probability of 1/8.
        5: sys_status <= GO;       // Probability of 5/8.
        2: sys_status <= PWAIT;    // Probability of 2/8.
      endcase
endprogram: pgm_rand
```

The weights of the branches need not be constants and can be arbitrary expressions but should evaluate to an integral value. Note that a randcase statement is a sequential statement and can appear anywhere sequential statements can, such as in tasks and initial statements.

8.5.5 Scope Randomize Function

The scope randomize function (*std::randomize*) that has been provided in the package *std* can be used to generate random values for data that does not belong to a class.

```
bit [15:0] alu_out, addr_in;
int qin, result;

result = randomize(alu_out, addr_in, qin);
  // Can call using std::randomize() as well.
```

The *randomize*() method generates random values for the three non-class variables *alu_out*, *addr_in* and *qin*. Inline constraints can be applied to the scope randomize function.

Here is such an example.

```
int num_match, num_fail, num_pass, is_pass;

is_pass = std::randomize(num_pass, num_fail) with
          ( num_pass + num_fail > 100;
            num_pass > 10;
            num_fail > 20;
          );
```

Random values are generated for *num_pass* and *num_fail* that meet the specified constraints.

8.5.6 Random Sequence Generation

SystemVerilog defines a random sequence generator that produces a stream of values based on a specified set of rules (grammar). These rules are described in a *randsequence* block, which is of the form:

```
randsequence ( start_nonterminal )
  nonterminal1: rule1;
  nonterminal2: rule2;
  . . .
endsequence
```

Rules are specified using nonterminals and terminals separated by the | (vertical bar) symbol. The | symbol implies a set of choices that the random sequence generator can make at random. A terminal is a code block, that is, a set of statements for execution. A nonterminal specifies a rule in terms of other nonterminals and terminals.

A randsequence block is a sequential statement and can thus appear in a procedural block. Whenever a randsequence block executes, it generates a rule-driven stream of random values or actions based upon the rules specified. Here is an example.

```
randsequence (start_nt)
  start_nt    : load_a compute save
  load_a      : mova_20 | mova_21;
  compute     : add | sub | mul;
  save        : { $display ("SAV"); };
```

```
    mova_20      : { $display ("MOVAh20"); };
    mova_21      : { $display ("MOVAh21"); };
    add          : { $display ("ADD"); };
    sub          : { $display ("SUB"); };
    mul          : { $display ("MUL"); };
endsequence
```

The starting nonterminal is *start_nt* and is defined as a sequence of three nonterminals *load*, *compute*, and *save*. Each of these nonterminals is decomposed further until the terminals that each have **$display** calls in their code blocks. The random sequence generator could generate the following sequence of values:

```
MOVAh20 SUB SAV
MOVAh20 MUL SAV
MOVAh21 ADD SAV
. . .
```

Randsequence blocks are useful in generating random sequences such as instructions for processors.

❑

Chapter 9

Assertions

This chapter describes how to write assertions in SystemVerilog. The assertion language is a complete language by itself. Describing the complete language in detail is beyond the scope of this book. However, what we will do is provide examples of common assertions. The idea being that these can provide a starting point for applying these immediately and can further be reused to formulate more complex assertions.

An assertion checks for a specified condition and provides a message if the condition fails. SystemVerilog provides two different kinds of assertions:

i. Immediate assertions.

ii. Concurrent assertions.

9.1 Immediate Assertions

There are two kinds of immediate assertions:

i. Simple immediate assertions.
ii. Deferred immediate assertions.

9.1.1 Simple Immediate Assertions

A *simple immediate assertion* is a sequential statement (used in a sequential block). There are three kinds of simple immediate assertion statements:

i. Immediate assert statement.
ii. Immediate assume statement.
iii. Immediate cover statement.

An *immediate assert* statement is an assertion that is checked at the time it is executed. If the assertion passes, a pass set of statements is executed; if the assertion fails, a fail set of statements is executed. It is of the form:

```
assert ( expression )
[ [ pass_statements ]
else
  fail_statements ]
```

Here is an example.

```
a_count: assert (count != 0)      // a_count is a label.
  $error ("Count is not zero");
else
  $error ("Count is 0");
```

Guideline: Label all assertions.

Labels are optional to an assertion statement, but a good recommendation is to label all assertions. Furthermore, labels can be used to enable or disable assertions.

When an assertion fails, the failure can be treated as:

i. a fatal runtime error,

ii. a regular runtime error,

iii. a warning, or

iv. a notification.

This is accomplished by using one of the system tasks **$fatal**, **$error**, **$warning** or **$info**. These system tasks have the same syntax as a **$display** task, but gives the opportunity for the tool to take an appropriate action in case of an assertion failure. All these system tasks print a tool-specific message indicating the severity of the failure and specific information about the failure such as file name and line number.

```
a_sumcheck: assert (sum > 5 && sum < 56)
else
  $fatal ("Not good: sum is outside of range");

// Assert read or write but not both:
event error_event;

a_rw: assert
  ((read == 0 && write == 1) || (read == 1 && write == 0))
else
  -> error_event;                  // Trigger an error event.
```

Guideline: Avoid using behavioral (design) code in the pass or fail set of statements.

```
a_nonzero: assert (a != 0 && b != 0)
  $info ("Both operands are non-zero.");
else
  $fatal (
    "One of the operands (%d, %d) is a 0", a, b);

logic [7:0] opcode;
. . .
a_isx:
assert (^opcode !== 1'bx)
else
  $error ("One of the bits of opcode is an x");
```

When an *else* part is missing in an assertion, an assertion failure is treated as a runtime error (a **$error** call is assumed).

An *immediate assume* statement specifies an assertion that is assumed to be true for formal verification. For simulation verification, the assertion should still hold and thus behaves exactly like an immediate assert statement. Here is an example of an immediate assume statement.

```
a_highbits0: assume (psp[15:12] == 4'b0000)
else
  $error ("Assumption not true");
```

9.1.2 Deferred Immediate Assertions

A *deferred immediate assertion* is like a simple immediate assertion except for the following:

i. A #0 is specified right after the keyword **assert**, **assume**, or **cover**, as the case may be.

ii. The optional pass statements or fail statements consists of only one subroutine call.

iii. The assertion is checked at the end of the time step[1] to ensure that all signals have settled to their steady state values. This helps avoid false assertion failures due to glitches.

Here is an example of a deferred immediate assertion.

```
a_in_range: assert #0 (abus[7:0] > 8'h3C);
```

A deferred immediate assertion can also appear as a concurrent statement. In such a case, it is treated as if it were contained in an always_comb statement. A deferred assertion can be disabled using a disable statement. This causes the assertion to be no longer active.

One recommendation is to use deferred immediate assertions in concurrent statements and combinational procedures (always_comb statement), while simple immediate assertions should be used in clocked procedures (always statement with clock event control).

1. Simplified representation without going into any detail of what comprises a time step.

```
module i_assert;
  // Deferred immediate assertion as a
  // concurrent statement:
  a_one_reset: assert #0 (rst_a || rst_b);

  // Deferred immediate assertion in a
  // combinational block:
  always_comb
    begin
      . . .
      a_enables: assert #0 (cena && wena);
    end

  // Simple immediate assertion in a clocked
  // procedural block:
  always @(posedge clk)
    begin
      . . .
      a_parity: assert (parity(sdata[7:0])== 1);
      . . .
    end
endmodule: i_assert
```

9.2 Concurrent Assertions

A *concurrent assertion* is a concurrent statement (same level as a module instantiation, always statement, initial statement, for example) that can check the behavior of an assertion over a period of time. Evaluation of a concurrent assertion is associated with a clock edge and the signals used in the assertion are sampled just before the clock edge; this ensures that all signals have attained their stable and race-free values.

A concurrent assertion can also appear as a sequential statement. We show an example of this later.

There are five kinds of concurrent assertion statement:

i. Assert property statement.

ii. Assume property statement.

iii. Cover property statement.

iv. Cover sequence statement.
v. Restrict property statement.

The *assert property* statement is used to ensure that a property (a property is a "fact" about the design) holds for a design. The syntax is of the form:

```
assert property ( property_specification )
  [ [ pass_statements ]
else
  fail_statements ]
```

If the property gets evaluated to true (note that this is typically over time, that is, over a number of clock cycles), the pass statements are executed; else the fail statements are executed. The system tasks **$fatal**, **$error**, **$warning** and **$info** can be used as part of the fail statements to provide diagnostic information when an assertion fails.

The *assume property* statement assumes that the property is true for that environment. It is considered as an assumption for formal verification. For simulation, the property must hold even though it is an assumption, and if it fails, it should be reported. The syntax is of the form:

```
assume property ( property_specification ) ;
```

The *cover property* statement monitors the property from a coverage perspective. Tools can collect information about the property. In this statement, if the property passes, the pass statements typically contain statements that collect statistics about the property. It is of the form:

```
cover property ( property_specification )
  [ pass_statements ] ;
```

The *cover sequence* statement monitors a sequence from a coverage perspective. The *restrict property* statement is used to constrain the design space for formal verification. It is similar to an assume property statement except that it is not checked in simulation.

```
restrict property ( property_specification ) ;
```

So what is a property specification?

i. It is in its simplest form, just an expression, or

ii. it can be a sequence, which is composed of expressions, or

iii. it can be a property, which in turn is composed of sequences and or expressions.

A concurrent assertion is evaluated only on clock ticks. Any changes between clock ticks are ignored. A clock tick corresponds to an event (**posedge** or **negedge**) on a clock or on any expression. See Figure 9-1. When monitoring asynchronous signals, a clock tick corresponds to a simulation time step. The clock tick for an assertion can be specified in a variety of ways, which we shall see in later examples.

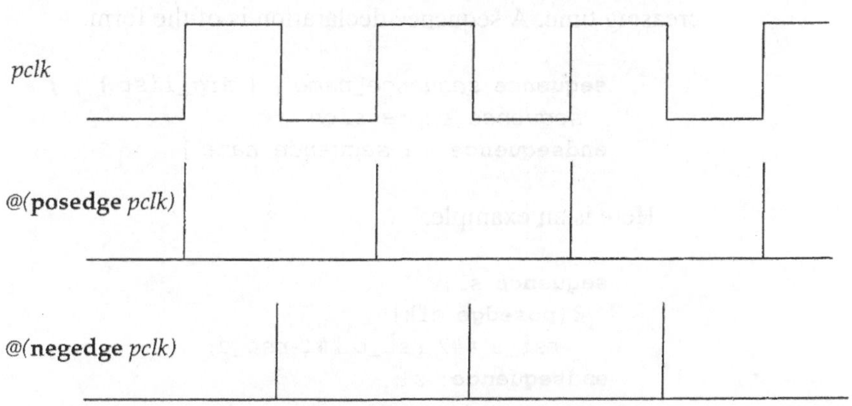

Figure 9-1 Clock ticks.

A concurrent assertion may appear in the design code or as part of testbench code including in a program or a checker, or in a separate file that is later bound to the design. Labels are optional to an assertion statement; however, it is a good idea to use labels for assertion statements, as the labels can be used to enable or disable the assertions.

Concurrent assertions can be used by a formal analysis tool, which can provide formal proofs; formal verification of assertions is beyond the scope of this text. We focus here only on the simulation semantics of concurrent assertions.

A concurrent assertion potentially fires on every clock tick. If an assertion say needs ten clock ticks to execute, it could potentially have ten different threads running in parallel.

We provide examples of assertions after the syntax for property and sequence declarations are described. Sequence and property declarations can occur within a module, an interface, a program block, a clocking block, a package, a checker or in the compilation-unit scope.

9.2.1 Sequence Declaration

Sequential behaviors can be used to describe a property. A *sequence declaration* provides the capability to describe a sequential behavior in a concise form by using a list of boolean expressions in a linear order of increasing time. A sequence declaration is of the form:

```
sequence sequence_name [ ( arg_list ) ] ;
  sequence_expression
endsequence [ : sequence_name ]
```

Here is an example.

```
sequence s1;
  @(posedge clk)
    rst_a ##2 rst_b ##1 rst_c;
endsequence: s1
```

The sequence name is *s1*. A clock tick corresponds to the rising edge of *clk*, that is, the sequence is checked only on the rising edges of *clk*. A linear sequence is defined using the ## operator. This operator defines delays in terms of clock ticks. So ##2 means two clock ticks. The above sequence specifies that after *rst_a* asserts, *rst_b* asserts two cycles later and *rst_c* asserts one subsequent cycle later.

A sequence matches or does not match. A sequence is said to match at a clock tick if the specified sequence has completely occurred (same meaning as *has been found*, or *a match occurs*). In the above sequence, the sequence matches at the clock tick when the complete sequence, *rst_a* followed two cycles later by *rst_b*, followed one cycle later by *rst_c*, has occurred. So a sequence has the notion of a start time and an end time. A sequence starts on every clock tick, but each sequence spans one or more clock ticks. Some sequences may end up not matching and some sequences end up matching the specified pattern. A sequence may have multiple matches when the match can occur within a range of cycles.

See Figure 9-2. A sequence starts on every clock tick, for example, sequence *s1_0* starts at time *t0*, sequence *s1_1* starts at time *t1*, sequence *s1_2* starts at time *t2*, and so on. Consider the *s1_0* sequence. Signal *rst_a* is asserted when the clock tick occurs at *t0*. Two ticks later, that is at *t2*, *rst_b* is asserted. One tick later, that is at *t3*, *rst_c* is asserted and thus the entire sequence matches and is marked as matched at time *t3*. The start time of this sequence *s1_0* is *t0* and the end time is *t3*. Similarly the sequence *s1_1* that starts at time *t1*, fails to match immediately since *rst_a* is false. The sequence *s1_2* that starts at time *t2*, passes the first expression at *t2*, the second expression at *t4*, but fails to match the third expression at time *t5*.

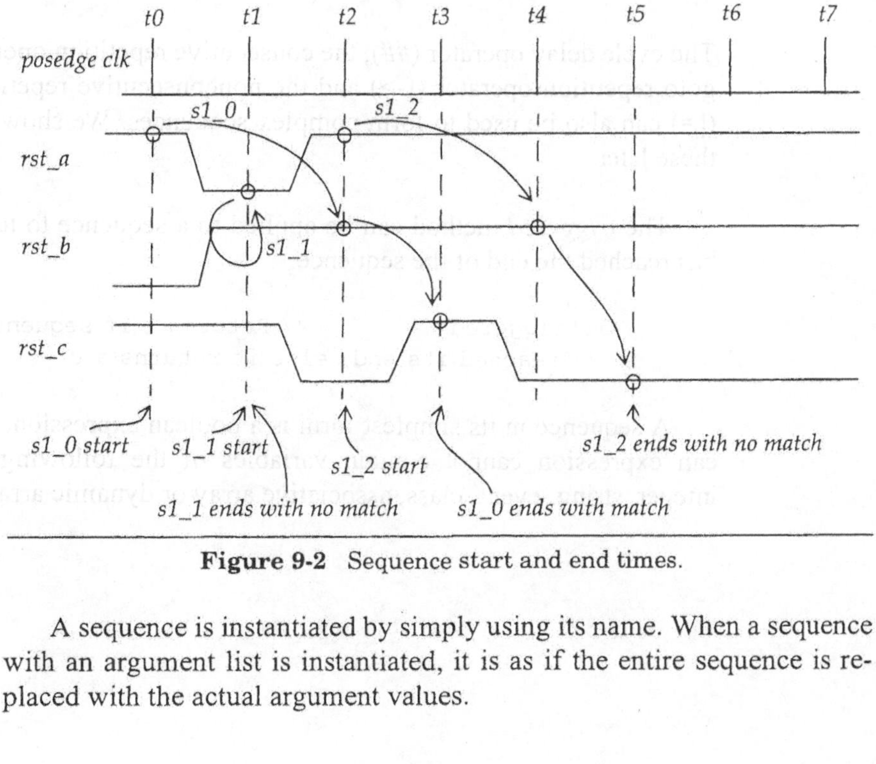

Figure 9-2 Sequence start and end times.

A sequence is instantiated by simply using its name. When a sequence with an argument list is instantiated, it is as if the entire sequence is replaced with the actual argument values.

A sequence can be combined to form more complex sequences.

- *seq1* **and** *seq2* : Matches if both *seq1* and *seq2* match. The end time is the end time of the sequence that completes last.
- *seq1* **or** *seq2* : Matches if either of the sequence match.
- *seq1* **intersect** *seq2* : Matches if both *seq1* and *seq2* match and if the end time of *seq1* is the same as the end time of *seq2*.
- **first_match**(*seq1*) : If *seq1* has multiple patterns to match, this command selects the first match that occurs and all other matches are discarded from future consideration for this particular sequence.
- *expr* **throughout** *seq1* : *expr* must be true at every clock tick during the evaluation of the sequence.
- *seq1* **within** *seq2* : The *seq1* occurs completely within *seq2*, that is, the start time and end time of *seq1* is between the start time and end time of *seq2*.

The cycle delay operator (##), the consecutive repetition operator ([*), the goto repetition operator ([->) and the nonconsecutive repetition operator ([=) can also be used to form complex sequences. We show examples of these later.

The *triggered* method can be applied to a sequence to test whether it has reached the end of the sequence.

```
s1.triggered            // Returns 1 if sequence s1 has
  // reached its end, else it returns a 0.
```

A sequence in its simplest form is a boolean expression. Such a boolean expression cannot contain variables of the following types: non-integer, string, event, class, associative array or dynamic array.

9.2.2 Property Declaration

A *property* is a fact about the design. By itself, it does not produce any result; it only describes a behavior of a design. A *property declaration* is of the form:

```
property property_name [ ( arg_list ) ] ;
  property_specification
endproperty [ : property_name ]
```

A property declaration can have optional formal arguments. Actual values are passed in when a property is instantiated; basically the property is replaced with the actual arguments.

A *property specification* is of the following form:

```
[ clocking_event ]
  [ disable iff ( expression ) ]
  property_expression
```

A *property expression* can be built using expressions, sequences and other properties. A property in its basic form is a sequence. More complex properties can be formed using the following operators.

- **strong** (*sequence_expression*)
- **weak** (*sequence_expression*)
- **not** *property_expression*
- *property_expr1* **and** *property_expr2*
- *property_expr1* **or** *property_expr2*
- **if** (*expression*) *property_expr1* [**else** *property_expr2*]
- **case (** *expression* **)** *property_case_items* **endcase**
- *sequence_expression* |=> *property_expression*
- *sequence_expression* |-> *property_expression*
- *sequence_expression* #-# *property_expression*
- *sequence_expression* #=# *property_expression*
- **nexttime** [*constant_expression*] *property_expression*

- **s_nexttime** [*constant_expression*] *property_expression*
- **always** [*constant_range*] *property_expression*
- **s_always** [*constant_range*] *property_expression*
- **eventually** [*constant_range*] *property_expression*
- **s_eventually** [*constant_range*] *property_expression*
- *property_expr1* **until** *property_expr2*
- *property_expr1* **s_until** *property_expr2*
- *property_expr1* **until_with** *property_expr2*
- *property_expr1* **s_until_with** *property_expr2*
- *property_expr1* **implies** *property_expr2*
- *property_expr1* **iff** *property_expr2*
- **accept_on** (*expression*) *property_expression*
- **reject_on** (*expression*) *property_expression*
- **sync_accept_on** (*expression*) *property_expression*
- **sync_reject_on** (*expression*) *property_expression*

While a property specification could be written directly in an assertion, writing property declarations and sequence declarations enables reuse of the properties and sequences in multiple concurrent assertions. A property that uses local variables must be declared before it is used in an assertion.

9.2.3 Assertion Types

Assertions can be classified into three categories:

i. Invariant assertions: Conditions that are true or never true. For example, read and write of a memory cannot occur together.

ii. Sequential assertions: Conditions that involve a pattern of values that occur over specific number of cycles. Example, a *request* must be followed by *grant*, and that must be followed by *busy*.

iii. Eventuality assertions: Condition followed by another condition that eventually should become true. There can be any number of clock cycles between the two conditions. For example, if *nreset* goes low, it must eventually go high.

9.2.4 Assertion Examples

Assertion 1: Assert that only one bit of *fsm_state* is high.

```
property p_onehot;
  @(posedge clk) $onehot(fsm_state[7:0]);
endproperty: p_onehot

assert_onehot: assert property (p_onehot)
else
  $info ("fsm_state is not one hot.");
```

The system function **$onehot** returns true (a 1 value) if exactly one bit in the expression is a 1. A similar function **$onehot0** returns a 1 if at most one bit in the expression is a 1. This is an example of an invariant assertion. The condition is checked on every clock tick.

Assertion 2: Check that at most one bit of *hgrant* is active at any one time.

```
assert_one: assert property
  ( @(posedge clk)
      disable iff (!nreset)
        $countones(hgrant) <= 1
  );
```

The *disable iff* clause disables the evaluation of the property as long as *nreset* is low. The number of ones in *hgrant* is checked on every clock tick and should not exceed 1, but this check is enabled only if *nreset* is 1.

The *disable iff* clause allows an asynchronous reset to be specified. A property can be disabled under certain conditions using the *disable iff* clause. When the condition with the *disable iff* is true, the assertion does not fire. A primary usage of the *disable iff* clause is to prevent false assertion failures while the design is under reset or is under control of some other asynchronous signals.

Assertion 3: Signal *req* should assert ten clocks after *reset* is deasserted.

```
sequence s_req_after_reset;
  @(posedge mclk)
    !reset ##10 req;
endsequence: s_req_after_reset

assert_req_reset: assert property (s_req_after_reset);
```

The linear sequence operator (##) is used to specify that *req* will occur ten clock ticks after *reset* goes to 0. However, there is a small caveat in this example. Note that an assertion fires on every clock tick. If *reset* is 1 on a clock tick, the assertion will fail; but this a false failure. We later see how to resolve this using the implication operator.

The clock tick definition can appear in a number of places. In this assertion, the clock tick definition appears within the sequence declaration.

Assertion 4: Signal *ack* should assert three clock cycles after *req* is asserted.

```
sequence s_ack_after_req;
  @(posedge sclk)
    req ##3 ack;
endsequence: s_ack_after_req

assert_req_ack: assert property (s_ack_after_req);
```

If the sequence were written as:

```
req ##0 ack;
```

the ##0 specifies that if the left hand side is true, then the right hand side is also true in the same clock tick.

Assertion 5: Signal *req* should assert ten cycles after *reset* is deasserted and *ack* should assert two cycles after *req* is asserted.

```
sequence s_reset_req_ack;
  @(posedge mclk)
    s_req_after_reset ##2 ack;
endsequence: s_reset_req_ack

assert_reset_req_ack:
assert property (s_reset_req_ack)
else
  $warning ("Sequence failed");
```

This assertion is described using a sequence within a sequence. The sequence *s_req_after_reset* is described in an earlier example.

Assertion 6: After the sequence *s_reset_req_ack*, either *ena* or *enb* asserts after five clock cycles.

```
assert_ena_enb: assert property
  ( @(posedge clk)
      s_reset_req_ack ##5 (ena || enb)
  );
```

The clock definition is in the concurrent assertion.

Assertion 7: Whenever *req* is asserted, *gnt* is asserted on the next clock or on the following clock cycle.

```
property p_req_gnt;
  @(posedge sysclk)
    req |-> ##[1:2] gnt;
endproperty: p_req_gnt

assert_req_gnt: assert property (p_req_gnt)
else
  $error ("gnt not after req in 1-2 clocks.");
```

The |-> is the *implication operator* that specifies to evaluate the right hand side sequence only if the left hand side sequence has been found. The left hand side is like a precondition to the evaluation of the right hand side. The left hand side is referred to as the *antecedent* and the right hand side is referred to as the *consequent*. The |=> is the non-overlapped implication operator while the |-> is the overlapped implication operator.

The expression *seq1* |-> *seq2* implies that if *seq1* matches in cycle *N*, then *seq2* must be started in the same clock cycle. If *seq1* does not match, then the operation returns a result of 1, that is, the assertion does not fail and is considered vacuous.

Guideline: Use the implication operators to avoid false assertion failures.

So the above assertion says that only if *req* is 1, check the consequent. If *req* is 0, do not do anything, the assertion does not fail; it is a vacuous success. It is equivalent to "*if req then ack else 1*".

The expression *seq1* |=> *seq2* implies that if *seq1* matches, *seq2* is checked on the following clock cycle.

Assertion 8: After an asynchronous reset, *fsm_state* goes to *RESET* in next clock cycle.

```
property p_to_reset;
  @(posedge clk)
    !nreset |=> fsm_state == RESET;
endproperty: p_to_reset;

assert_to_reset:
  assert property (p_to_reset)
  else
    $warning (
      "assert_to_reset: fsm_state is %d after reset.",
      fsm_state);
```

Assertion 9: Assert that state *S3* is entered from either states *S5* or *S0*.

```
property p_s3_s5_s0;
  @(posedge clk)
    disable iff (!nreset)
      mc_state == S3 |->
      ($past(mc_state) == S0 || $past(mc_state) == S5);
endproperty: p_s3_s5_s0
```

```
assert_s3_s5_s0: assert property (p_s3_s5_s0)
else
  $fatal ("Illegal transition.");
```

If *nreset* is 0, the sequence is not checked. If *nreset* is a 1, and *mc_state* is *S3*, then the previous state should have been either *S0* or *S5*. The previous state is checked using the system function **$past**, which returns the value of the expression at the previous clock tick.

Assertion 10: A write (active-low) must follow every read (active-high).

```
assert_read_write: assert property
  ( @(posedge clk)
    disable iff (!nreset)
      $rose(fifo_read) |=> $fell(fifo_write)
  )
else
  $info ("Write asserted before read.");
```

The system functions **$rose** and **$fell** are true if the value changed from the previous clock tick, from 0 to 1 for **$rose** and from 1 to 0 for **$fell**. Note that the above property is checked only when there is a rising edge on *fifo_read*. If the property were written without the **$rose**, such as:

```
fifo_read |=> $fell(fifo_write)
```

then this implies than the property is checked starting from every clock cycle whenever *fifo_read* is true.

Other than **$past**, **$rose** and **$fell**, the other sampled value functions are **$stable** and **$changed**. These system functions check whether the value of the expression changed between two consecutive clock ticks.

Assertion 11: Assume that after *req* is asserted, it is deasserted in the following cycle.

```
property p_req;
  @(posedge clk)
    req ##1 !req;
endproperty: p_req
```

```
assume_req: assume property (p_req);
```

The clock tick definition can be in a property declaration as well as in a sequence declaration.

While an assume property is used as an assumption for formal analysis, the assertion must hold true for simulation and a message is generated if the assertion is violated.

Assertion 12: Never the case that both *ena* and *enb* are asserted.

```
assert_reset_ena_enb: assert property
  ( @(posedge mclk)
      disable iff (!nreset)
        !(ena && enb)
  );
```

Assertion 13: After *req* asserts, at least one of *ack_a*, *ack_b* or *ack_c* asserts in one to four clock cycles.

```
assert_req_ack_abc:
  assert property
    ( @(posedge sclk)
        disable iff (!presetn)
          ($rose(req) |-> ##[1:4]
            (ack_a || ack_b || ack_c))
    );
```

Assertion 14: *reset* should never be an unknown value.

```
assert_reset_x: assert property ($isunknown(reset))
else
  $error ("Reset is an x");
```

The clock tick definition is specified elsewhere in the property's compilation-unit scope.

Assertion 15: Assume *prdata* is always greater than 31.

```
assume_prdata: assume property
  ( @(negedge armclk)
     (prdata > 31)
  );
```

Assertion 16: Assert that the parity of *prdata* is always true.

```
property p_parity;
  ^prdata[31:0];
endproperty: p_parity

assert_parity_prdata: assert property
  (@(negedge sysclk) p_parity);
```

The property has been written using a property declaration and the property is asserted.

Assertion 17: Memory read and write should never occur together.

```
assert_mem_rw:
  assert property
    ( @(posedge mem_clk)
        !(mem_read && mem_write)
    )
  else
    $error ("Read write violation");
```

Assertion 18: After *req* asserts, *ack* is asserted for three more clock ticks before *busy* is asserted within the next two cycles.

```
sequence s_req_ack_busy;
  @(posedge clk)
    req ##1 ack [*3] ##[1:2] busy;
  // Equivalent to:
  // req ##1 ack ##1 ack ##1 ack ##[1:2] busy
endsequence: s_req_ack_busy

assert property (s_req_ack_busy);
```

The [* is the *consecutive repetition* operator. It specifies a repetition of the left hand side. The sequence:

```
(req ##2 ack) [*2]
```

is equivalent to:

```
req ##2 ack ##1 req ##2 ack
```

The sequence:

```
(req ##2 ack) [*1:2]
```

is equivalent to one of:

```
req ##2 ack
req ##2 ack ##1 req ##2 ack
```

Assertion 19: gnt must be true at least four cycles later after *req* asserts.

```
assert_req_4_gnt: assert property
  ( @(posedge clk)
     disable iff (!presetn)
       req ##[4:$] gnt
  );
```

The $ can be used to specify a finite but unbounded range.

Assertion 20: After *req* asserts, *gnt* asserts on every clock cycle until *busy* asserts. *busy* should be checked on the negative edge of clock *pclk*.

```
sequence s_req_gnt_busy;
  @(posedge sclk)
    req ##1 gnt [*1:$] ##1 @(negedge pclk) busy;
endsequence: s_req_gnt_busy

assert_req_gnt_busy: assert property (s_req_gnt_busy);
```

This is an example of a sequence using multiple clocks. Each sequence can optionally have an explicit clock tick definition associated with it, if necessary, like *busy* does.

Assertion 21: After *req* asserts, *ack* is true for at least three non-consecutive clock cycles before *busy* asserts.

```
assert_non_conseq: assert property
  ( @(posedge uclk)
       req ##1 ack [->1:3] ##1 busy
  );
// Equivalent to "!ack !ack ack ack !ack ack busy"
```

The [-> is the *goto repetition* operator. It specifies a non-consecutive sequence. *ack* must be true in the last clock tick before *busy* is true.

Assertion 22: After *req* asserts, *ack* is true for at least two non-consecutive cycles, but need not be true before *busy* asserts.

```
assert_seq2: assert property
  ( @(negedge pclk)
       req ##1 ack [=1:2] ##1 busy
  );
// Equivalent to !ack !ack ack ack !ack busy
```

The [= is the *nonconsecutive repetition* operator. It has a similar behavior to the goto repetition operator ([->) except that *ack* need not be true before *busy* is true.

Assertion 23: Assert that the block is never in states *S0*, *S5* and *S7*, as these are illegal states.

```
assert_illegal: assert property
  ( @(posedge fclk)
       !(nxt_state == S0 ||
         nxt_state == S5 || nxt_state == S7)
  );
```

Assertion 24: After *req* occurs, *gnt* occurs in the next one to five clock cycles. Assume that such a property is true.

```
property prop1 (arg1, arg2, rstn, N);
  // opd1, opd2, rstn and N are formal arguments.
  @(posedge clk)
    disable iff (!rstn)
      arg1 ##[1:N] arg2;
endproperty: prop1

assume property (prop1(req, gnt, hresetn, 5));
```

This is an example of writing a *parameterized property.* The effect of passing actual arguments to formal arguments is as if the property were replaced with the actual arguments. A *parameterized sequence* can be described similarly.

Assertion 25: After *RESET,* it can only enter state *READY* or *RUN* on next cycle.

```
property p_next;
  @(negedge sclk)
    (pstate == RESET) |=>
      ((pstate == READY) || (pstate == RUN));
endproperty: p_next

assert_legal_state_transition:
  assert property (p_next);
```

Assertion 26: When data is ready to go into a pipeline, it will come out three to seven clock cycles later and will be incremented by five.

```
sequence s_temp_var;
  int td;                        // Temporary variable used.

  @(posedge clk)
    (ready, td = rdata) ##[3:7] (dout == (td+5));
endsequence: s_temp_var
```

A sequence expression can optionally have an assignment to a temporary variable. In this example, *ready* is the sequence and *rdata* is assigned to a temporary variable *td.* So when *ready* is asserted, save the value of *rdata* in *td*. The assertion uses this *td* value to check if *dout* has the value of *td+5* after three to seven clock ticks. Here is another example of a sequence using temporary variables.

```
sequence s_vars;
  int t1, t2;

  @(posedge clk)
    (req, t1 = pdata) ##2 (ack, t2 = pdata) ##5
      (busy && (wdata == t1 + t2));
endsequence: s_vars
```

When *req* is true, the value of *pdata* is saved in *t1*. When *ack* is true two cycles later, value of *pdata* is saved in *t2*. Five cycles later when *busy* becomes true, *wdata* should be the sum of *t1* and *t2*.

The above examples show the use of temporary variables within a sequence declaration. Such temporary variables can also be declared within a property declaration.

Assertion 27: As long as *test* signal is low, the sequence *s_abort* should not occur.

```
property p_test_abort;
  @(posedge clk)
    disable iff (test)
      not s_abort;
endproperty: p_test_abort

assert property (p_test_abort);
```

The sequence *s_abort* is declared elsewhere.

Assertion 28: When in state *ACK* and if *pready* is high, then *req* should be low for five clocks.

```
a_ack_check: assert property
  ( @(posedge clk)
      (hstate == ACK) && (pready == 1) |-> !req[*5]
  )
else
  $info ("Assertion failed.");
```

Assertion 29: If *req* changes from high to low between one rising clock and the next, *gnt* must be high on the following clock.

```
global clocking @(posedge clk); endclocking

property p_follow;
    $fell(req) |=> gnt;
endproperty: p_follow

assert property (p_follow);
```

The clock event is specified using the global clocking block. Note that the name of the global clocking block is optional and is not specified in this example. When a global clock is used, then a number of global clock sampled value functions are available for use. The past sampled value functions are **$past_gclk**, **$rose_gclk**, **$fell_gclk**, **$stable_gclk** and **$changed_gclk**. The future sampled value functions are **$future_gclk**, **$rising_gclk**, **$falling_gclk**, **$steady_gclk** and **$changing_gclk**.

Assertion 30: Assert that the state transitions *RED* to *YELLOW* and *RED* to *ORANGE* never occur.

```
assert_illegal_state: assert property
  ( @(posedge tclk)
      disable iff (!presetn)
        (cstate == RED) |=> !(cstate == YELLOW ||
         cstate == ORANGE)
  )
else
  $fatal ("assert_illegal: bad transition");
```

Assertion 31: A new bus cycle may not start for two cycles after an abort cycle occurs.

```
assert_bus_cycle: assert property
  ( @(posedge clk)
      $rose(abort_cycle) |-> !cycle_start[*2]
  );
```

Assertion 32: After *reset* asserts, *lock* asserts three to seven times, not necessarily in successive clocks and then *ready* asserts after four clock cycles. Assume that this property is true.

```
assume_lock: assume property
  ( @(negedge hclk)
      $rose(reset) |-> ##2 lock[->3:7] ##4 ready
  );
```

Assertion 33: Memory address should not change while chip enable is low.

```
assert_stable: assert property
  ( @(posedge clk)
      disable iff (!hresetn)
        mem_chip_enable == 0 |->
          $stable(mem_address)
  );
```

Assertion 34: Assert that memory output data is same as input data on next clock cycle, provided reset is low and chip enable is high.

```
assert_tracking: assert property
  ( @(posedge clk)
      disable iff (reset)
        enable |=> (mem_dout == $past(mem_din))
  );
```

The system function **$past** returns the value of the expression in the previous clock tick.

Assertion 35: Assert that the sequence *S0* to *S3* to *S5* to *S7* never occurs.

```
let in_s0 = mc_state == S0;
let in_s3 = mc_state == S3;
let in_s5 = mc_state == S5;
let in_s7 = mc_state == S7;

sequence s_illegal;
  in_s0 ##1 in_s3 ##1 in_s5 ##1 in_s7;
endsequence: s_illegal
```

```
property p_never;
  not (s_illegal);
endproperty: p_never

assert property (@(posedge hclk) p_never);
```

Assertion 36: Master must deassert *hbusreq* only when *htrans* has a value of *NONSEQ* or *SEQ*.

```
assert_hbusreq: assert property
  ( @(posedge hclk)
      disable iff (!hresetn)
        ($fell(hbusreq) |->
          (htrans == NONSEQ) || (htrans == SEQ))
  )
else
  $fatal ("htrans is %d", htrans);
```

Assertion 37: After a read request, *ack* is asserted eventually but after a minimum of five cycles.

```
property p_ack_eventually;
  read_req ##[5:$] ack;
endproperty: p_ack_eventually

always @(posedge clk)
  if (enable)
    assert property (p_ack_eventually);
```

The clock definition can come from a procedural block.

Concurrent assertions can appear in a procedural block (initial and always statement). If an assertion appears in an always statement, then the assertion is always checked. If the assertion appears in an initial statement, then the assertion is checked on only the first clock tick. The clock tick for a concurrent assertion in an always statement can be inferred from the event control specified for the always statement. A concurrent assertion that appears in a procedural block is called a *procedural concurrent assertion*. Such an assertion can be made inactive using the disable statement.

Assertion 38: Assume that *reset* starts low for one cycle, is high for five clock cycles and then goes low forever.

```
clocking c_reset @(posedge sclk);
  property p_reset;
     !reset ##1 reset[*5] |-> always(!reset);
  endproperty: p_reset
endclocking: c_reset

assume property (c_reset.p_reset);
```

The clock definition can come from a clocking block as well.

Assertion 39: Bus stays in *IDLE* state or transitions to only *SETUP* state.

```
default disable iff (!hresetn);

property p_valid_transition;
  @(posedge hclk)
      bus_state == IDLE |=>
        (bus_state == IDLE) || (bus_state == SETUP);
endproperty: p_valid_transition

assert_valid_transition:
assert property (p_valid_transition)
else
  $error ("assert_valid_transition: Bad transition.");
```

A *default disable* statement is used to specify a default disable condition for all assertions within the scope and subscopes.

Assertion 40: Variable takes only legal values of its enumeration type.

```
typedef enum {ST[4]} t_fsm;
t_fsm next_state;

clocking cb_a @(posedge clock); endclocking

// Default clocking statement:
default clocking cb_a;
```

```
assert_fsm_never_out_of_bounds:
assert property
  ( next_state == ST0 || next_state == ST1 ||
    next_state == ST2 || next_state == ST3
  );
```

The *default clocking* statement is used to specify the clocking block that in turn provides the clocking event for all assertions within its scope. A clock event specification is no longer required in the assert property statement.

Avoiding False Failures

An important point to remember in avoiding false failures is that an assertion is checked on every clock tick. So it is possible that in some cases, for example, where an assertion is a simple sequence such as,

```
req ##1 gnt ##2 !req
```

there could be false assertion failures reported. Some of the ways to avoid false failures are:

i. Use the *disable iff* clause or the default disable statement to disable the firing of the assertion.

ii. Use the implication operators so that the assertion is checked only if a condition occurs (antecedent matches).

iii. Use the sampled value functions such as **$rose** and **$fell**.

iv. Use the control system tasks described in the next section.

Some of the assertion examples presented in this section may suffer from this behavior. However the examples have been provided so that the semantics of the assertions could be understood under different scenarios.

9.2.5 Control System Tasks

Three system tasks are provided to control assertions.

i. **$assertoff()**: Stop checking specified assertions until *$asserton* is issued.

ii. **$assertkill()**: Abort the execution of the specified assertions.

iii. **$asserton()**: Renew execution of the specified assertions.

The arguments are the assertion labels and module names, plus a hierarchy level specifier. If no arguments are specified, the task applies to all assertions. Here are some examples.

```
// Turn off all assertions while nreset is active.
always @(negedge nreset)
  $assertoff();

// Turn on all assertions when nreset is no
//longer active.
always @(posedge nreset)
  $asserton();

// Turn on all assertions in specified module plus in
// all modules one level below:
$asserton (1, m_fifo); // m_fifo is name of a module.

// Turn off the two assertions:
$assertoff (0, assert_bus_cycle, assert_stable);

// Abort the specified assertion and all assertions
// in top-level of module m_counter:
$assertkill (0, m_counter, assert_req_ack);
```

It is possible to control the execution of the pass or the fail set of statements in an assertion or in an expect statement. This is accomplished using the following system tasks.

i. **$assertpasson()**: Enables the execution of the pass set of statements upon either a vacuous or a nonvacuous success.

ii. **$assertpassoff()**: Disables the execution of the pass set of statements upon either a vacuous or a nonvacuous success.

iii. **$assertfailon**(): Enables the execution of the fail set of statements upon assertion failure.

iv. **$assertfailoff**(): Disables the execution of the fail set of statements upon assertion failure.

v. **$assertnonvacuouson**(): Enables the execution of the pass set of statements for only a nonvacuous success.

vi. **$assertvacuousoff**(): Disables the execution of the pass set of statements for only a vacuous success.

The arguments to these system tasks are the hierarchy level specifier plus a list of assertion labels and module names.

9.2.6 Binding

It is possible to specify the assertions (including properties and sequences) in a separate file and bind these later to a module or specific module instances through bind directives. Semantically, this is same as writing an assertion external to a module using hierarchical path names.

```
// File: assertions.sv
module m_assertions;
  // Sequences, properties and assertions here.
endmodule: m_assertions

// File: mod_fifo.sv
module fifo;
  . . .
endmodule: fifo

// File: bind.sv
// In compilation-unit scope: compiled together
// with the above files.
bind fifo m_assertions u_m_assertions();
  // Binds the assertions in module
  // m_assertions to module fifo. The name of
  // the module instance is u_m_assertions.
```

Such binding allows the addition of assertions to design blocks without touching or modifying the design code. Basically the assertions are described in a separate file, and these are bound during simulation using bind directives.

The bind directives can be present in a module or in an interface or in the compilation-unit scope (as shown in last example). The bind directives can also be used to bind a module, interface or a program instance to a module or a module instance.

```
bind fifo: u1_fifo, u5_fifo
  gen_clks u_gen_clks (nreset, refclk);
```

This bind directive specifies to bind the module instance *u_gen_clks* (of module *gen_clks*) to the module instances *u1_fifo* and *u5_fifo* (of module *fifo*).

9.3 Expect Statement

An *expect statement* is just like an immediate assertion statement, except that it can block execution until the property succeeds. Its syntax is of the form:

```
expect ( property_specification )
  [ [ pass_statements ]
else
  fail_statements ]
```

If the property evaluation has not yet completed, the statement blocks and waits until the property has been evaluated. If it passes, then the pass set of statements are executed; if it fails, then the fail set of statements are executed.

9.4 Checker Construct

SystemVerilog provides a checker construct to encapsulate assertions and its associated code. A checker is a design element, that is, it is at the same level as a module, and thus can appear in a separate file. It can serve as a verification library unit. Here is the syntax of a checker declaration.

```
checker checker_name [ ( checker_port_list ) ] ;
  // Assertion, property, sequence declarations.
  // Variable declarations.
  // Initial, always, final statements.
  // Checker declarations and instantiations.
endchecker [ : checker_name ]
```

A module, interface or a program cannot be declared or instantiated within a checker. In addition, no nets can be declared within a checker. Variables declared within a checker are called *checker variables* and can be assigned values using only nonblocking assignments. Here is an example of a checker declaration.

```
checker check_39 (logic hclk, hreset, t_bus bus_state);
  logic [3:0] bad_count = 0;          // Checker variable.

  property p_valid_transition;
    @(posedge hclk)
      disable iff (!hresetn)
        bus_state == IDLE |=>
          (bus_state == IDLE) || (bus_state == SETUP);
  endproperty: p_valid_transition

  assert_valid_transition:
  assert property (p_valid_transition)
  else
    begin
      $error (
        "assert_valid_transition: Bad transition.");
      bad_count <= bad_count + 1;
    end
endchecker: check_39
```

A checker declaration can also appear inside a module, interface, program, package, or within another checker.

A checker instantiation format is much like that of a module instantiation.

```
checker_name inst_name [ ( checker_port_connections ) ];
```

Here is an example.

```
check_39 c_check39 ( .hclk(clk), .hreset(reset),
                     .bus_state(mstate));
```

A checker instance can appear as a concurrent statement (static checker instance) or as a sequential statement (procedural checker instance).

❑

Appendix A

Syntax Reference

This appendix presents the complete syntax[1] of the SystemVerilog language.

A.1 *Keywords*

Following are the keywords of the SystemVerilog language. Note that only lower case names are keywords. The keywords marked with * are added for SystemVerilog (the non-* ones were present in the Verilog HDL language).

accept_on*	**alias ***	**always**	**always_comb***
always_ff*	**always_latch**	**and**	**assert***
assign	**assume***	**automatic**	

1. Reprinted here with permission from IEEE Std 1800-2009, Copyright © 2009, IEEE, All rights reserved.

Guideline: Do not use signal names that differ only in case with any keyword.

before*	begin	bind*	bins*
binsof*	bit*	break*	buf
bufif0	bufif1	byte*	
case	casex	casez	cell
chandle*	checker*	class*	clocking*
cmos	config	const*	constraint*
context*	continue*	cover*	covergroup*
coverpoint*	cross*		
deassign	default	defparam	design
disable	dist*	do*	
edge	else	end	endcase
endchecker*	endclass*	endclocking*	endconfig
endfunction	endgenerate	endgroup*	endinterface*
endmodule	endpackage*	endprimitive	endprogram*
endproperty*	endspecify	endsequence*	endtable
endtask	enum*	event	eventually*
expect*	export*	extends*	extern*
final*	first_match*	for	force
foreach	forever	fork	forkjoin*
function			
generate	genvar	global*	
highz0	highz1		
if	iff*	ifnone	ignore_bins*
illegal_bins*	implies*	import*	incdir
include	initial	inout	input
inside*	instance	int*	integer
interface*	intersect*		
join	join_any*	join_none*	
large	let*	liblist	library
local*	localparam	logic*	longint*
macromodule	matches*	medium	modport*
module			
nand	negedge	new*	nexttime*
nmos	nor	noshowcancelled	
not	notif0	notif1	null*

or	output		
package*	packed*	parameter	pmos
posedge	primitive	priority*	program*
property*	protected*	pull0	pull1
pulldown	pullup	pulsestyle_onevent	
pulsestyle_ondetect		pure*	
rand*	randc*	randcase*	randsequence*
rcmos	real	realtime	ref*
reg	reject_on*	release	repeat
restrict*	return*	rnmos	rpmos
rtran	rtranif0	rtranif1	
s_always*	s_eventually*	s_nexttime*	s_until*
s_until_with*	scalared	sequence*	shortint*
shortreal*	showcancelled	signed	small
solve*	specify	specparam	static*
string*	strong*	strong0	strong1
struct*	super*	supply0	supply1
sync_accept_on*		sync_reject_on*	
table	tagged*	task	this*
throughout*	time	timeprecision*	timeunit*
tran	tranif0	tranif1	tri
tri0	tri1	triand	trior
trireg	type*	typedef*	
union*	unique*	unique0*	unsigned
until*	until_with*	untyped*	use
uwire			
var*	vectored	virtual*	void*
wait	wait_order*	wand	weak*
weak0	weak1	while	wildcard*
wire	with*	within*	wor
xnor	xor		

A.2 Syntax Conventions

The following conventions are used in describing the syntax, which is described using the Backus-Naur Form (BNF).

i. The syntax rules are organized in an alphabetical order by their left-hand nonterminal name.

ii. Reserved words, operators and punctuation marks that are part of the syntax appear in **boldface**.

iii. A name in *italics* prefixed to a nonterminal name represents the semantic meaning associated with that nonterminal name.

iv. The vertical bar symbol, non-bold, (|) separates alternative items.

v. Square brackets, non-bold, ([. . .]) denote optional items.

vi. Curly braces, non-bold, ({ . . . }) identify an item that is repeated zero or more times.

vii. Square brackets, parentheses, and curly braces and other characters (such as **,** **;**) appearing in bold (**[...]**, **(...)**, **{ ... }**) indicate characters that are part of the syntax.

viii. The starting nonterminal name for the SystemVerilog source is *source_text.* The starting nonterminal name for a library map file is *library_text.*

ix. The terminal names used in this grammar appear in upper case.

A.3 The Syntax

action_block ::=
    statement_or_null
  | [statement] **else** statement_or_null

actual_arg_expr ::= event_expression | $

always_construct ::=
  always_keyword
    statement

always_keyword ::= **always** | **always_comb** | **always_latch** | **always_ff**

anonymous_program ::=
  program ; { anonymous_program_item } **endprogram**

```
anonymous_program_item ::=
      task_declaration
    | function_declaration
    | class_declaration
    | covergroup_declaration
    | class_constructor_declaration
    | ;
ansi_port_declaration ::=
      [ net_port_header | interface_port_header ]
        port_identifier { unpacked_dimension } [ = constant_expression ]
    | [ variable_port_header ] port_identifier
        { variable_dimension } [ = constant_expression ]
    | [ port_direction ] . port_identifier ( [ expression ] )
array_identifier ::= identifier
array_manipulation_call ::=
    array_method_name { attribute_instance }
      [ ( list_of_arguments ) ] [ with ( expression ) ]
array_method_name ::= method_identifier | unique | and | or | xor
array_pattern_key ::= constant_expression | assignment_pattern_key
array_range_expression ::=
      expression
    | expression : expression
    | expression +: expression
    | expression -: expression
assertion_item ::=
      concurrent_assertion_item
    | deferred_immediate_assertion_item
assertion_item_declaration ::=
      property_declaration
    | sequence_declaration
    | let_declaration
assertion_variable_declaration ::=
    var_data_type list_of_variable_decl_assignments ;
assert_property_statement ::=
    assert property ( property_spec ) action_block
assignment_operator ::=
    = | += | -= | *= | /= | %= | &= | |= | ^= | <<= | >>= | <<<= | >>>=
assignment_pattern ::=
      '{ expression { , expression } }
    | '{ structure_pattern_key : expression
        { , structure_pattern_key : expression } }
    | '{ array_pattern_key : expression { , array_pattern_key : expression } }
    | '{ constant_expression { expression { , expression } } }
```

assignment_pattern_expression ::=
[assignment_pattern_expression_type] assignment_pattern

assignment_pattern_expression_type ::=
ps_type_identifier
| ps_parameter_identifier
| integer_atom_type
| type_reference

assignment_pattern_key ::= simple_type | **default**

assignment_pattern_net_lvalue ::= '{ net_lvalue { , net_lvalue } }

assignment_pattern_variable_lvalue ::=
'{ variable_lvalue { , variable_lvalue } }

associative_dimension ::= [data_type] | [*]

assume_property_statement ::=
assume property (property_spec) action_block

attribute_instance ::= (* attr_spec { , attr_spec } *)

attr_name ::= identifier

attr_spec ::= attr_name [= constant_expression]

base_expression ::= expression

binary_base ::= **'[s|S]b** | **'[s|S]B**

binary_digit ::= x_digit | z_digit | **0** | **1**

binary_module_path_operator ::= == | != | && | || | & | | | ^ | ^~ | ~^

binary_number ::= [size] binary_base binary_value

binary_operator ::=
+ | - | * | / | %
| == | != | === | !== | ==? | !=? | && | || | ** | < | <= | > | >=
| & | | | ^ | ^~ | ~^ | >> | << | >>> | <<< | -> | <->

binary_value ::= binary_digit { _ | binary_digit }

bind_directive ::=
bind bind_target_scope
[: bind_target_instance_list] bind_instantiation ;
| **bind** bind_target_instance bind_instantiation ;

bind_instantiation ::=
program_instantiation
| module_instantiation
| interface_instantiation
| checker_instantiation

bind_target_instance ::= hierarchical_identifier constant_bit_select

bind_target_instance_list ::= bind_target_instance { , bind_target_instance }

bind_target_scope ::= module_identifier | interface_identifier

bins_expression ::=
    variable_identifier
  | cover_point_identifier [. bins_identifier]

bins_keyword ::= **bins** | **illegal_bins** | **ignore_bins**

bins_or_empty ::=
    { { attribute_instance } { bins_or_options ; } }
  | ;

bins_or_options ::=
    coverage_option
  | [**wildcard**] bins_keyword bin_identifier
      [[[expression]]] = { open_range_list } [**iff** (expression)]
  | [**wildcard**] bins_keyword bin_identifier [[ ]] = trans_list
      [**iff** (expression)]
  | bins_keyword bin_identifier [[[expression]]] =
      default [**iff** (expression)]
  | bins_keyword bin_identifier = **default_sequence** [**iff** (expression)]

bins_selection ::=
  bins_keyword bin_identifier = select_expression [**iff** (expression)]

bins_selection_or_option ::=
    { attribute_instance } coverage_option
  | { attribute_instance } bins_selection

bin_identifier ::= identifier

bit_select ::= { [expression] }

block_comment ::= /* comment_text */

block_event_expression ::=
    block_event_expression **or** block_event_expression
  | **begin** hierarchical_btf_identifier
  | **end** hierarchical_btf_identifier

block_identifier ::= identifier

block_item_declaration ::=
    { attribute_instance } data_declaration
  | { attribute_instance } local_parameter_declaration ;
  | { attribute_instance } parameter_declaration ;
  | { attribute_instance } overload_declaration
  | { attribute_instance } let_declaration

block_reg_declaration ::=
  reg [**signed**] [range] list_of_block_variable_identifiers ;

block_variable_type ::=
    variable_identifier
  | variable_identifier dimension { dimension }

blocking_assignment ::=
    variable_lvalue = delay_or_event_control expression
  | nonrange_variable_lvalue = dynamic_array_new
  | [implicit_class_handle . | class_scope | package_scope]
      hierarchical_variable_identifier select = class_new
  | operator_assignment

boolean_abbrev ::=
    consecutive_repetition
  | non_consecutive_repetition
  | goto_repetition

built_in_method_call ::=
    array_manipulation_call
  | randomize_call

case_expression ::= expression

case_generate_construct ::=
  case (constant_expression)
    case_generate_item
    { case_generate_item }
  endcase

case_generate_item ::=
    constant_expression { , constant_expression } :
      generate_block
  | **default** [:] generate_block

case_inside_item ::=
    open_range_list : statement_or_null
  | **default** [:] statement_or_null

case_item ::=
    case_item_expression { , case_item_expression } : statement_or_null
  | **default** [:] statement_or_null

case_item_expression ::= expression

case_keyword ::= **case** | **casez** | **casex**

case_pattern_item ::=
    pattern [&&& expression] : statement_or_null
  | **default** [:] statement_or_null

case_statement ::=
    [unique_priority] case_keyword (case_expression)
      case_item { case_item } **endcase**
  | [unique_priority] case_keyword (case_expression) **matches**
      case_pattern_item { case_pattern_item } **endcase**
  | [unique_priority] **case** (case_expression) **inside**
      case_inside_item { case_inside_item } **endcase**

cast ::= casting_type ' (expression)

casting_type ::= simple_type | constant_primary | signing | **string** | **const**

cell_clause ::= **cell** [library_identifier **.**] cell_identifier

cell_identifier ::= identifier

charge_strength ::= **(small)** | **(medium)** | **(large)**

checker_always_construct ::= **always** statement

checker_declaration ::=
  checker checker_identifier [**(** [checker_port_list] **)**] **;**
    { checker_or_generate_item }
  endchecker [**:** checker_identifier]

checker_generate_item ::=
    loop_generate_construct
  | conditional_generate_construct
  | generate_region
  | elaboration_system_task

checker_identifier ::= identifier

checker_instantiation ::=
  checker_identifier name_of_instance
    ([list_of_checker_port_connections] **) ;**

checker_or_generate_item ::=
    checker_or_generate_item_declaration
  | initial_construct
  | checker_always_construct
  | final_construct
  | assertion_item
  | checker_generate_item

checker_or_generate_item_declaration ::=
    [**rand**] data_declaration
  | function_declaration
  | assertion_item_declaration
  | covergroup_declaration
  | overload_declaration
  | genvar_declaration
  | clocking_declaration
  | **default clocking** clocking_identifier **;**
  | **default disable iff** expression_or_dist **;**
  | **;**

checker_port_item ::=
  { attribute_instance } property_formal_type port_identifier
    { variable_dimension } [**=** property_actual_arg]

checker_port_list ::= checker_port_item { **,** checker_port_item }

checktime_condition ::= mintypmax_expression

class_constraint ::=
  constraint_prototype
  | constraint_declaration

class_constructor_declaration ::=
  function [class_scope] **new** [**(** [tf_port_list] **)**] **;**
    { block_item_declaration }
    [**super . new** [**(** list_of_arguments **)**] **;**]
    { function_statement_or_null }
  endfunction [**: new**]

class_constructor_prototype ::= **function new (** [tf_port_list] **) ;**

class_declaration ::=
  [**virtual**] **class** [lifetime] class_identifier [parameter_port_list]
    [**extends** class_type [(list_of_arguments)]] **;**
    { class_item }
  endclass [**:** class_identifier]

class_identifier ::= identifier

class_item ::=
  { attribute_instance } class_property
  | { attribute_instance } class_method
  | { attribute_instance } class_constraint
  | { attribute_instance } class_declaration
  | { attribute_instance } covergroup_declaration
  | local_parameter_declaration **;**
  | parameter_declaration **;**
  | **;**

class_item_qualifier ::= **static | protected | local**

class_method ::=
  { method_qualifier } task_declaration
  | { method_qualifier } function_declaration
  | **extern** { method_qualifier } method_prototype **;**
  | { method_qualifier } class_constructor_declaration
  | **extern** { method_qualifier } class_constructor_prototype

class_new ::= **new** [**(** list_of_arguments **)** | expression]

class_property ::=
  { property_qualifier } data_declaration
  | **const** { class_item_qualifier } data_type const_identifier
    [= constant_expression] **;**

class_qualifier ::= [**local ::**] [implicit_class_handle **.** | class_scope]

class_scope ::= class_type **::**

class_type ::=
  ps_class_identifier [parameter_value_assignment]
    { **::** class_identifier [parameter_value_assignment] }

class_variable_identifier ::= variable_identifier

clocking_declaration ::=
[**default**] **clocking** [clocking_identifier] clocking_event ;
{ clocking_item }
endclocking [: clocking_identifier]
| **global clocking** [clocking_identifier] clocking_event ;
endclocking [: clocking_identifier]

clocking_decl_assign ::= signal_identifier [= expression]

clocking_direction ::=
input [clocking_skew]
| **output** [clocking_skew]
| **input** [clocking_skew] **output** [clocking_skew]
| **inout**

clocking_drive ::=
clockvar_expression <= [cycle_delay] expression

clocking_event ::=
@ identifier
| @ (event_expression)

clocking_identifier ::= identifier

clocking_item ::=
default default_skew ;
| clocking_direction list_of_clocking_decl_assign ;
| { attribute_instance } assertion_item_declaration

clocking_skew ::=
edge_identifier [delay_control]
| delay_control

clockvar ::= hierarchical_identifier

clockvar_expression ::= clockvar select

cmos_switch_instance ::=
[name_of_instance] (output_terminal , input_terminal ,
ncontrol_terminal , pcontrol_terminal)

cmos_switchtype ::= **cmos** | **rcmos**

combinational_body ::=
table
combinational_entry { combinational_entry }
endtable

combinational_entry ::= level_input_list : output_symbol ;

comment ::= one_line_comment | block_comment

comment_text ::= { ANY_ASCII_CHARACTER }

concatenation ::= { expression { , expression } }

concurrent_assertion_item ::=
    [block_identifier :] concurrent_assertion_statement
  | checker_instantiation

concurrent_assertion_item_declaration ::=
    property_declaration
  | sequence_declaration

concurrent_assertion_statement ::=
    assert_property_statement
  | assume_property_statement
  | cover_property_statement
  | cover_sequence_statement
  | restrict_property_statement

conditional_expression ::=
  cond_predicate ? { attribute_instance } expression **:** expression

conditional_generate_construct ::=
    if_generate_construct
  | case_generate_construct

conditional_statement ::=
  [unique_priority] **if (** cond_predicate **)** statement_or_null
    { **else if (** cond_predicate) statement_or_null }
    [**else** statement_or_null]

cond_pattern ::= expression **matches** pattern

cond_predicate ::=
  expression_or_cond_pattern { **&&&** expression_or_cond_pattern }

config_declaration ::=
  config config_identifier ;
    { local_parameter_declaration **;** }
    design_statement
    { config_rule_statement }
  endconfig [: config_identifier]

config_identifier ::= identifier

config_rule_statement ::=
    default_clause liblist_clause ;
  | inst_clause liblist_clause ;
  | inst_clause use_clause ;
  | cell_clause liblist_clause ;
  | cell_clause use_clause ;

consecutive_repetition ::=
    [* const_or_range_expression]
  | [*]
  | [+]

constant_assignment_pattern_expression ::=
  assignment_pattern_expression

```
constant_base_expression ::= constant_expression

constant_bit_select ::= { [ constant_expression ] }

constant_cast ::= casting_type ' ( constant_expression )

constant_concatenation ::= { constant_expression { , constant_expression } }

constant_expression ::=
      constant_primary
    | unary_operator { attribute_instance } constant_primary
    | constant_expression binary_operator { attribute_instance }
        constant_expression
    | constant_expression ? { attribute_instance }
        constant_expression : constant_expression

constant_function_call ::= function_subroutine_call

constant_indexed_range ::=
      constant_expression +: constant_expression
    | constant_expression -: constant_expression

constant_let_expression ::= let_expression

constant_mintypmax_expression ::=
      constant_expression
    | constant_expression : constant_expression : constant_expression

constant_multiple_concatenation ::=
    { constant_expression constant_concatenation }

constant_param_expression ::=
    constant_mintypmax_expression | data_type | $

constant_part_select_range ::=
      constant_range
    | constant_indexed_range

constant_primary ::=
      primary_literal
    | ps_parameter_identifier constant_select
    | specparam_identifier [ [ constant_range_expression ] ]
    | genvar_identifier
    | [ package_scope | class_scope ] enum_identifier
    | constant_concatenation [ [ constant_range_expression ] ]
    | constant_multiple_concatenation [ [ constant_range_expression ] ]
    | constant_function_call
    | constant_let_expression
    | ( constant_mintypmax_expression )
    | constant_cast
    | constant_assignment_pattern_expression
    | type_reference

constant_range ::= constant_expression : constant_expression
```

constant_range_expression ::=
    constant_expression
  | constant_part_select_range

constant_select ::= [{ . member_identifier constant_bit_select } .
  member_identifier] constant_bit_select [[constant_part_select_range]]

constraint_block ::= { { constraint_block_item } }

constraint_block_item ::=
    solve solve_before_list **before** solve_before_list ;
  | constraint_expression

constraint_declaration ::=
  [**static**] **constraint** constraint_identifier constraint_block

constraint_expression ::=
    expression_or_dist ;
  | expression -> constraint_set
  | **if** (expression) constraint_set [**else** constraint_set]
  | **foreach** (ps_or_hierarchical_array_identifier [loop_variables])
      constraint_set

constraint_identifier ::= identifier

constraint_prototype ::=
  [constraint_prototype_qualifier] [**static**] **constraint**
    constraint_identifier ;

constraint_prototype_qualifier ::= **extern** | **pure**

constraint_set ::=
    constraint_expression
  | { { constraint_expression } }

const_identifier ::= identifier

const_or_range_expression ::=
    constant_expression
  | cycle_delay_const_range_expression

continuous_assign ::=
    assign [drive_strength] [delay3] list_of_net_assignments ;
  | **assign** [delay_control] list_of_variable_assignments ;

controlled_reference_event ::= controlled_timing_check_event

controlled_timing_check_event ::=
  timing_check_event_control specify_terminal_descriptor
    [&&& timing_check_condition]

coverage_option ::=
    option.member_identifier = expression
  | **type_option.**member_identifier = constant_expression

coverage_event ::=
  clocking_event
  | **with function sample** ([tf_port_list])
  | @@ (block_event_expression)

coverage_spec ::=
  cover_point
  | cover_cross

coverage_spec_or_option ::=
  { attribute_instance } coverage_spec
  | { attribute_instance } coverage_option ;

covergroup_declaration ::=
  covergroup covergroup_identifier [([tf_port_list])] [coverage_event] ;
    { coverage_spec_or_option }
  endgroup [: covergroup_identifier]

covergroup_identifier ::= identifier

covergroup_variable_identifier ::= variable_identifier

cover_cross ::=
  [cross_identifier :] **cross** list_of_coverpoints
    [**iff** (expression)] select_bins_or_empty

cover_point ::=
  [cover_point_identifier :] **coverpoint** expression
    [**iff** (expression)] bins_or_empty

cover_point_identifier ::= identifier

cover_property_statement ::=
  cover property (property_spec) statement_or_null

cover_sequence_statement ::=
  cover sequence ([clocking_event] [**disable iff** (expression_or_dist)]
    sequence_expr) statement_or_null

cross_identifier ::= identifier

cross_item ::=
  cover_point_identifier
  | variable_identifier

current_state ::= level_symbol

cycle_delay ::=
  ## integral_number
  | ## identifier
  | ## (expression)

cycle_delay_const_range_expression ::=
  constant_expression : constant_expression
  | constant_expression : $

cycle_delay_range ::=
    ## constant_primary
  | ## [const_delay_const_range_expression]
  | ## [*]
  | ## [+]

c_identifier ::= [**a-z A-Z _**] { [**a-z A-Z 0-9 _**] }

data_declaration ::=
    [**const**] [**var**] [lifetime] data_type_or_implicit
      list_of_variable_decl_assignments ;
  | type_declaration
  | package_import_declaration
  | virtual_interface_declaration

data_event ::= timing_check_event

data_source_expression ::= expression

data_type ::=
    integer_vector_type [signing] { packed_dimension }
  | integer_atom_type [signing]
  | non_integer_type
  | struct_union [**packed** [signing]] { struct_union_member
      { struct_union_member } } { packed_dimension }
  | **enum** [enum_base_type] { enum_name_declaration
      { , enum_name_declaration } } { packed_dimension }
  | **string**
  | **chandle**
  | **virtual** [**interface**] interface_identifier
  | [class_scope | package_scope] type_identifier { packed_dimension }
  | class_type
  | **event**
  | ps_covergroup_identifier
  | type_reference

data_type_or_implicit ::=
    data_type
  | implicit_data_type

data_type_or_void ::=
    data_type
  | **void**

decimal_base ::= '[**s**|**S**]**d** | '[**s**|**S**]**D**

decimal_digit ::= **0** | **1** | **2** | **3** | **4** | **5** | **6** | **7** | **8** | **9**

decimal_number ::=
    unsigned_number
  | [size] decimal_base unsigned_number
  | [size] decimal_base x_digit { _ }
  | [size] decimal_base z_digit { _ }

default_clause ::= **default**

default_skew ::=
  input clocking_skew
  | **output** clocking_skew
  | **input** clocking_skew **output** clocking_skew

deferred_immediate_assertion_item ::=
  [block_identifier **:**] deferred_immediate_assertion_statement

deferred_immediate_assertion_statement ::=
  deferred_immediate_assert_statement
  | deferred_immediate_assume_statement
  | deferred_immediate_cover_statement

deferred_immediate_assert_statement :=
  assert #0 (expression) action_block

deferred_immediate_assume_statement ::=
  assume #0 (expression) action_block

deferred_immediate_cover_statement ::=
  cover #0 (expression) statement_or_null

defparam_assignment ::=
  hierarchical_parameter_identifier = constant_mintypmax_expression

delayed_data ::=
  terminal_identifier
  | terminal_identifier [constant_mintypmax_expression]

delayed_reference ::=
  terminal_identifier
  | terminal_identifier [constant_mintypmax_expression]

delay2 ::=
  # delay_value
  | # (mintypmax_expression [, mintypmax_expression])

delay3 ::=
  # delay_value
  | # (mintypmax_expression [, mintypmax_expression
    [, mintypmax_expression]])

delay_control ::=
  # delay_value
  | # (mintypmax_expression)

delay_or_event_control ::=
  delay_control
  | event_control
  | **repeat** (expression) event_control

delay_value ::=
    unsigned_number
  | real_number
  | ps_identifier
  | time_literal
  | **1step**

description ::=
    module_declaration
  | udp_declaration
  | interface_declaration
  | program_declaration
  | package_declaration
  | { attribute_instance } package_item
  | { attribute_instance } bind_directive
  | config_declaration

design_statement ::= **design** { [library_identifier **.**]cell_identifier } **;**

dimension ::=
    [dimension_constant_expression **:** dimension_constant_expression]

dimension_constant_expression ::= constant_expression

disable_statement ::=
    disable hierarchical_task_identifier **;**
  | **disable** hierarchical_block_identifier **;**
  | **disable fork ;**

dist_item ::=
    value_range [dist_weight]

dist_list ::=
    dist_item { , dist_item }

dist_weight ::=
    := expression
  | :/ expression

dpi_function_import_property ::= **context** | **pure**

dpi_function_proto ::= function_prototype

dpi_import_export ::=
    import dpi_spec_string [dpi_function_import_property]
      [c_identifier =] dpi_function_proto **;**
  | **import** dpi_spec_string [dpi_task_import_property]
      [c_identifier =] dpi_task_proto **;**
  | **export** dpi_spec_string [c_identifier =] **function** function_identifier **;**
  | **export** dpi_spec_string [c_identifier =] **task** task_identifier **;**

dpi_spec_string ::= **"DPI-C"** | **"DPI"**

dpi_task_import_property ::= **context**

dpi_task_proto ::= task_prototype

drive_strength ::=
    (strength0 , strength1)
  | (strength1 , strength0)
  | (strength0 , **highz1**)
  | (strength1 , **highz0**)
  | (**highz1** , strength0)
  | (**highz0** , strength1)

dynamic_array_new ::=
  new [expression] [(expression)]

dynamic_array_variable_identifier ::= variable_identifier

edge_control_specifier ::=
  edge [edge_descriptor { , edge_descriptor }]

edge_descriptor ::=
    01
  | **10**
  | z_or_x zero_or_one
  | zero_or_one z_or_x

edge_identifier ::=
  posedge | **negedge** | **edge**

edge_indicator ::=
    (level_symbol level_symbol)
  | edge_symbol

edge_input_list ::=
  { level_symbol } edge_indicator { level_symbol }

edge_sensitive_path_declaration ::=
    parallel_edge_sensitive_path_description = path_delay_value
  | full_edge_sensitive_path_description = path_delay_value

edge_symbol ::= **r** | **R** | **f** | **F** | **p** | **P** | **n** | **N** | *****

elaboration_system_task ::=
    $**fatal** [(finish_number [, list_of_arguments])] ;
  | $**error** [([list_of_arguments])] ;
  | $**warning** [([list_of_arguments])] ;
  | $**info** [([list_of_arguments])] ;

empty_queue ::= { }

enable_gate_instance ::=
  [name_of_instance] (output_terminal , input_terminal ,
    enable_terminal)

enable_gate_type ::=
  bufif0 | **bufif1** | **notif0** | **notif1**

enable_terminal ::= expression

end_edge_offset ::= mintypmax_expression

enum_base_type ::=
    integer_atom_type [signing]
  | integer_vector_type [signing] [packed_dimension]
  | type_identifier [packed_dimension]

enum_identifier ::= identifier

enum_name_declaration ::=
  enum_identifier [[integral_number [: integral_number]]]
    [= constant_expression]

error_limit_value ::= limit_value

escaped_arrayed_identifier ::= escaped_identifier [range]

escaped_identifier ::=
  \ { ANY_ASCII_CHARACTER_EXCEPT_WHITE_SPACE } white_space

event_based_flag ::= constant_expression

event_control ::=
    @ hierarchical_event_identifier
  | @ (event_expression)
  | @ *
  | @ (*)
  | @ ps_or_hierarchical_sequence_identifier

event_declaration ::= **event** list_of_event_identifiers ;

event_expression ::=
    [edge_identifier] expression [**iff** expression]
  | sequence_instance [**iff** expression]
  | event_expression **or** event_expression
  | event_expression , event_expression
  | (event_expression)

event_identifier ::= identifier

event_trigger ::=
    -> hierarchical_event_identifier ;
  | ->> [delay_or_event_control] hierarchical_event_identifier ;

exp ::= **e** | **E**

expect_property_statement ::= **expect** (property_spec) action_block

expression ::=
    primary
  | unary_operator { attribute_instance } primary
  | inc_or_dec_expression
  | (operator_assignment)
  | expression binary_operator { attribute_instance } expression
  | conditional_expression
  | inside_expression
  | tagged_union_expression

expression1 ::= expression

expression2 ::= expression

expression3 ::= expression

expression_or_cond_pattern ::=
  expression
  | cond_pattern

expression_or_dist ::= expression [**dist** { dist_list }]

extern_constraint_declaration ::=
  [**static**] **constraint** class_scope constraint_identifier constraint_block

extern_tf_declaration ::=
  extern method_prototype ;
  | **extern forkjoin** task_prototype ;

file_path_spec ::= file_path

final_construct ::= **final** function_statement

finish_number ::= **0** | **1** | **2**

fixed_point_number ::= unsigned_number **.** unsigned_number

formal_identifier ::= identifier

formal_list_item ::= formal_identifier [= actual_arg_expr]

for_initialization ::=
  list_of_variable_assignments
  | for_variable_declaration { , for_variable_declaration }

for_step ::= for_step_assignment { , for_step_assignment }

for_step_assignment ::=
  operator_assignment
  | inc_or_dec_expression
  | function_subroutine_call

for_variable_declaration ::=
  data_type variable_identifier = expression
    { , variable_identifier = expression }

full_edge_sensitive_path_description ::=
  ([edge_identifier] list_of_path_inputs [polarity_operator] *>
    (list_of_path_outputs [polarity_operator] : data_source_expression))

full_path_description ::=
  (list_of_path_inputs [polarity_operator] *> list_of_path_outputs)

function_blocking_assignment ::= variable_lvalue = expression

function_body_declaration ::=
  function_data_type_or_implicit [interface_identifier . | class_scope]
    function_identifier ;
      { tf_item_declaration }
      { function_statement_or_null }
  endfunction [: function_identifier]

```
    | function_data_type_or_implicit [ interface_identifier . | class_scope ]
        function_identifier ( [ tf_port_list ] ) ;
        { block_item_declaration }
        { function_statement_or_null }
      endfunction [ : function_identifier ]
function_call ::=
    hierarchical_function_identifier { attribute_instance }
      ( expression { , expression } )
function_case_item ::=
      expression { , expression } : function_statement_or_null
    | default [ : ] function_statement_or_null
function_case_statement ::=
      case ( expression ) function_case_item { function_case_item }
      endcase
    | casez ( expression ) function_case_item { function_case_item }
      endcase
    | casex ( expression ) function_case_item { function_case_item }
      endcase
function_conditional_statement ::=
      if ( expression ) function_statement_or_null
        [ else function_statement_or_null ]
    | function_if_else_if_statement
function_data_type ::= data_type | void
function_data_type_or_implicit ::=
      data_type_or_void
    | implicit_data_type
function_declaration ::= function [ lifetime ] function_body_declaration
function_identifier ::= identifier
function_if_else_if_statement ::=
    if ( expression ) function_statement_or_null
      { else if ( expression ) function_statement_or_null }
      [ else function_statement_or_null ]
function_item_declaration ::=
      block_item_declaration
    | { attribute_instance } tf_input_declaration ;
function_loop_statement ::=
      forever function_statement
    | repeat ( expression ) function_statement
    | while ( expression ) function_statement
    | for ( variable_assignment ; expression ; variable_assignment )
        function_statement
```

function_port_list ::=
    { attribute_instance } tf_input_declaration
        { , { attribute_instance } tf_input_declaration }

function_prototype ::=
    function data_type_or_void function_identifier ([tf_port_list])

function_seq_block ::=
    begin [: block_identifier { block_item_declaration }]
        { function_statement } **end**

function_statement ::= statement

function_statement_or_null ::=
    function_statement
    | { attribute_instance } ;

function_subroutine_call ::= subroutine_call

gate_instance_identifier ::= arrayed_identifier

gate_instantiation ::=
    cmos_switchtype [delay3] cmos_switch_instance
        { , cmos_switch_instance } ;
    | enable_gatetype [drive_strength] [delay3] enable_gate_instance
        { , enable_gate_instance } ;
    | mos_switchtype [delay3] mos_switch_instance
        { , mos_switch_instance } ;
    | n_input_gatetype [drive_strength] [delay2] n_input_gate_instance
        { , n_input_gate_instance } ;
    | n_output_gatetype [drive_strength] [delay2]
        n_output_gate_instance { , n_output_gate_instance } ;
    | pass_en_switchtype [delay2] pass_enable_switch_instance
        { , pass_enable_switch_instance } ;
    | pass_switchtype pass_switch_instance { , pass_switch_instance } ;
    | **pulldown** [pulldown_strength] pull_gate_instance
        { , pull_gate_instance } ;
    | **pullup** [pullup_strength] pull_gate_instance { , pull_gate_instance } ;

generated_instantiation ::= **generate** { generate_item } **endgenerate**

generate_block ::=
    generate_item
    | [generate_block_identifier :] **begin** [: generate_block_identifier]
        { generate_item }
    end [: generate_block_identifier]

generate_block_identifier ::= identifier

generate_block_or_null ::= generate_block | ;

generate_case_statement ::=
    case (constant_expression) genvar_case_item
        { genvar_case_item } **endcase**

generate_conditional_statement ::=
    if (constant_expression) generate_item_or_null [**else**
        generate_item_or_null]

generate_item ::=
        module_or_generate_item
    | interface_or_generate_item
    | checker_or_generate_item

generate_item_or_null ::= generate_item | ;

generate_loop_statement ::=
    for (genvar_assignment ; constant_expression ; genvar_assignment)
        begin : generate_block_identifier { generate_item } **end**

generate_region ::=
    generate { generate_item } **endgenerate**

genvar_assignment ::= genvar_identifier = constant_expression

genvar_case_item ::=
        constant_expression { , constant_expression } : generate_item_or_null
    | **default** [:] generate_item_or_null

genvar_declaration ::= **genvar** list_of_genvar_identifiers ;

genvar_expression ::= constant_expression

genvar_function_call ::=
    genvar_function_identifier { attribute_instance }
        (constant_expression { , constant_expression })

genvar_function_identifier ::= identifier /* Hierarchy disallowed */

genvar_identifier ::= identifier

genvar_initialization ::= [**genvar**] genvar_identifier = constant_expression

genvar_iteration ::=
        genvar_identifier assignment_operator genvar_expression
    | inc_or_dec_operator genvar_identifier
    | genvar_identifier inc_or_dec_operator

goto_repetition ::= **[->** const_or_range_expression **]**

hex_base ::= **'[s|S]h** | **'[s|S]H**

hex_digit ::=
        x_digit | z_digit
    | **0** | **1** | **2** | **3** | **4** | **5** | **6** | **7** | **8** | **9**
    | **a** | **b** | **c** | **d** | **e** | **f** | **A** | **B** | **C** | **D** | **E** | **F**

hex_number ::= [size] hex_base hex_value

hex_value ::= hex_digit { _ | hex_digit }

hierarchical_array_identifier ::= hierarchical_identifier

hierarchical_block_identifier ::= hierarchical_identifier

hierarchical_btf_identifier ::=
hierarchical_tf_identifier
| hierarchical_block_identifier
| hierarchical_identifier [class_scope] method_identifier

hierarchical_dynamic_array_variable_identifier ::=
hierarchical_variable_identifier

hierarchical_event_identifier ::= hierarchical_identifier

hierarchical_function_identifier ::= hierarchical_identifier

hierarchical_identifier ::= [**$root** .] { identifier constant_bit_select . } identifier

hierarchical_instance ::=
name_of_instance ([list_of_port_connections])

hierarchical_net_identifier ::= hierarchical_identifier

hierarchical_parameter_identifier ::= hierarchical_identifier

hierarchical_property_identifier ::= hierarchical_identifier

hierarchical_sequence_identifier ::= hierarchical_identifier

hierarchical_task_identifier ::= hierarchical_identifier

hierarchical_tf_identifier ::= hierarchical_identifier

hierarchical_variable_identifier ::= hierarchical_identifier

identifier := simple_identifier | escaped_identifier

identifier_list ::= identifier { , identifier }

if_else_if_statement ::=
if (expression) statement_or_null
{ **else if** (expression) statement_or_null }
[**else** statement_or_null]

if_generate_construct ::=
if (constant_expression) generate_block
[**else** generate_block]

immediate_assertion_statement ::=
simple_immediate_assertion_statement
| deferred_immediate_assertion_statement

implicit_class_handle ::= **this** | **super** | **this . super**

implicit_data_type ::= [signing] { packed_dimension }

import_export ::= **import** | **export**

include_statement ::= **include** file_path_spec ;

inc_or_dec_expression ::=
inc_or_dec_operator { attribute_instance } lvariable_lvalue
| variable_lvalue { attribute_instance } inc_or_dec_operator

inc_or_dec_operator ::= ++ | --

indexed_range ::=
expression +: constant_expression
| expression -: constant_expression

index_variable_identifier ::= identifier

init_val ::= **1'b0** | **1'b1** | **1'bx** | **1'bX** | **1'B0** | **1'B1** | **1'Bx** | **1'BX** | **1** | **0**

initial_construct ::=
initial
statement_or_null

inout_declaration ::= **inout** net_port_type list_of_port_identifiers

inout_port_identifier ::= identifier

inout_terminal ::= net_lvalue

input_declaration ::=
input net_port_type list_of_port_identifiers
| **input** variable_port_type list_of_variable_identifiers

input_identifier ::=
input_port_identifier
| inout_port_identifier
| interface_identifier **.** port_identifier

input_port_identifier ::= identifier

input_terminal ::= expression

inside_expression ::= expression **inside** { open_range_list }

inst_clause ::= **instance** inst_name

inst_name ::= topmodule_identifier { **.** instance_identifier }

instance_identifier ::= identifier

integer_declaration ::= **integer** list_of_variable_identifiers **;**

integer_atom_type ::= **byte** | **shortint** | **int** | **longint** | **integer** | **time**

integer_type ::= integer_vector_type | integer_atom_type

integer_vector_type ::= **bit** | **logic** | **reg**

integral_number ::= decimal_number | octal_number
| binary_number | hex_number

interface_ansi_header ::=
{ attribute_instance } **interface** [lifetime] interface_identifier
{ package_import_declaration } [parameter_port_list]
[list_of_port_declarations] **;**

interface_declaration ::=
interface_nonansi_header [timeunits_declaration]
{ interface_item } **endinterface** [**:** interface_identifier]
| interface_ansi_header [timeunits_declaraton]
{ non_port_interface_item } **endinterface** [**:** interface_identifier]

| { attribute_instance } **interface** interface_identifier **(.*) ;**
[timeunits_declaration] { interface_item }
endinterface [**:** interface_identifier]
| **extern** interface_nonansi_header
| **extern** interface_ansi_header

interface_identifier ::= identifier

interface_instance_identifier ::= identifier

interface_instantiation ::=
interface_identifier [parameter_value_assignment]
hierarchical_instance { **,** hierarchical_instance } **;**

interface_item ::= port_declaration | non_port_interface_item

interface_nonansi_header ::=
{ attribute_instance } **interface** [lifetime] interface_identifier
{ package_import_declaration } [parameter_port_list] list_of_ports **;**

interface_or_generate_item ::=
{ attribute_instance } module_common_item
| { attribute_instance } modport_declaration
| { attribute_instance } extern_tf_declaration

interface_port_declaration ::=
interface_identifier list_of_interface_identifiers
| interface_identifier **.** modport_identifier list_of_interface_identifiers

interface_port_header ::=
interface_identifier [**.** modport_identifier]
| **interface** [**.** modport_identifier]

join_keyword ::= **join** | **join_any** | **join_none**

jump_statement ::=
return [expression] **;**
| **break ;**
| **continue ;**

let_actual_arg ::= expression

let_declaration ::=
let let_identifier [**(** [let_port_list] **)**] **=** expression **;**

let_expression ::=
[package_scope] let_identifier [**(** [let_list_of_arguments] **)**]

let_formal_type ::= data_type_or_implicit

let_identifier ::= identifier

let_list_of_arguments ::=
[let_actual_arg] { **,** [let_actual_arg] }
{ **,** **.** identifier **(** [let_actual_arg] **)** }
| **.** identifier **(** [let_actual_arg] **)** { **,** **.** identifier **(** [let_actual_arg] **)** }

let_port_item ::=
{ attribute_instance } let_formal_type port_identifier
{ variable_dimension } [= expression]

let_port_list ::= let_port_item { , let_port_item }

level_input_list ::= level_symbol { level_symbol }

level_symbol ::= **0** | **1** | **x** | **X** | **?** | **b** | **B**

liblist_clause ::= **liblist** { library_identifier }

library_declaration ::=
library library_identifier file_path_spec { , file_path_spec }
[**-incdir** file_path_spec { , file_path_spec }] **;**

library_description ::=
library_declaration
| include_statement
| config_declaration
| ;

library_identifier ::= identifier

library_text ::= { library_description }

lifetime ::= **static** | **automatic**

limit_value ::= constant_mintypmax_expression

list_of_arguments ::=
[expression] { , [expression] } { , . identifier ([expression]) }
| . identifier ([expression]) { , . identifier ([expression]) }

list_of_block_variable_identifiers ::=
block_variable_type { , block_variable_type }

list_of_checker_port_connections ::=
ordered_checker_port_connection
{ , ordered_checker_port_connection }
| named_checker_port_connection
{ , named_checker_port_connection }

list_of_clocking_decl_assign ::=
clocking_decl_assign { , clocking_decl_assign }

list_of_coverpoints ::= cross_item , cross_item { , cross_item }

list_of_defparam_assignments ::=
defparam_assignment { , defparam_assignment }

list_of_event_identifiers ::=
event_identifier [dimension { dimension }]
{ , event_identifier [dimension { dimension }] }

list_of_formals ::= formal_list_item { , formal_list_item }

list_of_genvar_identifiers ::= genvar_identifier { , genvar_identifier }

```
list_of_interface_identifiers ::=
    interface_identifier { unpacked_dimension }
      { , interface_identifier { unpacked_dimension } }
list_of_module_connections ::=
      ordered_port_connection { , ordered_port_connection }
    | named_port_connection { , named_port_connection }
list_of_net_assignments ::= net_assignment { , net_assignment }
list_of_net_decl_assignments ::=
    net_decl_assignment { , net_decl_assignment }
list_of_net_identifiers ::=
    net_identifier [ dimension { dimension } ]
      { , net_identifier [ dimension { dimension } ] }
list_of_parameter_assignments ::=
      ordered_parameter_assignment { , ordered_parameter_assignment }
    | named_parameter_assignment { , named_parameter_assignment }
list_of_param_assignments ::= param_assignment { , param_assignment }
list_of_path_delay_expressions ::=
      t_path_delay_expression
    | trise_path_delay_expression , tfall_path_delay_expression
    | trise_path_delay_expression , tfall_path_delay_expression ,
        tz_path_delay_expression
    | t01_path_delay_expression , t10_path_delay_expression ,
        t0z_path_delay_expression , tz1_path_delay_expression ,
        t1z_path_delay_expression , tz0_path_delay_expression
    | t01_path_delay_expression , t10_path_delay_expression ,
        t0z_path_delay_expression , tz1_path_delay_expression ,
        t1z_path_delay_expression , tz0_path_delay_expression ,
        t0x_path_delay_expression , tx1_path_delay_expression ,
        t1x_path_delay_expression , tx0_path_delay_expression ,
        txz_path_delay_expression , tzx_path_delay_expression
list_of_path_inputs ::=
    specify_input_terminal_descriptor { , specify_input_terminal_descriptor }
list_of_path_outputs ::=
    specify_output_terminal_descriptor
      { , specify_output_terminal_descriptor }
list_of_port_connections ::=
      ordered_port_connection { , ordered_port_connection }
    | named_port_connection { , named_port_connection }
list_of_port_declarations ::=
    ( [ { attribute_instance } ansi_port_declaration
      { , {attribute_instance } ansi_port_declaration } ] )
```

```
list_of_port_identifiers ::=
    port_identifier { unpacked_dimension }
      { , port_identifier { unpacked_dimension } }
list_of_ports ::= ( port { , port } )
list_of_real_identifiers ::= real_type { , real_type }
list_of_specparam_assignments ::=
    specparam_assignment { , specparam_assignment }
list_of_tf_variable_identifiers ::=
    port_identifier { variable_dimension } [ = expression ]
      { , port_identifier { variable_dimension } [ = expression ] }
list_of_type_assignments ::= type_assignment { , type_assignment }
list_of_udp_port_identifiers ::= port_identifier { , port_identifier }
list_of_variable_assignments ::=
    variable_assignment { , variable_assignment }
list_of_variable_decl_assignments ::=
    variable_decl_assignment { , variable_decl_assignment }
list_of_variable_identifiers ::=
    variable_identifier { variable_dimension }
      { , variable_identifier { variable_dimension } }
list_of_variable_port_identifiers ::=
    port_identifier { variable_dimension } [ = constant_expression ]
      { , port_identifier { variable_dimension } [ = constant_expression ] }
list_of_virtual_interface_decl ::=
    variable_identifier [ = interface_instance_identifier ]
      { , variable_identifier [ = interface_instance_identifier ] }
local_parameter_declaration ::=
      localparam data_type_or_implicit list_of_param_assignments
    | localparam type list_of_type_assignments
long_comment ::= /* comment_text */
loop_generate_construct ::=
    for ( genvar_initialization ; genvar_expression ; genvar_iteration )
      generate_block
loop_statement ::=
      forever statement_or_null
    | repeat ( expression ) statement_or_null
    | while ( expression ) statement_or_null
    | for ( for_initialization ; expression ; for_step ) statement_or_null
    | do statement_or_null while ( expression ) ;
    | foreach ( ps_or_hierarchical_array_identifier [ loop_variables ] )
        statement
loop_variables ::= [ index_variable_identifier ] { , [ index_variable_identifier ] }
```

```
lsb_constant_expression ::= constant_expression

member_identifier ::= identifier

memory_identifier ::= identifier

method_call ::= method_call_root . method_call_body

method_call_body ::=
        method_identifier { attribute_instance } [ ( list_of_arguments ) ]
    |   built_in_method_call

method_call_root ::= primary | implicit_class_handle

method_identifier ::= identifier

method_prototype ::= task_prototype | function_prototype

method_qualifier ::=
        [ pure ] virtual
    |   class_item_qualifier

mintypmax_expression ::=
        expression
    |   expression : expression : expression

modport_clocking_declaration ::= clocking clocking_identifier

modport_declaration ::= modport modport_item { , modport_item } ;

modport_identifier ::= identifier

modport_item ::=
    modport_identifier ( modport_ports_declaration
      { , modport_ports_declaration } )

modport_ports_declaration ::=
        { attribute_instance } modport_simple_ports_declaration
    |   { attribute_instance } modport_tf_ports_declaration
    |   { attribute_instance } modport_clocking_declaration

modport_simple_port ::=
        port_identifier
    |   . port_identifier ( [ expression ] )

modport_simple_ports_declaration ::=
    port_direction modport_simple_port { , modport_simple_port }

modport_tf_port ::=
        method_prototype
    |   tf_identifier

modport_tf_ports_declaration ::=
    import_export modport_tf_port { , modport_tf_port }

module_ansi_header ::=
    { attribute_instance } module_keyword [ lifetime ] module_identifier
      { package_import_declaration} [ parameter_port_list ]
      [ list_of_port_declarations ] ;
```

module_common_item ::=
  module_or_generate_item_declaration
  | interface_instantiation
  | program_instantiation
  | assertion_item
  | bind_directive
  | continuous_assign
  | net_alias
  | initial_construct
  | final_construct
  | always_construct
  | loop_generate_construct
  | conditional_generate_construct
  | elaboration_system_task

module_declaration ::=
  module_nonansi_header [timeunits_declaration] { module_item }
  endmodule [: module_identifier]
  | module_ansi_header [timeunits_declaration]
    { non_port_module_item }
  endmodule [: module_identifier]
  | { attribute_instance } module_keyword [lifetime]
    module_identifier **(.*) ;** [timeunits_declaration] { module_item }
  endmodule [: module_identifier]
  | **extern** module_nonansi_header
  | **extern** module_ansi_header

module_identifier ::= identifier

module_instance ::= name_of_instance **(** [list_of_port_connections] **)**

module_instance_identifier ::= arrayed_identifier

module_instantiation ::=
  module_identifier [parameter_value_assignment] hierarchical_instance
    { , hierarchical_instance } ;

module_item ::=
  port_declaration ;
  | non_port_module_item

module_item_declaration ::=
  parameter_declaration
  | input_declaration
  | output_declaration
  | inout_declaration
  | net_declaration
  | reg_declaration
  | integer_declaration
  | real_declaration
  | time_declaration
  | realtime_declaration

```
          | event_declaration
          | task_declaration
          | function_declaration
module_keyword ::= module | macromodule
module_nonansi_header ::=
          { attribute_instance } module_keyword [ lifetime ] module_identifier
            { package_import_declaration } [ parameter_port_list ] list_of_ports ;
module_or_generate_item ::=
            { attribute_instance } parameter_override
          | { attribute_instance } gate_instantiation
          | { attribute_instance } udp_instantiation
          | { attribute_instance } module_instantiation
          | { attribute_instance } module_common_item
module_or_generate_item_declaration ::=
            package_or_generate_item_declaration
          | genvar_declaration
          | clocking_declaration
          | default clocking clocking_identifier ;
          | default disable iff expression_or_dist ;
module_or_interface_or_generate_item ::=
            module_or_generate_item
          | interface_or_generate_item
module_parameter_port_list ::=
          # ( parameter_declaration { , parameter_declaration } )
module_path_concatenation ::=
          { module_path_expression { , module_path_expression } }
module_path_conditional_expression ::=
          module_path_expression ? { attribute_instance }
            module_path_expression : module_path_expression
module_path_expression ::=
            module_path_primary
          | unary_module_path_operator { attribute_instance }
              module_path_primary
          | module_path_expression binary_module_path_operator
              { attribute_instance } module_path_expression
          | module_path_conditional_expression
module_path_mintypmax_expression ::=
            module_path_expression
          | module_path_expression : module_path_expression
              : module_path_expression
module_path_multiple_concatenation ::=
          { constant_expression module_path_concatenation }
```

module_path_primary ::=
number
| identifier
| module_path_concatenation
| module_path_multiple_concatenation
| function_subroutine_call
| (module_path_mintypmax_expression)

mos_switch_instance ::=
[name_of_instance] (output_terminal , input_terminal , enable_terminal)

mos_switchtype ::= **nmos** | **pmos** | **rnmos** | **rpmos**

msb_constant_expression ::= constant_expression

multiple_concatenation ::= { expression concatenation }

n_input_gate_instance ::=
[name_of_instance] (output_terminal , input_terminal { , input_terminal })

n_input_gatetype ::= **and** | **nand** | **or** | **nor** | **xor** | **xnor**

n_output_gate_instance ::=
[name_of_instance] (output_terminal { , output_terminal } , input_terminal)

n_output_gatetype ::= **buf** | **not**

name_of_gate_instance ::= gate_instance_identifier [range]

name_of_instance ::= instance_identifier { unpacked_dimension }

name_of_system_function ::= $identifier

name_of_udp_instance ::= udp_instance_identifier [range]

named_checker_port_connection ::=
{ attribute_instance } . port_identifier [([property_actual_arg])]
| { attribute_instance } . *

named_parameter_assignment ::=
. parameter_identifier ([param_expression])

named_port_connection ::=
{ attribute_instance } . port_identifier [([expression])]
| { attribute_instance } .*

ncontrol_terminal ::= expression

net_alias ::=
alias net_lvalue = net_lvalue { = net_lvalue } ;

net_assignment ::=
net_lvalue = expression

net_concatenation ::=
{ net_concatenation_value { , net_concatenation_value } }

net_concatenation_value ::=
hierarchical_net_identifier
| hierarchical_net_identifier [expression] { [expression] }
| hierarchical_net_identifier [expression] { [expression] }
[range_expression]
| hierarchical_net_identifier [range_expression]
| net_concatenation

net_decl_assignment ::=
net_identifier { unpacked_dimension } [= expression]

net_declaration ::=
net_type [drive_strength | charge_strength] [**vectored** | **scalared**]
data_type_or_implicit [delay3] list_of_net_decl_assignments ;

net_identifier ::= identifier

net_lvalue ::=
ps_or_hierarchical_net_identifier constant_select
| { net_lvalue { , net_lvalue } }
| [assignment_pattern_expression_type]
assignment_pattern_net_lvalue

net_port_header ::= [port_direction] net_port_type

net_port_type ::= [net_type] data_type_or_implicit

net_type ::=
supply0 | **supply1** | **tri** | **triand** | **trior** | **trireg** |
tri0 | **tri1** | **uwire** | **wire** | **wand** | **wor**

next_state ::=
output_symbol | -

nonblocking_assignment ::=
variable_lvalue <= [delay_or_event_control] expression

nonrange_select ::=
[{ . member_identifier bit_select } . member_identifier] bit_select

nonrange_variable_lvalue ::=
[implicit_class_handle . | package_scope]
hierarchical_variable_identifier nonrange_select

non_consecutive_repetition ::=
[= const_or_range_expression]

non_integer_type ::=
shortreal | **real** | **realtime**

non_port_interface_item ::=
generate_region
| interface_or_generate_item
| program_declaration
| interface_declaration
| timeunits_declaration

non_port_module_item ::=
  generate_region
  | module_or_generate_item
  | specify_block
  | { attribute_instance } specparam_declaration
  | program_declaration
  | module_declaration
  | interface_declaration
  | timeunits_declaration

non_port_program_item ::=
  { attribute_instance } continuous_assign
  | { attribute_instance } module_or_generate_item_declaration
  | { attribute_instance } initial_construct
  | { attribute_instance } final_construct
  | { attribute_instance } concurrent_assertion_item
  | { attribute_instance } timeunits_declaration
  | program_generate_item

non_zero_decimal_digit ::= **1** | **2** | **3** | **4** | **5** | **6** | **7** | **8** | **9**

non_zero_unsigned_number ::=
  non_zero_decimal_digit { _ | decimal_digit }

notifier ::= variable_identifier

number ::= integral_number | real_number

octal_base ::= **'[s|S]o** | **'[s|S]O**

octal_digit ::= x_digit | z_digit | **0** | **1** | **2** | **3** | **4** | **5** | **6** | **7**

octal_number ::= [size] octal_base octal_value

octal_value ::= octal_digit { _ | octal_digit }

one_line_comment ::= // comment_text **\n**

open_range_list ::= open_value_range { , open_value_range }

open_value_range ::= value_range

operator_assignment ::= variable_lvalue assignment_operator expression

ordered_checker_port_connection ::=
  { attribute_instance } [property_actual_arg]

ordered_parameter_assignment ::= param_expression

ordered_port_connection ::= { attribute_instance } [expression]

output_declaration ::=
  output net_port_type list_of_port_identifiers
  | **output** variable_port_type list_of_variable_port_identifiers

output_identifier ::=
  output_port_identifier
  | inout_port_identifier
  | interface_identifier . port_identifier

output_port_identifier ::= identifier

output_symbol ::= **0** | **1** | **x** | **X**

output_terminal ::= net_lvalue

output_variable_type ::= **integer** | **time**

overload_declaration ::= **bind** overload_operator **function** data_type
function_identifier (overload_proto_formals) ;

overload_operator ::= + | ++ | - | -- | * | ** | / | % | == | != | < | <= | > | >= | =

overload_proto_formals ::= data_type { , data_type }

package_declaration ::=
{ attribute_instance } **package** package_identifier ;
[timeunits_declaration] { { attribute_instance } package_item }
endpackage [: package_identifier]

package_export_declaration ::=
export * :: * ;
| **export** package_import_item { , package_import_item } ;

package_identifier ::= identifier

package_import_declaration ::=
import package_import_item { , package_import_item } ;

package_import_item ::=
package_identifier :: identifier
| package_identifier :: *

package_item ::=
package_or_generate_item_declaration
| anonymous_program
| package_export_declaration
| timeunits_declaration

package_or_generate_item_declaration ::=
net_declaration
| data_declaration
| task_declaration
| function_declaration
| checker_declaration
| dpi_import_export
| extern_constraint_declaration
| class_declaration
| class_constructor_declaration
| local_parameter_declaration ;
| parameter_declaration ;
| covergroup_declaration
| overload_declaration
| assertion_item_declaration
| ;

package_scope ::= package_identifier **::** | **$unit ::**

packed_dimension ::=
    [constant_range **]**
  | unsized_dimension

par_block ::=
    fork [**:** block_identifier]
      { block_item_declaration } { statement_or_null }
    join_keyword [**:** block_identifier]

parallel_edge_sensitive_path_description ::=
    ([edge_identifier] specify_input_terminal_descriptor
      [polarity_operator] **=>** **(** specify_output_terminal_descriptor
      [polarity_operator] **:** data_source_expression **))**

parallel_path_description ::=
    (specify_input_terminal_descriptor [polarity_operator] **=>**
      specify_output_terminal_descriptor **)**

param_assignment ::=
    parameter_identifier { unpacked_dimension }
      [**=** constant_param_expression]

param_expression ::= mintypmax_expression | data_type

parameter_declaration ::=
    parameter data_type_or_implicit list_of_param_assignments
  | **parameter type** list_of_type_assignments

parameter_identifier ::= identifier

parameter_override ::= **defparam** list_of_param_assignments **;**

parameter_port_declaration ::=
    parameter_declaration
  | local_parameter_declaration
  | data_type list_of_param_assignments
  | **type** list_of_type_assignments

parameter_port_list ::=
    # (list_of_param_assignments { **,** parameter_port_declaration } **)**
  | **# (** parameter_port_declaration { **,** parameter_port_declaration } **)**
  | **#()**

parameter_value_assignment ::= **# (** [list_of_parameter_assignments] **)**

part_select_range ::= constant_range | indexed_range

pass_en_switchtype ::= **tranif0** | **tranif1** | **rtranif1** | **rtranif0**

pass_enable_switch_instance ::=
    [name_of_instance] **(** inout_terminal **,** inout_terminal **,** enable_terminal **)**

pass_switch_instance ::=
    [name_of_instance] **(** inout_terminal **,** inout_terminal **)**

pass_switchtype ::= **tran** | **rtran**

```
path_declaration ::=
      simple_path_declaration ;
    | edge_sensitive_path_declaration ;
    | state_dependent_path_declaration ;

path_delay_expression ::= constant_mintypmax_expression

path_delay_value ::=
      list_of_path_delay_expressions
    | ( list_of_path_delay_expressions )

pattern ::=
      . variable_identifier
    | .*
    | constant_expression
    | tagged member_identifier [ pattern ]
    | '{ pattern { , pattern } }
    | '{ member_identifier : pattern { , member_identifier : pattern } }

pcontrol_terminal ::= expression

polarity_operator ::= + | –

port ::=
      [ port_expression ]
    | . port_identifier ( [ port_expression ] )

port_declaration ::=
      { attribute_instance } inout_declaration
    | { attribute_instance } input_declaration
    | { attribute_instance } output_declaration
    | { attribute_instance } ref_declaration
    | { attribute_instance } interface_port_declaration

port_direction ::= input | output | inout | ref

port_expression ::=
      port_reference
    | { port_reference { , port_reference } }

port_identifier ::= identifier

port_reference ::= port_identifier constant_select

primary ::=
      primary_literal
    | [ class_qualifier | package_scope ] hierarchical_identifier select
    | empty_queue
    | concatenation [ [ range_expression ] ]
    | multiple_concatenation [ [ range_expression ] ]
    | function_subroutine_call
    | let_expression
    | ( mintypmax_expression )
    | cast
    | assignment_pattern_expression
```

```
      | streaming_concatenation
      | sequence_method_call
      | this
      | $
      | null

primary_literal ::=
      number | time_literal | unbased_unsized_literal | string_literal

procedural_assertion_statement ::=
        concurrent_assertion_statement
      | immediate_assertion_statement
      | checker_instantiation

procedural_continuous_assignment ::=
        assign variable_assignment
      | deassign variable_lvalue
      | force variable_assignment
      | force net_assignment
      | release variable_lvalue
      | release net_lvalue

procedural_timing_control ::=
      delay_control | event_control | cycle_delay

procedural_timing_control_statement ::=
      procedural_timing_control statement_or_null

production ::=
      [ data_type_or_void ] production_identifier
        [ ( tf_port_list ) ] : rs_rule { | rs_rule } ;

production_identifier ::= identifier

production_item ::=
      production_identifier [ ( list_of_arguments ) ]

program_ansi_header ::=
      { attribute_instance } program [ lifetime ] program_identifier
        { package_import_declaration } [ parameter_port_list ]
        [ list_of_port_declarations ] ;

program_declaration ::=
        program_nonansi_header [ timeunits_declaration ] { program_item }
        endprogram [ : program_identifier ]
      | program_ansi_header
          [ timeunits_declaration ] { non_port_program_item }
        endprogram [ : program_identifier ]
      | { attribute_instance } program program_identifier ( .* ) ;
          [ timeunits_declaration ] { program_item }
        endprogram [ : program_identifier ]
      | extern program_nonansi_header
      | extern program_ansi_header
```

program_generate_item ::=
loop_generate_construct
| conditional_generate_construct
| generate_region
| elaboration_system_task

program_identifier ::= identifier

program_instantiation ::=
program_identifier [parameter_value_assignment]
hierarchical_instance { , hierarchical_instance } ;

program_item ::=
port_declaration ;
| non_port_program_item

program_nonansi_header ::=
{ attribute_instance } **program** [lifetime] program_identifier
{ package_import_declaration } [parameter_port_list] list_of_ports ;

property_actual_arg ::=
property_expr
| sequence_actual_arg

property_case_item ::=
expression_or_dist { , expression_or_dist } **:** property_statement
| **default** [**:**] property_statement

property_declaration ::=
property property_identifier [**(** [tf_port_list] **)**] **;**
{ assertion_variable_declaration }
property_statement_spec
endproperty [**:** property_identifier]

property_expr ::=
sequence_expr
| **strong** **(** sequence_expr **)**
| **weak** **(** sequence_expr **)**
| **(** property_expr **)**
| **not** property_expr
| property_expr **or** property_expr
| property_expr **and** property_expr
| sequence_expr |-> property_expr
| sequence_expr |=> property_expr
| property_statement
| sequence_expr # - # property_expr
| sequence_expr # = # property_expr
| **nexttime** property_expr
| **nexttime** [constant_expression] property_expr
| **s_nexttime** property_expr
| **s_nexttime** [constant_expression] property_expr
| **always** property_expr

| **always** [cycle_delay_const_range_expression] property_expr
| **s_always** [constant_range] property_expr
| **s_eventually** property_expr
| **eventually** [constant_range] property_expr
| **s_eventually** [cycle_delay_const_range_expression] property_expr
| property_expr **until** property_expr
| property_expr **s_until** property_expr
| property_expr **until_with** property_expr
| property_expr **s_until_with** property_expr
| property_expr **implies** property_expr
| property_expr **iff** property_expr
| **accept_on** (expression_or_dist) property_expr
| **reject_on** (expression_or_dist) property_expr
| **sync_accept_on** (expression_or_dist) property_expr
| **sync_reject_on** (expression_or_dist) property_expr
| property_instance
| clocking_event property_expr

property_formal_type ::=
sequence_formal_type
| **property**

property_identifier ::= identifier

property_instance ::=
ps_or_hierarchical_property_identifier
[([property_list_of_arguments])]

property_list_of_arguments ::=
[property_actual_arg] { , [property_actual_arg] }
{ , . identifier ([property_actual_arg]) }
| . identifier ([property_actual_arg])
{ , . identifier ([property_actual_arg]) }

property_lvar_port_direction ::= **input**

property_port_item ::=
{ attribute_instance } [**local** [property_lvar_port_direction]]
property_formal_type port_identifier { variable_dimension }
[= property_actual_arg]

property_port_list ::= property_port_item { , property_port_item }

property_qualifier ::= random_qualifier | class_item_qualifier

property_spec ::=
[clocking_event] [**disable iff** (expression_or_dist)] property_expr

property_statement ::=
property_expr ;
| **case** (expression_or_dist) property_case_item
{ property_case_item } **endcase**
| **if** (expression_or_dist) property_expr [**else** property_expr]

property_statement_spec ::=
[clocking_event] [**disable iff** (expression_or_dist)]
property_statement

ps_class_identifier ::= [package_scope] class_identifier

ps_covergroup_identifier ::= [package_scope] covergroup_identifier

ps_identifier ::= [package_scope] identifier

ps_or_hierarchical_array_identifier::=
[implicit_class_handle **.** | class_scope | package_scope]
hierarchical_array_identifier

ps_or_hierarchical_net_identifier ::= [package_scope] net_identifier |
hierarchical_net_identifier

ps_or_hierarchical_property_identifier ::=
[package_scope] property_identifier | hierarchical_property_identifier

ps_or_hierarchical_sequence_identifier ::=
[package_scope] sequence_identifier | hierarchical_sequence_identifier

ps_or_hierarchical_tf_identifier ::=
[package_scope] tf_identifier | hierarchical_tf_identifier

ps_parameter_identifier ::=
[package_scope | class_scope] parameter_identifier
| { generate_block_identifier [[constant_expression]] **.**}
parameter_identifier

ps_type_identifier ::= [**local ::** | package_scope] type_identifier

pull_gate_instance ::= [name_of_instance] **(** output_terminal **)**

pulldown_strength ::=
(strength0 **,** strength1 **)**
| **(** strength1 **,** strength0 **)**
| **(** strength0 **)**

pullup_strength ::=
(strength0 **,** strength1 **)**
| **(** strength1 **,** strength0 **)**
| **(** strength1 **)**

pulsestyle_declaration ::=
pulsestyle_onevent list_of_path_outputs **;**
| **pulsestyle_ondetect** list_of_path_outputs **;**

pulse_control_specparam ::=
PATHPULSE$ = **(** reject_limit_value [**,** error_limit_value] **)**
| **PATHPULSE$**specify_input_terminal_descriptor
/**no space; continue**/ $specify_output_terminal_descriptor =
(reject_limit_value [**,** error_limit_value] **)**[1]

---

1. For example, **PATHPULSE**CLKQ = (5, 3).

queue_dimension ::= [$ [: constant_expression]]

randcase_item ::= expression : statement_or_null

randcase_statement ::=
  randcase randcase_item { randcase_item } **endcase**

randomize_call ::=
  randomize { attribute_instance } [([variable_identifier_list | **null**])]
    [**with** [([identifier_list])] constraint_block]

random_qualifier ::= **rand** | **randc**

randsequence_statement ::=
  randsequence ([production_identifier])
    production { production }
  endsequence

range ::= [msb_constant_expression : lsb_constant_expression]

range_expression ::=
    expression
  | part_select_range

range_list ::= value_range { , value_range }

range_or_type ::= range | **integer** | **real** | **realtime** | **time**

real_declaration ::= **real** list_of_real_identifiers ;

real_identifier ::= identifier

real_number ::=
    fixed_point_number
  | unsigned_number [. unsigned_number] exp [sign]
    unsigned_number

realtime_declaration ::= **realtime** list_of_real_identifiers ;

real_type ::=
    real_identifier [= constant_expression]
  | real_identifier dimension { dimension }

reference_event ::= timing_check_event

ref_declaration ::= **ref** variable_port_type list_of_port_identifiers

reg_declaration ::= **reg** [**signed**] [range] list_of_variable_identifiers ;

reject_limit_value ::= limit_value

remain_active_flag ::= constant_mintypmax_expression

repeat_range ::=
    expression
  | expression : expression

restrict_property_statement ::=
  restrict property (property_spec) ;

rs_case ::= **case** (expression) rs_case_item { rs_case_item } **endcase**

rs_case_item ::=
    case_item_expression { , case_item_expression } : production_item ;
  | **default** [:] production_item ;

rs_code_block ::= { { data_declaration } { statement_or_null } }

rs_if_else ::= **if** (expression) production_item [**else** production_item]

rs_prod ::=
    production_item
  | rs_code_block
  | rs_if_else
  | rs_repeat
  | rs_case

rs_production_list ::=
    rs_prod { rs_prod }
  | **rand join** [(expression)] production_item
      production_item { production_item }

rs_repeat ::= **repeat** (expression) production_item

rs_rule ::= rs_production_list [:= weight_specification [rs_code_block]]

scalar_constant ::= **1'b0** | **1'b1** | **1'B0** | **1'B1** | **'b0** | **'b1** | **'B0** | **'B1** | **1** | **0**

scalar_timing_check_condition ::=
    expression
  | ~ expression
  | expression == scalar_constant
  | expression === scalar_constant
  | expression != scalar_constant
  | expression !== scalar_constant

select ::=
  [{ . member_identifier bit_select } . member_identifier]
    bit_select [[part_select_range]]

select_bins_or_empty ::= { { bins_selection_or_option ; } } | ;

select_condition ::=
  binsof (bins_expression) [**intersect** { open_range_list }]

select_expression ::=
    select_condition
  | ! select_condition
  | select_expression && select_expression
  | select_expression | | select_expression
  | (select_expression)

seq_block ::=
  begin [: block_identifier]
    { block_item_declaration } { statement_or_null }
  end [: block_identifier]

seq_input_list ::= level_input_list | edge_input_list

```
sequence_abbrev ::= consecutive_repetition

sequence_actual_arg ::=
      event_expression
    | sequence_expr

sequence_declaration ::=
    sequence sequence_identifier [ ( [ sequence_port_list ] ) ] ;
      { assertion_variable_declaration }
      sequence_expr ;
    endsequence [ : sequence_identifier ]

sequence_expr ::=
      cycle_delay_range sequence_expr
        { cycle_delay_range sequence_expr }
    | sequence_expr cycle_delay_range sequence_expr
        { cycle_delay_range sequence_expr }
    | expression_or_dist [ boolean_abbrev ]
    | sequence_instance [ sequence_abbrev ]
    | ( sequence_expr { , sequence_match_item } ) [ sequence_abbrev ]
    | sequence_expr and sequence_expr
    | sequence_expr intersect sequence_expr
    | sequence_expr or sequence_expr
    | first_match ( sequence_expr { , sequence_match_item } )
    | expression_or_dist throughout sequence_expr
    | sequence_expr within sequence_expr
    | clocking_event sequence_expr

sequence_formal_type ::=
      data_type_or_implicit
    | sequence
    | event
    | untyped

sequence_identifier ::= identifier

sequence_instance ::=
    ps_or_hierarchical_sequence_identifier
      [ ( [ sequence_list_of_arguments ] ) ]

sequence_list_of_arguments ::=
      [ sequence_actual_arg ] { , [ sequence_actual_arg ] }
        { , . identifier ( [ sequence_actual_arg ] ) }
    | . identifier ( [ sequence_actual_arg ] )
        { , . identifier ( [ sequence_actual_arg ] ) }

sequence_lvar_port_direction ::= input | inout | output

sequence_match_item ::=
      operator_assignment
    | inc_or_dec_expression
    | subroutine_call
```

```
sequence_method_call ::= sequence_instance . method_identifier

sequence_port_item ::=
    { attribute_instance } [ local [ sequence_lvar_port_direction ] ]
      sequence_formal_type port_identifier { variable_dimension }
      [ = sequence_actual_arg ]

sequence_port_list ::= sequence_port_item { , sequence_port_item }

sequential_body ::=
    [ udp_initial_statement ]
    table
      sequential_entry
      { sequential_entry }
    endtable

sequential_entry ::= seq_input_list : current_state : next_state ;

short_comment ::= // comment_text \n

showcancelled_declaration ::=
      showcancelled list_of_path_outputs ;
    | noshowcancelled list_of_path_outputs ;

sign ::= + | -

signal_identifier ::= identifier

signing ::=
      signed
    | unsigned

simple_identifier¹ ::= [ a-z A-Z _ ] { [ a-z A-Z _ $ 0-9 ] }

simple_immediate_assertion_statement ::=
      simple_immediate_assert_statement
    | simple_immediate_assume_statement
    | simple_immediate_cover_statement

simple_immediate_assert_statement ::=
    assert ( expression ) action_block

simple_immediate_assume_statement ::=
    assume ( expression ) action_block

simple_immediate_cover_statement :=
    cover ( expression ) statement_or_null

simple_path_declaration ::=
      parallel_path_description = path_delay_value
    | full_path_description = path_delay_value
```

1. A `simple_identifier` shall start with an alpha or underscore character, shall have at least one character, and shall not have any spaces.

simple_type ::=
  integer_type
  | non_integer_type
  | ps_type_identifier
  | ps_parameter_identifier

size ::= non_zero_unsigned_number

slice_size ::= simple_type | constant_expression

solve_before_list ::= solve_before_primary { , solve_before_primary }

solve_before_primary ::=
  [implicit_class_handle **.** | class_scope] hierarchical_identifier select

source_text ::= [timeunits_declaration] { description }

specify_block ::=
  specify
    { specify_item }
  endspecify

specify_input_terminal_descriptor ::=
  input_identifier [[constant_range_expression]]

specify_item ::=
  specparam_declaration
  | pulsestyle_declaration
  | showcancelled_declaration
  | path_declaration
  | system_timing_check

specify_output_terminal_descriptor ::=
  output_identifier [[constant_range_expression]]

specify_terminal_descriptor ::=
  specify_input_terminal_descriptor
  | specify_output_terminal_descriptor

specparam_assignment ::=
  specparam_identifier = constant_mintypmax_expression
  | pulse_control_specparam

specparam_declaration ::=
  specparam [packed_dimension] list_of_specparam_assignments ;

specparam_identifier ::= identifier

stamptime_condition ::= mintypmax_expression

start_edge_offset ::= mintypmax_expression

state_dependent_path_declaration ::=
  if (module_path_expression) simple_path_declaration
  | **if** (module_path_expression) edge_sensitive_path_declaration
  | **ifnone** simple_path_declaration

statement ::= [block_identifier **:**] { attribute_instance } statement_item

```
statement_item ::=
        blocking_assignment ;
      | nonblocking_assignment ;
      | procedural_continuous_assignment ;
      | case_statement
      | conditional_statement
      | inc_or_dec_expression ;
      | subroutine_call_statement
      | disable_statement
      | event_trigger
      | loop_statement
      | jump_statement
      | par_block
      | procedural_timing_control_statement
      | seq_block
      | wait_statement
      | procedural_assertion_statement
      | clocking_drive ;
      | randsequence_statement
      | randcase_statement
      | expect_property_statement
statement_or_null ::=
        statement
      | { attribute_instance } ;
streaming_concatenation ::=
    { stream_operator [ slice_size ] stream_concatenation }
stream_expression ::= expression [ with [ array_range_expression ] ]
stream_concatenation ::= { stream_expression { , stream_expression } }
stream_operator ::= >> | <<
strength0 ::= supply0 | strong0 | pull0 | weak0
strength1 ::= supply1 | strong1 | pull1 | weak1
string_literal ::= " { ANY_ASCII_CHARACTERS } "
structure_pattern_key ::= member_identifier | assignment_pattern_key
struct_union ::= struct | union [ tagged ]
struct_union_member ::=
    { attribute_instance } [ random_qualifier ] data_type_or_void
        list_of_variable_decl_assignments ;
subroutine_call ::=
        tf_call
      | system_tf_call
      | method_call
      | [ std :: ] randomize_call
```

```
subroutine_call_statement ::=
        subroutine_call ;
    | void ' ( function_subroutine_call ) ;

system_tf_call ::=
        system_tf_identifier [ ( list_of_arguments ) ]
    | system_tf_identifier ( data_type [ . expression ] )

system_tf_identifier ::= $[ a-z A-Z 0-9 _ $ ] { [ a-z A-Z 0-9 _ $ ] }

system_timing_check ::=
        $setup_timing_check
    | $hold_timing_check
    | $setuphold_timing_check
    | $recovery_timing_check
    | $removal_timing_check
    | $recrem_timing_check
    | $skew_timing_check
    | $timeskew_timing_check
    | $fullskew_timing_check
    | $period_timing_check
    | $width_timing_check
    | $nochange_timing_check

tagged_union_expression ::= tagged member_identifier [ expression ]

task_body_declaration ::=
        [ interface_identifier . | class_scope ] task_identifier ;
          { tf_item_declaration } { statement_or_null }
        endtask [ : task_identifier ]
    | [ interface_identifier . | class_scope ] task_identifier ( [ tf_port_list ] ) ;
          { block_item_declaration } { statement_or_null }
        endtask [ : task_identifier ]

task_declaration ::= task [ lifetime ] task_body_declaration

task_enable ::= hierarchical_task_identifier [ ( expression { , expression } ) ] ;

task_identifier ::= identifier

task_item_declaration ::=
        block_item_declaration
    | { attribute_instance } tf_input_declaration ;
    | { attribute_instance } tf_output_declaration ;
    | { attribute_instance } tf_inout_declaration ;

task_port_item ::=
        { attribute_instance } tf_input_declaration
    | { attribute_instance } tf_output_declaration
    | { attribute_instance } tf_inout_declaration

task_port_list ::= task_port_item { , task_port_item }

task_port_type ::= time | real | realtime | integer
```

task_prototype ::= **task** task_identifier ([tf_port_list])

terminal_identifier ::= identifier

text_macro_identifier ::= simple_identifier

tf_call ::=
  ps_or_hierarchical_tf_identifier { attribute_instance }
    [(list_of_arguments)]

tf_identifier ::= identifier

tf_inout_declaration ::=
    inout [**reg**] [**signed**] [range] list_of_port_identifiers
  | **inout** [task_port_type] list_of_port_identifiers

tf_input_declaration ::=
    input [**reg**] [**signed**] [range] list_of_port_identifiers
  | **input** [task_port_type] list_of_port_identifiers

tf_item_declaration ::=
    block_item_declaration
  | tf_port_declaration

tf_output_declaration ::=
    output [**reg**] [**signed**] [range] list_of_port_identifiers
  | **output** [task_port_type] list_of_port_identifiers

tf_port_declaration ::=
  { attribute_instance } tf_port_direction [**var**] data_type_or_implicit
    list_of_tf_variable_identifiers ;

tf_port_direction ::= port_direction | **const ref**

tf_port_item ::=
  { attribute_instance } [tf_port_direction] [**var**] data_type_or_implicit
    [port_identifier { variable_dimension } [= expression]]

tf_port_list ::= tf_port_item { , tf_port_item }

threshold ::= constant_expression

timecheck_condition ::= mintypmax_expression

timestamp_condition ::= mintypmax_condition

timeunits_declaration ::=
    timeunit time_literal [/ time_literal] ;
  | **timeprecision** time_literal ;
  | **timeunit** time_literal **; timeprecision** time_literal ;
  | **timeprecision** time_literal **; timeunit** time_literal ;

time_declaration ::= **time** list_of_variable_identifiers ;

time_literal ::=
    unsigned_number time_unit
  | fixed_point_number time_unit

time_unit ::=
  s | **ms** | **us** | **ns** | **ps** | **fs**

timing_check_condition ::=
  scalar_timing_check_condition
  | (scalar_timing_check_condition)

timing_check_event ::=
  [timing_check_event_control] specify_terminal_descriptor
  [&&& timing_check_condition]

timing_check_event_control ::=
  posedge
  | **negedge**
  | **edge**
  | edge_control_specifier

timing_check_limit ::= expression

tfall_path_delay_expression ::= path_delay_expression

topmodule_identifier ::= identifier

trans_item ::= range_list

trans_list ::= (trans_set) { , (trans_set) }

trans_range_list ::=
  trans_item
  | trans_item [* repeat_range]
  | trans_item [-> repeat_range]
  | trans_item [= repeat_range]

trans_set ::= trans_range_list { => trans_range_list }

trise_path_delay_expression ::= path_delay_expression

txz_path_delay_expression ::= path_delay_expression

tx0_path_delay_expression ::= path_delay_expression

tx1_path_delay_expression ::= path_delay_expression

type_assignment ::= type_identifier [= data_type]

type_declaration :=
  typedef data_type type_identifier { variable_dimension } ;
  | **typedef** interface_instance_identifier
    constant_bit_select . type_identifier type_identifier ;
  | **typedef** [**enum** | **struct** | **union** | **class**] type_identifier ;

type_identifier ::= identifier

type_reference ::=
  type (expression)
  | **type** (data_type)

tzx_path_delay_expression ::= path_delay_expression

tz0_path_delay_expression ::= path_delay_expression

tz1_path_delay_expression ::= path_delay_expression

tz_path_delay_expression ::= path_delay_expression

t0x_path_delay_expression ::= path_delay_expression

t0z_path_delay_expression ::= path_delay_expression

t01_path_delay_expression ::= path_delay_expression

t1x_path_delay_expression ::= path_delay_expression

t1z_path_delay_expression ::= path_delay_expression

t10_path_delay_expression ::= path_delay_expression

t_path_delay_expression := path_delay_expression

udp_ansi_declaration ::=
  { attribute_instance } **primitive** udp_identifier
  (udp_declaration_port_list) ;

udp_body ::=
  combinational_body
  | sequential_body

udp_declaration ::=
  udp_nonansi_declaration udp_port_declaration
   { udp_port_declaration }
   udp_body
  endprimitive [: udp_identifier]
  | udp_ansi_declaration
   udp_body
  endprimitive [: udp_identifier]
  | **extern** udp_nonansi_declaration
  | **extern** udp_ansi_declaration
  | { attribute_instance } **primitive** udp_identifier (.*) ;
   { udp_port_declaration }
   udp_body
  endprimitive [: udp_identifier]

udp_declaration_port_list ::=
  udp_output_declaration , udp_input_declaration
   { , udp_input_declaration }

udp_identifier ::= identifier

udp_initial_statement ::= **initial** output_port_identifier = init_val ;

udp_input_declaration ::=
  { attribute_instance } **input** list_of_udp_port_identifiers

udp_instance ::=
  [name_of_instance] (output_terminal , input_terminal
   { , input_terminal })

udp_instance_identifier ::= arrayed_identifier

udp_instantiation ::=
  udp_identifier [drive_strength] [delay2] udp_instance
    { , udp_instance } ;

udp_nonansi_declaration ::=
  { attribute_instance } **primitive** udp_identifier (udp_port_list) ;

udp_output_declaration ::=
  { attribute_instance } **output** port_identifier
  | { attribute_instance } **output reg** port_identifier
    [= constant_expression]

udp_port_declaration ::=
  udp_output_declaration ;
  | udp_input_declaration ;
  | udp_reg_declaration ;

udp_port_list ::=
  output_port_identifier , input_port_identifier { , input_port_identifier }

udp_reg_declaration ::= { attribute_instance } **reg** variable_identifier

unary_module_path_operator ::= ! | ~ | & | ~& | | | ~| | ^ | ~^ | ^~

unary_operator ::= + | - | ! | ~ | & | ~& | | | ~| | ^ | ~^ | ^~

unbased_unsized_literal ::= '**0** | '**1** | 'z_or_x

unique_priority ::= **unique** | **unique0** | **priority**

unique_priority_if_statement ::=
  [unique_priority] **if** (cond_predicate) statement_or_null
    { **else if** (cond_predicate) statement_or_null }
    [**else** statement_or_null]

unpacked_dimension ::=
  [constant_range]
  | [constant_expression]

unsigned_number ::= decimal_digit { _ | decimal_digit }

unsized_dimension ::= [ ]

use_clause ::=
  use [library_identifier **.**] cell_identifier [**: config**]
  | **use** named_parameter_assignment
    { , named_parameter_assignment } [**: config**]
  | **use** [library_identifier **.**] cell_identifier named_parameter_assignment
    { , named_parameter_assignment } [**: config**]

value_range ::= expression | [expression : expression]

variable_assignment ::= variable_lvalue = expression

variable_concatenation ::=
  { variable_concatenation_value { , variable_concatenation_value } }

variable_concatenation_value ::=
  hierarchical_variable_identifier

| hierarchical_variable_identifier [expression] { [expression] }
| hierarchical_variable_identifier [expression] { [expression] }
[range_expression]
| hierarchical_variable_identifier [range_expression]
| variable_concatenation

variable_decl_assignment ::=
variable_identifier { variable_dimension } [= expression]
| dynamic_array_variable_identifier unsized_dimension
{ variable_dimension } [= dynamic_array_new]
| class_variable_identifier [= class_new]

variable_dimension ::=
unsized_dimension
| unpacked_dimension
| associative_dimension
| queue_dimension

variable_identifier ::= identifier

variable_identifier_list ::= variable_identifier { , variable_identifier }

variable_lvalue ::=
[implicit_class_handle . | package_scope]
hierarchical_variable_identifier select
| { variable_lvalue { , variable_lvalue } }
| [assignment_pattern_expression_type]
assignment_pattern_variable_lvalue
| streaming_concatenation

variable_port_header ::= [port_direction] variable_port_type

variable_port_type ::= var_data_type

variable_type ::=
variable_identifier [= constant_expression]
| variable_identifier dimension { dimension }

var_data_type ::=
data_type
| **var** data_type_or_implicit

virtual_interface_declaration ::=
virtual [**interface**] interface_identifier [parameter_value_assignment]
[. modport_identifier] list_of_virtual_interface_decl ;

wait_statement ::=
wait (expression) statement_or_null
| **wait fork ;**
| **wait_order** (hierarchical_identifier { , hierarchical_identifier })
action_block

weight_specification ::=
integral_number

```
    | ps_identifier
    | ( expression )
white_space ::= space | tab | newline | eof
x_digit ::= x | X
z_digit ::= z | Z | ?
zero_or_one ::= 0 | 1
z_or_x ::= x | X | z | Z
$fullskew_timing_check ::=
    $fullskew ( reference_event , data_event , timing_check_limit ,
      timing_check_limit [ , [ notifier ] [ , [ event_based_flag ]
      [ , [ remain_active_flag ] ] ] ] ) ;
$hold_timing_check ::=
    $hold ( reference_event , data_event , timing_check_limit [ , [ notifier ] ] ) ;
$nochange_timing_check ::=
    $nochange ( reference_event , data_event , start_edge_offset ,
      end_edge_offset [ , [ notifier ] ] ) ;
$period_timing_check ::=
    $period ( controlled_reference_event , timing_check_limit
      [ , [ notifier ] ] ) ;
$recovery_timing_check ::=
    $recovery ( reference_event , data_event ,
      timing_check_limit [ , [ notifier ] ] ) ;
$recrem_timing_check ::=
    $recrem ( reference_event , data_event ,
      timing_check_limit , timing_check_limit [ , [ notifier ]
      [ , [ timestamp_condition ] [ , [ timecheck_condition ]
      [ , [ delayed_reference ] [ , [ delayed_data ] ] ] ] ] ] ) ;
$removal_timing_check ::=
    $removal ( reference_event , data_event ,
      timing_check_limit [ , [ notifier ] ] ) ;
$setuphold_timing_check ::=
    $setuphold ( reference_event , data_event ,
      timing_check_limit , timing_check_limit [ , [ notifier ]
      [ , [ timestamp_condition ] [ , [ timecheck_condition ]
      [ , [ delayed_reference ] [ , [ delayed_data ] ] ] ] ] ] ) ;
$setup_timing_check ::=
    $setup ( data_event , reference_event ,
      timing_check_limit [ , [ notifier ] ] ) ;
$skew_timing_check ::=
    $skew ( reference_event , data_event ,
      timing_check_limit [ , [ notifier ] ] ) ;
```

```
$timeskew_timing_check ::=
    $timeskew ( reference_event , data_event ,
      timing_check_limit [ , [ notifier ] [ , [ event_based_flag ]
      [ , [ remain_active_flag ] ] ] ] ) ;
$width_timing_check ::=
    $width ( controlled_reference_event , timing_check_limit ,
      threshold [ , [ notifier ] ] ) ;
```

❑

Bibliography

1. Bergeron J., *Writing Testbenches using SystemVerilog*, Springer, MA, ISBN 978-0-387-29221-2, 2006.
2. Cohen B., S. Venkataramanan, A. Kumari, and L. Piper, *SystemVerilog Assertions Handbook for Dynamic and Formal Verification, 2nd Edition*, VhdlCohen Publishing, CA, ISBN 878-0-9705394-8-7, 2010.
3. Glasser M., *Open Verification Methodology Cookbook*, Springer, MA, ISBN 978-1-441-90967-1, 2009.
4. *IEEE Standard for SystemVerilog: Unified Hardware Design, Specification and Verification Language*, IEEE Std 1800-2009, IEEE, 2009.
5. OVM: http://www.ovmworld.org.
6. Spear C., *SystemVerilog For Verification: A Guide to Learning the Testbench Language Features*, Springer, MA, ISBN 978-0-387-76529-7, 2008.
7. Sutherland S., S. Davidmann and P. Flake, *SystemVerilog for Design: A Guide to Using SystemVerilog for Hardware Design and Modeling, 2nd edition*, Springer, MA, ISBN 978-0-387-33399-1, 2006.
8. SystemVerilog: http://www.systemverilog.org.
9. VMM: http://vmmcentral.org.

❑

Index

❑